The Complete Idiot's Guide Reference Card

Principles for Creating the Perfect Resume

Set aside at least three hours (that's an average length of time to complete a resume if all goes smoothly). Before you start, tear out this card and tape it to your computer, on the wall next to your desk, or someplace where you'll see it throughout the process.

Once you've used the Five Resume Commandments below to craft your perfect resume, turn this card over and use the Top Ten Checklist to make sure you covered everything.

The Five Resume Commandments

I. *Thou shalt not write about your past; thou shalt write about your future!* Your resume should paint a picture of you at your next job. Without realizing it, the reader of your resume will be "tricked" into envisioning you working for him or her.

II. *Thou shalt not confess.* In other words, you don't have to "tell all." Stick to what's relevant and marketable.

III. *Thou shalt not write job descriptions; thou shalt write about achievements.* Talk about your experience in terms of your achievements instead of monotonous job descriptions.

IV. *Thou shalt not write about stuff you don't want to do again.* Promote only the skills you enjoy using.

V. *Thou shalt not lie.* You can be creative, but always be honest.

alpha
books

The Top Ten Checklist for Creating the Perfect Resume

Here's a handy checklist to make sure you don't forget anything important on your resume. Take your pencil in hand (or get out a box of gold stars) and give yourself credit for each one of the items on this list that you've completed:

1. Your name appears in the top center or on the upper right-hand side (not in the upper left-hand corner) of the page.

2. Your resume starts with a brief and clear job objective statement or a strong indication of what position you are seeking.

3. Everything on your resume supports your job objective.

4. Achievements, rather than job descriptions, are stressed.

5. Achievement statements start with action verbs and do not contain vague terms such as "responsible for."

6. There are no paragraphs anywhere on the resume. Bulleted statements make achievements quick and easy to read.

7. Statements and sections are prioritized so that the most impressive information comes first.

8. Your resume fits on no more than two pages. The exception to the two-page limit applies to resumes (also called curriculum vitas) for the academic and scientific communities.

9. If you have a two-page resume, "Continued" appears on the bottom of page one, and your name and "Page Two" appears at the top of the second page.

10. There are no misspellings, grammatical errors, or other mistakes.

The

COMPLETE

IDIOT'S

GUIDE TO

the Perfect

Resume

by Susan Ireland

alpha
books

A Division of Macmillan General Reference
A Simon & Schuster Macmillan Company
1633 Broadway, New York, 10019

International Standard Book Number: 0-02-861093-8
Library of Congress Catalog Card Number: 96-085363

98 97   8   7   6   5   4

Interpretation of the printing code: the rightmost number of the first series of numbers is the year of the book's printing; the rightmost number of the second series of numbers is the number of the book's printing. For example, a printing code of 96-1 shows that the first printing occurred in 1996.

Printed in the United States of America

Publisher
Theresa Murtha

Editor
Nancy Mikhail

Copy/Production Editor
Lynn Northrup

Cover Designer
Mike Freeland

Illustrator
Judd Winick

Designer
Kim Scott

Production Supervisor
Laurie Casey

Indexer
Debra Myers

Production Team
*Angela Calvert, Daniel Caparo, Kim Cofer, Terrie Deemer,
Aleata Howard, Erich Richter, Megan Wade*

Contents at a Glance

Contents

Introduction

Success in finding your ideal job depends largely upon having a dynamite resume!

Drastic changes are taking place in the way resumes are reviewed by managers and human resource professionals. Would you believe that the number of applicants per job has increased to such a point that each resume is given only about eight seconds—maybe less—to grab the reader's attention?

In some organizations, resumes are never even read by human eyes. They're put into a resume scanner and electronically entered into a database for automated selection. Some companies want resumes sent to them through electronic mail.

Knowing how to create a resume for this new job market could make or break your job search. But don't panic! Just follow the guidelines in this book and you'll get your resume considered by a hiring manager of any job you sincerely believe you're qualified for.

As a professional resume writer who has helped over 3,000 job seekers, I've seen how well-written resumes (not boilerplate forms) lead to promising interviews and job offers. I've also seen how a carefully crafted resume can help a job seeker (like you) get through the seemingly impossible task of finding career satisfaction—in other words, a position where you go to work with a smile on your face because you enjoy your job and come home with a paycheck that supports your lifestyle.

Since helping you craft a top-notch resume is the goal of *The Complete Idiot's Guide to the Perfect Resume*, let's talk about what's inside.

Part 1, "Before You Start," explains why you need a good resume and what a good resume can do for you. You'll also find in this section the "Five Resume Commandments"—my secrets to a compelling resume.

Part 2, "Navigating Your Way," is where you'll find my straightforward, nine-step resume-writing process. Before you know it, you'll be finished with your resume.

Part 3, "So, You Need a Special Resume," shows you variations on a typical resume, including achievement resumes, hybrid resumes, and curriculum vitas.

Part 4, "Keeping Up With Technology," teaches you about resume scanning and using on-line services for your job search. You'll learn how to create a successful electronic resume that won't get lost in cyberspace!

As the proud owner of *The Complete Idiot's Guide to the Perfect Resume*, consider me your personal resume coach. Imagine that I'm sitting right at your elbow as you work at your desk or kitchen table. My job is to guide you through the entire process as you:

➤ Develop a winning resume strategy.

➤ Write each line to get the most out of your qualifications.

➤ Create a great format for your resume.

➤ Distribute your new resume to employers.

To illustrate my points, I've included lots of resumes from real job seekers that reflect goals and challenges similar to what you're facing. Their solutions may spark some ideas that you can use for *your* resume.

The secret to success in using this book is to relax and take one step at a time. You'll be surprised how painless the process is!

Signposts Along the Way

You'll notice the following sidebars throughout the book. They mark some special points I want you to be sure to catch.

Commandments

Each of these boxes refers to one of the five commandments that I fully explain in Chapter 2. They are scattered throughout this book so you'll understand how to apply the rules while you write your resume.

Definition
This sidebar provides the meaning of technical terms and words peculiar to resume writing.

Tip
These boxes offer inside advice and great suggestions on how you can get ahead of your competition.

Warning
These sidebars help you avoid unnecessary errors or save you from missing opportunities.

Getting More Help

What if, despite all the great advice in this book, you get stuck? At any point, my resume writing service, Dynamite!! Resumes, can come to your rescue.

Dynamite!! Resume Writing Service

From anywhere in the United States, you can have your resume written professionally through my Dynamite!! Resume Writing Service. One of my associates will compose and produce your resume, working with you by telephone, fax,
e-mail, and regular mail. For those of you who live in the San Francisco area, you can have your resume written during a one-on-one session.

Dynamite!! Resume Critique Service

Once you've written your resume, use my Dynamite!! Resume Critique Service to be sure you have the most effective job search tool possible. A professional resume writer will examine your resume and give you a half-hour critique by phone. (Believe me, we pack a lot of information into our half-hour sessions.)

For a recorded message about Dynamite!! Resumes, call this toll-free number: (888) 296-2200.

Special Thanks from the Publisher to the Technical Reviewer

The Complete Idiot's Guide to the Perfect Resume was reviewed by an expert who not only checked the technical accuracy of what you'll learn in this book, but also provided invaluable insight and suggestions to ensure that you receive everything you need to know when creating your own resume.

Our special thanks are extended to Marilyn Miller, who has worked for Random House's college division for more than 12 years, where she edited business, English, writing, and communication books. Currently, she is a freelance writer. Her most recent project is the *New York Times Library Book of American History*, which she is co-authoring with Marian Faux.

Dedication

To my Dad, who taught me at an early age the value of building character through work.

Acknowledgments

Many thanks to my friends and allies: Yana Parker, Tad Gage, Brad Whitaker, Greg Herman, Vickie Zenoff, Robyn Kliger, Jane Conger, Andrée Abecassis (my agent at Ann Elmo Agency), Nancy Mikhail (my editor), Lynn Northrup (my copy/production editor), Anne Sparks, Robin Holt, and my other colleagues and clients at Alumnae Resources Career Center in San Francisco, and, of course, Mom.

Foreword

One of the most important tools in a job search is the resume, that piece of paper or on-line screen that contains your employment history—and also your hopes and dreams for getting the job you want.

No wonder you panic at the thought of putting one together!

And you're absolutely right to be concerned about your resume: It can make the difference in whether you get the job interview, and ultimately, the job.

If you're uptight about the business of resume writing—and who wouldn't be—help is on the way. It's right here in Susan Ireland's comprehensive book that doesn't miss a beat when it comes to resumes.

Ms. Ireland is an expert resume writer; a professional who earns her living by helping job seekers create successful ones. What I like most about *The Complete Idiot's Guide to the Perfect Resume* is that in addition to the author's on-target advice and analysis, it also includes real-life resumes used successfully by real-life job seekers. Whether it's your first or your 50th resume, you'll be eased into writing a top-notch one by Ms. Ireland's relaxed and friendly approach.

You'll find yourself smiling at her good humor—even if you're scared silly about compiling your work history into one brief page (two pages are okay but only if absolutely necessary, Ms. Ireland says; unless you're creating a curriculum vita).

With her insightful advice, you'll be able to produce a winning resume...and the winner will be you!

Carol Kleiman

Carol Kleiman is a nationally syndicated Jobs columnist for *The Chicago Tribune*. She is the author of *The 100 Best Jobs for the 1990s & Beyond* and *The Career Coach: Carol Kleiman's Inside Tips to Getting and Keeping the Job You Want*.

Part 1
Before You Start

It's been a long hard day at the office for Ms. Hiring Manager. Her eyes are glazed over from looking at 75 resumes, trying to find the right person for an opening in her department. She's about to put on her coat and head for home when something on her desk catches her eye. It's a resume—yours. "At last!" she announces, after spending less than a minute scanning the page. "Someone who fits the bill!"

That's the kind of immediate recognition you can expect from your resume once you grasp and employ the concepts presented in this part. So before you actually put your pencil to paper (or fingers to the keyboard, for those of you working on computers), let's discuss the principles behind a dynamite resume.

After reading this section, you'll be miles ahead of your competition. In fact, the principles in Part 1 alone are well worth the price of this book.

So, turn the page and find out what most job seekers don't know about writing a job-winning resume!

Chapter 1

A Resume for All Reasons

In This Chapter

➤ How a good resume can make your job search successful

➤ Knowing where you want to work will help you get there quicker

➤ Your resume can help you champion job interviews

➤ Start negotiating for bigger bucks

➤ Get your network working

So you need a resume, huh? Are you a virgin resume writer? Or have you just blown the dust off your old resume and decided that it's time to upgrade it onto a computer disk? Either way, you've probably been putting off the writing because it feels like a big job and you'd rather be out playing golf or even mowing the lawn. Think of all the things you could have done if you had really followed through on those excuses: "I can't do my resume right now, I have to paint the house, wash my car, pay the bills..." Well, I'm going to help you get this "chore" out of the way so you can move on to more fun things in your life.

Why Do You Need a Resume?

The reason you need a resume is that you're probably looking for a job or planning to change positions in the near future. Maybe it's your first job out of school, a move up the career ladder, a promotion within your company, a career change, or a job to save you from an imminent or recent layoff. Before you start writing your resume, let's talk about how a great resume makes your job search more successful.

Your Personal Road Map

Definition
The most common meaning of the word *resume* is a short account of one's professional experience and qualifications, typically used by a job applicant. However, resumes are also used for projects that don't involve a job search, such as business plans, school applications, and consulting proposals.

The very process of writing your resume helps you put your job search in perspective. To sell yourself to an employer, your resume should be focused on a *job objective* (more about that in Chapter 2). That means you have to figure out where you're headed on your career path (or at least what your next step is). Uh-oh! You're scratching your head. If you feel completely lost with this "where am I going" thing, don't panic! There's lots of help available. Take some time to do what many job changers do—see a career counselor or consult a career guidance book. A good one to try is *The Complete Idiot's Guide to Getting the Job You Want.*

Once you know what your job objective is, it's easy for you to take inventory of your skills and present your favorite and most marketable ones. Now, that's a powerful package—a resume that says what you want and why you should have it!

Win Interviews

For most people, the resume's most important job is to solicit interviews. It's your brochure or marketing piece to potential employers. Because your resume may stand against hundreds of other resumes in competition for a job, it needs to present you in the best light possible. (I know, I know—that's why you bought this book!)

Tip

Write your resume with the idea that it's a marketing piece for your future (instead of a boring description of your past). This "marketing approach" to creating your resume is the surest way to convince an employer that you're a promising candidate for the job. (There's more on this "future" concept in Chapter 2.)

Answer Tough Interview Questions

A resume also prepares you for job interviews. Just the process of putting your resume together will help you figure out the answers to interview questions such as:

➤ What makes you think you'll do well in this new job?

➤ What achievement are you proud of that relates to this new position?

➤ Why do you think you'd fit into our company culture?

➤ What do you consider your biggest strengths and weaknesses?

➤ How has your previous work experience prepared you for this position?

➤ What kinds of challenges have you faced in past positions and how did you handle them?

Don't worry if you don't know the answers to these questions right now. You'll have a handle on them by the time you finish writing your resume, with the help of the exercises in Part 2.

Set the Tone for the Interview

What you decide to put on your resume will suggest the topics for discussion during the interview. In other words, it's your chance to say, "Hey, let's talk about my strengths. Here's what I'm really good at..."

Tip

If a job announcement says, "Include salary history with resume," what should you do? I recommend that you avoid mentioning your exact salary figure until the interview, when you can discuss it in person. But in order to comply with the ad's salary history request and get past the initial screening process, you should include a brief sentence in your cover letter, referring to your salary. See Chapter 11 to learn how to appropriately address the salary issue in your cover letter.

Write Your Own Recommendation

Once you've had a successful interview, your interviewer may need to get hiring approval from someone higher up the ladder. And if you've armed your interviewer with a dynamite resume, the recommendation has a better chance of being approved.

Start Salary Negotiations Now!

Believe it or not, salary negotiations start with your resume. Even though you don't include monetary expectations on your resume, the bargaining begins by the way your resume presents you. Here is some information that prospective employers can gather from your resume:

➤ How much experience you have

➤ How old you appear to be

➤ How focused you are in your career objective

Ready, Set, Network!

Once you have your resume in hand, you're ready to exploit one of the most powerful job-search tools: *networking.* The importance of networking can't be overestimated.

Definition

Networking: Picture a carefully crafted net (like a fishing net), with you (the job hunter) in the center, reaping the benefits of all that falls into your net. Made of invisible "threads" that extend from you to all the people you know, to the people those people know, and so on, your network becomes a conduit for ideas, favors, and information for your job search. With a strong net-work, you could be the recipient of a big job search payoff!

Here's a story that demonstrates that point. Dave got laid off from his job at a software development firm. One weekday morning when he went outside his home to pick up the newspaper, he struck up a conversation with the garbage collector who was making his rounds in the neighborhood. "What are you doing home at this time of day?" asked the collector. Dave explained that he had been laid off, to which the collector asked, "What kind of work do you do?" Pretty soon the garbage collector was telling Dave that he should speak to a woman who lived around the corner who worked for a software company. You can fill in the rest of the story—Dave gave the neighbor his resume and he ended up with a new job at her company.

This story may seem hard to believe, but opportunity *does* come in unexpected ways. So arm yourself with your resume and use it to stimulate networking. Circulate it among your friends, relatives, and business associates. They may know someone who knows someone who knows of the perfect job for you!

The Least You Need to Know

➤ Writing a resume is like drawing your personal map—it states clearly what your next career move will be.

➤ Creating a strong resume helps you articulate your skills and attributes—a must for a successful interview.

➤ A good resume opens the door for a job interview.

➤ A strong, well-thought-out resume starts you off on the right foot when negotiating your salary.

➤ Use your resume to establish a valuable job-search network.

Chapter 2

Winning Concepts— The Five Resume Commandments

Writing the perfect resume takes a little time and concentration, but when it's over you'll feel as if you've just won the lottery (well, maybe not that good, but pretty good). Trust me, it's worth it. I've seen lots of people walk away with finished resumes, saying they never knew they could look so good on paper; never thought their work history could appear so plausible; or never thought they would look qualified for something they've never done in the past.

Before you boot up your computer or get out your quill and inkwell (or your chisel and stone tablet, if you're Fred Flintstone), I want to impart a few tricks that even most professional resume writers don't know about. (Bet on it, your competition surely doesn't!) These concepts can make the difference between presenting a boring resume that just sits on someone's desk (or even worse, gets thrown away) and one that demands, "Read me, read me! Call me, Call me!"

To show you how important I think these resume tips are, I've dubbed them "The Five Resume Commandments."

> The Five Resume Commandments
>
> I. Thou shalt not write about your past; thou shalt write about your future!
>
> II. Thou shalt not confess.
>
> III. Thou shalt not write job descriptions; thou shalt write about achievements.
>
> IV. Thou shalt not write about stuff you don't want to do again.
>
> V. Thou shalt not lie.

Now let's look at each one of these commandments to understand why they are so important.

The 1st Commandment: Thou Shalt Not Write About Your Past; Thou Shalt Write About Your Future!

"My resume is about my future?" you ask. "But it talks about my work history and what I did at my previous jobs. Doesn't that mean it's about my past?"

That's exactly what most people think. But the secret to getting a new and exciting job is to *build your resume around your future, not your past.* So, before you even start writing your resume, you need to plan what kind of work you want to do next.

What will the employer think of your future-oriented resume? At first glance she may assume she's reading about your past, but as she gets drawn into it, *she'll find herself imagining you working for her.* And that's what will make her want to call you for an interview.

Tip

YOU'RE HIRED.

Create a resume that's about your future by imagining that you're an artist with an empty canvas (such as your computer screen) in front of you. Your assignment is to paint a picture of yourself at your next job, using any of the following four tools:

➤ Your *experience* (such as previous job titles, volunteer work, or school projects)

➤ Your *skill areas* (such as management, computer knowledge, or sales)

➤ Your *concerns* (such as the environment, homelessness, or human rights)

➤ Your *personality* (such as dependability, sense of humor, or ability to communicate)

The 2nd Commandment: Thou Shalt Not Confess

"Father, forgive me for I have sinned." If your resume sounds anything like that, you might as well go to the employer and declare, "Here are all the reasons you shouldn't hire me."

Your resume is not a confessional—you don't have to "tell all." Pick through all your information and choose only what's relevant to your job objective.

Tip

To decide whether or not to put something on your resume, ask yourself these questions:

➤ Does it support my job objective?

➤ Does it cast me in the best light possible with regard to experience, ability, age, and personality?

The following resumes show you how to apply this commandment. By the way, on all the resumes in this book, I've included the year in which the resume was written to give you a sense of the job seeker's state of employment (or unemployment) at that time. Also, knowing when the resume was written helps you understand what year the word "present" refers to in a job hunter's work history.

➤ Don't appear overqualified for the job.

Sharon Collar was having trouble finding a position as a marketing director. She needed a job desperately and decided to go for a position as an administrative assistant. If she put "MBA" under Education, she knew she would look overqualified for a clerical job. Take a look at her resume on the following page. You'll notice that she decided not to include her degree to improve her chances of getting an interview.

Remember: *Not* disclosing information is different than lying.

Tip

When an employer first receives your resume, you have only *eight seconds* to convince him to read your resume in detail. We're talking about a quick scan by a very busy manager! For that reason, it's vital that you order your material according to how relevant it is to your job objective.

Prioritizing correctly will make your resume scream out, "I'm the one you're looking for!" You'll hear more about this concept in Chapters 6 and 9.

Sharon Collar

431 University Avenue
Berkeley, CA 94211
(510) 663-2197

JOB OBJECTIVE

Administrative Assistant

HIGHLIGHTS OF QUALIFICATIONS

- Seven years combined administrative and research experience.

- Adept at handling sensitive business issues with discretion and professionalism.

- Cited as one of the top administrative assistants at Franklin Meyer Corporation.

PROFESSIONAL EXPERIENCE

1993-pres.   **Franklin Meyer Corporation,** Oakland, CA
ADMINISTRATIVE ASSISTANT

- Charged with organizing and generating correspondence for major clients involved in confidential government activities.

- Re-designed the office computer system, enabling 125% more work to be processed.

- Commended for creating weekly "Dress-Down Day," which brought a friendlier and more cooperative atmosphere to the workplace.

- Prepared legal and business documents using word processing and spreadsheet applications.

1989-1993   **University of California,** Berkeley, CA
RESEARCH ASSISTANT

- Conducted bibliographic research that contributed to paper delivered at the National Ape Behavior Institute in Washington, D.C.

- Word processed voluminous notes and provided accurate transcriptions of university and professional lectures.

- Translated French scientific text and compiled readers for undergraduate and graduate classes.

EDUCATION

B.A., Business Administration
University of California, Berkeley, 1988

Sharon didn't list her MBA because she didn't want to appear overqualified for the job she is applying for.

Resume written in 1996.

➤ Get your priorities straight.

Sylvia Benson had been a secretary and receptionist for a number of years and wanted to move into the field of human resources. In preparing for her career change, she had gone back to college and gotten her degree in human resources—all while continuing her occupation as a secretary.

Notice how Sylvia prioritized information on her resume on the following page to make the most marketable items pop out at the reader. Since her degree was more marketable than her work history, she decided to show it off by positioning her Education section near the top of her resume. By doing so, she got bonus points from the reader, who quickly saw that she was a new graduate in human resources who had worked her way through school. Sylvia then deemphasized her former job titles by placing her Work History at the bottom of the page and listing the job titles after the company names.

Tip

Sometimes the "Thou shalt not confess" commandment can give relief to job seekers who have something they'd rather not talk about. For example:

➤ A death in the family

➤ An illness, injury, or disability

➤ A foiled business venture

➤ Rehabilitation for emotional or substance abuse

Create a work history on your resume that doesn't mention any such "off-limits for discussion" events. If you need to justify a gap in your work history due to one of the above reasons, mention other, more positive things you did during that time. That way, an interviewer won't even think to ask a question about an awkward issue.

➤ Delete information that isn't relevant to your job objective, as long as you don't create gaps in your work history.

For the last two years, Vickie Habas spent most of her time managing a family crisis that she decided was not appropriate to put on her resume. During that time span, she did some freelance catalog production for an individual she knew from a previous job.

Notice how Vickie constructed the Work History on her resume without mentioning her personal situation, even though it actually consumed about 80 percent of her time and energy. Vickie's resume is shown later in this chapter.

Sylvia Benson

82 Pacific Grove Circle • Daly City, CA 94115 • (415) 832-9983

JOB OBJECTIVE

A position in Human Resources

SUMMARY OF QUALIFICATIONS

- Five years experience in business office work with recent assignments in personnel administration.
- Competent project manager with an eye for added results.
- Eager to pursue a career in human resources.

EDUCATION

M.S., Human Resources, San Francisco State University, 1995

Sylvia moved her Education section toward the top of her resume because her degree is highly relevant to her job objective.

RELEVANT ACCOMPLISHMENTS

PERSONNEL ADMINISTRATION

- Processed a minimum of 100 applications per week, using a database to file and sort data accessed by 13 managers. (Handel and Fredrick Associates)
- Conducted orientations for new hires: explained company policies and gave employee tours of company. (Transplants Nursery)
- Coordinated payroll data by compiling information from time card machine and tallying employee vacation calendars. (Handel and Fredrick Associates)

PROJECT MANAGEMENT

- Completely redesigned the mail system to expedite sorting and delivery. (San Francisco Opera Company)
- Managed a 4,000-piece direct mail effort that met seasonal marketing deadlines despite heavy in-house workloads. (Handel and Fredrick Associates)
- Initiated a company-wide recycling program that resulted in excellent publicity for the firm. (Transplants Nursery)

WORK HISTORY

1993-present	Handel and Fredrick Associates, Daly City, CA
	Executive Secretary
1990-1993	San Francisco Opera Company, San Francisco, CA
	Administrative Assist.
1988-1990	Transplants Nursery, San Bruno, CA
	Receptionist

Because her job titles are not directly relevant to her job objective, Sylvia placed her Work History at the end of the resume.

Resume written in 1996.

Vickie Habas

431 Deleware St.
Toledo, OH 36519
232-739-0931

JOB OBJECTIVE

Catalog Production Director

SUMMARY OF QUALIFICATIONS

- Seven years as a catalog production professional, working in corporate and independent settings.
- Degree in journalism with additional training at daily news publication.
- Noted for accelerating production through strong managerial skills.

PROFESSIONAL EXPERIENCE

Here's how Vickie explained the time when she was going through a family crisis and working at her profession part-time.

1995-pres.   **Francine Palender** (independent artist), Toledo, OH
BROCHURE PRODUCTION SPECIALIST

- Designed and coordinated production of a four-color brochure that portrayed the artist's talent in three media: paint on canvas, ceramics, and bronze.

1988-95   **Fulbright Paper Industries,** Toledo, OH
CATALOG PRODUCTION COORDINATOR

- Managed full production of a 360-page catalog distributed to more than 5000 retailers and 79 distributors.
- Coordinated deadlines among five departments that sprinted from creative to shipping in less than two months per run.
- Supervised 26 artists and technicians; handled relations with at least 12 vendors.
- Represented the Production Department at management meetings.
- Instructed local college interns in print production techniques and systems.

1987-88   **University of Ohio Press,** Toledo, OH
PRINT PRODUCTION INTERN

- Gained hands-on experience in every aspect of print production, working under the press' most senior printer.
- Frequently assisted in technically demanding assignments for major clients.
- Received "Intern of the Month" award four times.

EDUCATION AND AFFILIATIONS

B.A., Journalism, University of Ohio, Toledo, 1986
Junior year abroad in Paris for work-study program at prominent newspaper

American Printers Association
International Paper and Print Production Institute

Resume written in 1996.

➤ Understate experience when necessary.

Patrick Buckner had 15 years of experience as an auditor. He thought that if he put "15 years as an accounting professional" in his Summary of Qualifications section, he might seem too high-powered since the job announcement asked for five to seven years of experience. As you can see from his resume on the following page, Patrick decided to write "More than seven years as an accounting professional." Patrick's revised statement is true (since 15 years is certainly more than seven years) and makes him look more suitable for the job he is seeking.

Definition
Over and *more than* are two terms that are often confused. On your resume, use "more than" to mean "in excess of." For instance, use "more than 10 years of experience" instead of "over 10 years of experience."

The 2nd commandment comes in handy in Part 2 of this book, when you figure out how far back to go in your work history; what to say about gaps in your employment; whether or not to present your volunteer work; and some other issues you may not have thought of. Until then, I hope this commandment gives you some peace of mind knowing that you really don't have to write a complete autobiography.

The 3rd Commandment: Thou Shalt Not Write About Job Descriptions; Thou Shalt Write About Achievements

If you were an employer, what three questions would you ask a job candidate? Probably something like:

➤ Do you have any experience?

➤ Are you good at what you do?

➤ Do you like this kind of work?

Don't be shy—tell the employer "yes" to all of these questions by writing about *achievements instead of job duties* on your resume. Achievement statements are the most powerful way to say "I'm good at what I do!"

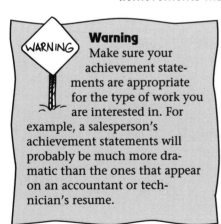

Warning
Make sure your achievement statements are appropriate for the type of work you are interested in. For example, a salesperson's achievement statements will probably be much more dramatic than the ones that appear on an accountant or technician's resume.

The two resumes for Marlene Kruse appear later in this chapter. The first is a job description resume (blah!); the second is an achievement-oriented resume (yes!). See how much more enticing the second one is? Marlene's achievement statements at once say what she has done, that she's good at what she does, and that she believes in and likes her work. She has given the reader three good reasons to call her for an interview.

I'll expand on this commandment in Chapter 9, when you actually write your achievement statements. At this point, I want you to get the concept of using your resume to brag a little (or a lot) about your successes.

PATRICK BUCKNER, CPA
497 St. Anne Blvd.
Walnut Creek, CA 94772
(510) 834-9642

OBJECTIVE

Audit Manager

> Patrick translated his 15 years of experience as "More than seven years" to match the job announcement.

SUMMARY OF QUALIFICATIONS

- More than seven years as an accounting professional with particular strength in conducting audits.
- Skilled at gaining cooperation from internal and external professionals.
- Experienced consultant to executive management regarding sensitive financial issues.

PROFESSIONAL EXPERIENCE

1995-pres.   Operations Auditor
Franklin Pierce Manufacturing, Lafayette, CA

- Realized $28,000 in three months for the company by discovering two major "unnoticed" past due collections.
- Audited expense reports to verify compliance with company and governmental policies.
- Implemented CEO and CFO directed projects to restructure accounting procedures.

1990-1995   Senior Internal Auditor
Danson Union, Walnut Creek, CA

- Conducted quarterly and annual audits for main headquarters and 12 branch offices.
- Guided management through setup of accounting departments in three new business units located in different states.
- Facilitated external audits that showed 100% compliance with professional standards.
- Authored analysis sections of SEC annual 10K and quarterly 10Q corporate reports.
- Designated Sr. Internal Auditor after three months with company as Internal Auditor.

1988-1990   Accountant
Anderson CPA & Associates, San Francisco, CA

- Provided auditing services to corporate clients engaged in international import and export.
- Served as financial consultant to two of the nation's largest banking institutions.
- Prepared federal and state tax forms for a wide range of corporate structures

EDUCATION AND CERTIFICATION

B.S., Accounting, San Jose State University, San Jose, CA
CPA since 1986

> Resume written in 1996.

(A Boring Job Description Resume)

MARLENE KRUSE
Marketing Communications Director

882 Chestnut Street
San Francisco, CA 94212
(415) 686-2056

SUMMARY OF QUALIFICATIONS

- 12 years in marketing with recent experience as Director, Marketing Communications for the largest manufacturer in its classification.
- Creative thinker whose ideas have directly increased profitability.
- Manage multiple projects at once, with strict adherence to time and budget constraints.

PROFESSIONAL EXPERIENCE

1990-pres. BANANA REPUBLIC, San Francisco
Director of Marketing Communications, 1994-present
Director of Public Relations/Licensing Coordinator, 1991-1994
Public Relations Consultant, 1990

- Created sales collateral (including videos) and ran the creative aspects for advertising campaign.
- Developed and managed a national publicity program.
- Authored and designed press kits.
- Developed GWPs (gift with purchase).
- Collaborated with Duke University Medical Center to design a promotion.
- Currently developing a merchandise strategy for a TV program.
- Analyzed competition, oversaw product development, approved prototypes, and managed business relations with licensees.
- Designed merchandise packaging and displays, and negotiated with licensees and retailers to use these visuals.

Don't use boring job descriptions like these! (Yawn!)

1987-1990 GREY ADVERTISING, INC., New York City
Creative Services Director

- Directed the New York office.
- Supervised staff and managed photographic production.
- Set and allocated production budgets.

1983-1987 BANANA REPUBLIC, San Francisco
Media Coordinator

- Developed and implemented advertising campaigns. Managed creative development and execution. Monitored media budget.
- Started company catalog.

EDUCATION

B.A., Information and Communication Studies, minor in Business Administration
California State University, Santa Cruz

Multimedia Program, California State University, San Francisco, currently enrolled

Resume written in 1995.

(A Dynamite Achievement Resume)

MARLENE KRUSE
Marketing Communications Director

882 Chestnut Street
San Francisco, CA 94212
(415) 686-2056

SUMMARY OF QUALIFICATIONS

- 12 years in marketing with recent experience as Director, Marketing Communications for the largest manufacturer in its classification.
- Creative thinker whose ideas have directly increased profitability.
- Manage multiple projects at once, with strict adherence to time and budget constraints.

PROFESSIONAL EXPERIENCE

1990-pres. BANANA REPUBLIC, San Francisco
Director of Marketing Communications, 1994-present
Director of Public Relations/Licensing Coordinator, 1991-1994
Public Relations Consultant, 1990

- Created sales collateral (including videos) and ran the creative for national advertising campaign that established Banana Republic as the manufacturer of quality products.
- Developed and managed a national publicity program that increased retail sales more than 5% and dramatically enhanced brand recognition.
- Authored and designed the first press kit that clearly defined the company's image and product range.
- Enhanced product value and increased sales by developing GWPs (gift with purchase).
- To position company as an advocate for women's health, collaborated with Duke University Medical Center to design a promotion that shared proceeds.
- Currently developing a merchandise strategy for an hour-long QVC-TV program to air Christmas 1995.
- Analyzed competition, oversaw product development, approved prototypes, and managed business relations with national and international licensees.
- Designed merchandise packaging and displays, and successfully negotiated with licensees and retailers to utilize these visuals to maintain consistent image.

(Use powerful achievements like these!)

1987-1990 GREY ADVERTISING, INC., New York City
Creative Services Director

- Directed the New York office for this national full-service advertising company.
- Supervised staff and managed high-volume photographic production.
- Set and allocated over 200 production budgets that ranged from $30K to $150K each.

1983-1987 BANANA REPUBLIC, San Francisco
Media Coordinator

- Developed and implemented advertising campaigns. Managed all phases of creative development and execution. Monitored media budget.
- Started company catalog that achieved circulation of over .5 million in two years.

EDUCATION

B.A., Information and Communication Studies, minor in Business Administration
California State University, Santa Cruz
Multimedia Program, California State University, San Francisco, currently enrolled

(Resume written in 1995.)

17

The 4th Commandment: Thou Shalt Not Write About Stuff You Don't Want to Do Again

When you think about it, writing your resume is like writing your next job description, since everything you put in your resume suggests what you're eager to do in your new job. *Never write about duties that you don't want to do again,* no matter how good you are at them!

Here's an example. When George was after an accounting position at a CPA firm, he specifically did *not* want to supervise any staff. Even though in his previous job he had been in charge of a department and had been commended for his ability to build team spirit under adverse conditions, he was determined not to repeat that situation in his next job. In his resume, he spoke about his many accounting achievements, but never once mentioned that he had managed anyone. Consequently, he attracted an accounting job he loves with no supervisory responsibilities.

I'll remind you about this commandment as you go through the steps in Part 2. For now, just keep in mind that *you* are in the seat of power. You get to create your future by choosing what to put in and leave out of your resume!

The 5th Commandment: Thou Shalt Not Lie

I guess I'm beginning to sound like your mother, aren't I? I've got to say it anyway: Never tell a lie on your resume.

Just in case you're wondering what kinds of lies I'm talking about, here are some that frequently appear on resumes and are apt to get caught by employers:

➤ Stating experience at a particular place of employment where you've never worked

➤ Misrepresenting the level of responsibility you've held (not using an accurate job title)

➤ Listing a school that you didn't attend

➤ Claiming to have a degree that you didn't obtain

➤ Taking credit for someone else's achievement

➤ Overstating skill levels in a technical field

Lying on your resume can cause more damage to your career than you may realize. Here are three good reasons to create a resume that contains only the truth:

➤ *A lie on your resume can undermine your self-confidence during a job interview.* If you're anything like me, just knowing that the interviewer might ask a question about your fib probably makes you nervous. And to make matters worse, if your anxiety is noticed, it will most likely make a bad impression on your potential employer.

➤ *Once you are hired, a falsehood on your resume can be grounds for termination.* If your resume is examined as part of your promotion review, you could lose your job if someone finds a lie. Or, if your employer wants an excuse to fire you, he could investigate details on your resume with the hope of finding a lie.

➤ *A lie on your resume may indicate that you don't believe you are qualified for the job.* Maybe you need to rethink your job objective, or perhaps you need counseling to build your self-esteem.

The Least You Need to Know

➤ Make sure to write about your future, not about your past.

➤ You don't have to "tell all" in your resume. Stick to what's relevant and marketable.

➤ Write about your achievements!

➤ Don't write about anything you don't want to do again.

➤ Be creative but honest in your resume.

Part 2
Navigating Your Way

Picture Christopher Columbus standing at the bow of his ship looking out at the horizon, about to embark upon his famous voyage of 1492. Not knowing how vast the Atlantic Ocean was or exactly what he was getting into, my guess is he had a major anxiety attack—a normal response to a seemingly impossible task. To keep his sanity, he must have taken this monumental trip one knot at a time until he finally spotted land some 34 days after setting sail.

I'm going to assume that, like Columbus, you're feeling a little overwhelmed as you set out to "put your life on paper." Most job seekers do. To help you keep your stress level down, I've broken the process into manageable pieces, which I talk about in this part of the book.

Turn the page and read about the first of nine steps for writing your resume. Set aside about three hours (that's an average length of time to complete a resume if all goes smoothly). Follow each step, and, like Columbus, you'll get to your destination. If you get stuck on one step, don't worry about it. Just go on to the next and come back to the hard one later. (Hopefully it won't take you 34 days!)

Chapter 3

Step One—You Gotta Have a Strategy

In This Chapter

➤ Communicate more effectively by saying less

➤ Never use paragraphs in your resume format

➤ Get your message across with a good resume layout

There's no question—good marketing strategy is the key to success for almost every product or service. Why else would corporations spend big bucks on research to determine what marketing techniques draw the greatest response? (Ah yes, those memorable direct mail pieces!) They're constantly testing designs, words, and distribution to be sure every advertising dollar is spent wisely. A lot of thought is put into each promotion before it's produced.

Likewise, you need to take a good look at your situation and figure out the best strategy for marketing yourself through your resume. In this chapter, you'll discover how to rope in your potential employer before he or she reads even one word of your resume.

Less Is More

Ah, the oxymoron that works so well in marketing: Less is more. Let's consider why it has withstood the test of time.

When it comes to things we all value, time sits near the top of the list, along with wealth and health. We say things like, "Time is money" and "It's not worth my time." Since time is at a premium in today's hectic world, it stands to reason that a promotional piece that takes less time to read is more likely to get read than a lengthy one. Therefore, less is more—more effective at grabbing the reader's attention.

Here's another advantage to the "less is more" theory: By distilling all of your skills and experience into a minimum of words on a single sheet of paper, you automatically put down only the very best stuff. So less is more in the sense that even though you provide less information, it's all high-quality information—making the resume more impressive.

In today's job market, your resume has only about *eight seconds* to catch an employer's attention. That's right! In eight seconds an employer scans your resume and decides whether he or she will invest more time to consider you as a job candidate. The secret to passing the eight-second test is to make your resume look quick and inviting to read. That's why I recommend having a one-page resume if possible. Having a one-pager says "I'm organized and I'm not a motor-mouth."

But for those who have a really beefy career history or lengthy list of "must read" accomplishments, one page just isn't enough. If you're one of those people, go for it—just don't exceed two pages unless you're sure the reader is expecting more. (For instance, if you're applying for an academic or scientific position, you might have a seven- or eight-pager.)

> **YOU'RE HIRED.** **Tip**
> If your resume is just a little more than a page, do your best to get it down to one page, using your editing and computer graphics skills. Then ask yourself, "Does it look easy to read?" If the print is too small or dense, you're better off with a two-page resume that's inviting to read.

> **YOU'RE HIRED.** **Tip**
> For a two-page resume, be sure to put "continued" at the bottom of page 1, and your name and "page 2" at the top of page 2. It's better not to staple the pages together, since you want to encourage the reader to hold the pages side-by-side for easy referencing.

No Paragraphs!

One of the biggest obstacles to getting a resume read by a busy manager is dense paragraphs. Many resumes have long paragraphs, undoubtedly filled with juicy information. The problem is, nobody wants to read a long paragraph when they're in a hurry. A paragraph demands too much time to read.

> **Tip**
>
> Think of your resume as a valuable piece of real estate in Manhattan where every increment of space should be capitalized. Just as land is used for buildings, signs, and pathways, use the space on your resume for headings, phrases, and lists. And just as landscaping and parks are appreciated in congested urban areas, white space gives relief to the resume reader's eye.

So you'll do the reader (and yourself) a favor by using bullet points to break your material into bite-sized pieces. A *bullet point* is a graphic symbol (•) used to highlight a statement. A bullet statement says, "Here's an independent thought that's quick and easy to read," whereas a paragraph implies that one has to read the whole thing to get the full meaning.

For the best effect, start each accomplishment statement on a new line so that all the bullet points line up on the left, like this:

- Made classroom presentations to students K-8, demonstrating the importance of art to man's physical and mental survival.

- Tutored high school students of Project Read, integrating reading and writing to offer new perspectives and respect for their own life stories.

- Conducted cultural field trips to sites including businesses, performing arts centers, and museums.

In case you're not convinced that bullet statements are a good idea, take a look at JoAnna's resume on the next two pages. You'll see the same resume in two graphic layouts: the first uses bullet points to break up the blocks of print; the second uses paragraphs. Which do you think looks quicker to read?

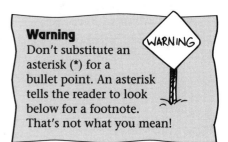

Warning
Don't substitute an asterisk (*) for a bullet point. An asterisk tells the reader to look below for a footnote. That's not what you mean!

JoAnna West
47 Lindwood Street • Daly City, CA 94115 • (415) 883-7291

JOB OBJECTIVE
Catalog and Brochure Production Specialist

SUMMARY OF QUALIFICATIONS

- 14 years managing production of collectors' catalogs that built annual sales to $10 million.
- "An inspired catalog. I would expect no less from you." — Bernard Osher, Chairman, Butterfield & Butterfield.
- Skilled contract negotiator.
- Published writer.

Bullet points make JoAnna's achievements stand out.

PROFESSIONAL EXPERIENCE

Present   **Catalog Production Contractor,** San Francisco, CA

- Currently producing a four-color catalog of fine signature pieces owned by a private jewelry collector.

1980-1993   **Director of Fine Jewelry Department/Catalog Production**
BUTTERFIELD & BUTTERFIELD, San Francisco, CA

Managed the consignment, marketing, and sales of the $10 million jewelry department of this major auction house selling fine arts, furniture, and decorative art.

- Designed and produced 68, 80-page, four-color and black & white catalogs that raised the standard of catalog production throughout the company.
  - Achieved a 100% record of deadline and budget compliance by creating and implementing a standard format for streamlined catalog production.
  - Led production team of graphics director, photographers, catalogers, and marketing director.
  - Wrote, edited, and proofread catalogs, press releases, and brochures.
- Authored article and provided photographs published in *Antiques & Fine Art* magazine. Wrote in-depth articles for company newsletter with circulation of 60,000.
- Increased profitability 35% through tough negotiations with suppliers, contractors, and legal counsel.
- Lectured to symposium audiences of up to 500 at Stanford University and University of San Francisco.
- Dramatically increased pool of international dealers through private showings in New York, Los Angeles, and Houston. Represented company in Hong Kong and Beijing.

Incorporating subbullets makes this text even more inviting to read.

1974-1980   **Montessori Teacher**
ST. BRIGID'S SCHOOL, San Francisco, CA

- Developed essential organizational and diplomacy skills that have proven valuable throughout my career.

EDUCATION

B.A., English, Queens College, Flushing, NY
Montessori Diploma, Montessori Education Center, Palo Alto, CA
Graduate Gemologist, Gemological Institute of America, Santa Monica, CA

— Portfolio available —

JoAnna West

47 Lindwood Street • Daly City, CA 94115 • (415) 883-7291

JOB OBJECTIVE

Catalog and Brochure Production Specialist

SUMMARY OF QUALIFICATIONS

(This paragraph looks like it would take too long to read.)

14 years managing production of collectors' catalogs that built annual sales to $10 million. "An inspired catalog. I would expect no less from you." — Bernard Osher, Chairman, Butterfield & Butterfield. Skilled contract negotiator. Published writer.

PROFESSIONAL EXPERIENCE

Present   **Catalog Production Contractor,** San Francisco, CA

Currently producing a four-color catalog of fine signature pieces owned by a private jewelry collector.

1980-1993   **Director of Fine Jewelry Department/Catalog Production**
BUTTERFIELD & BUTTERFIELD, San Francisco, CA

(Notice how dense and uninteresting this paragraph looks.)

Managed the consignment, marketing, and sales of the $10 million jewelry department of this major auction house selling fine arts, furniture, and decorative art. Designed and produced 68, 80-page, four-color and black & white catalogs that raised the standard of catalog production throughout the company. Achieved a 100% record of deadline and budget compliance by creating and implementing a standard format for streamlined catalog production. Led production team of graphics director, photographers, catalogers, and marketing director. Wrote, edited, and proofread catalogs, press releases, and brochures. Authored article and provided photographs published in *Antiques & Fine Art* magazine. Wrote in-depth articles for company newsletter with circulation of 60,000. Increased profitability 35% through tough negotiations with suppliers, contractors, and legal counsel. Lectured to symposium audiences of up to 500 at Stanford University and University of San Francisco. Dramatically increased pool of international dealers through private showings in New York, Los Angeles, and Houston. Represented company in Hong Kong and Beijing.

1974-1980   **Montessori Teacher**
ST. BRIGID'S SCHOOL, San Francisco, CA

Developed essential organizational and diplomacy skills that have proven valuable throughout my career.

EDUCATION

B.A., English, Queens College, Flushing, NY
Montessori Diploma, Montessori Education Center, Palo Alto, CA
Graduate Gemologist, Gemological Institute of America, Santa Monica, CA

— Portfolio available —

(Resume written in 1994.)

Format, Format, Format

In real estate, the adage is "location, location, location." Well, in resume writing it's "format, format, format." If you use the right format, the reader can spot you as a top-notch candidate in less than eight seconds.

There are two basic resume formats: *chronological* and *functional*. Check out the following guidelines, templates, and samples for these two types of resumes. Once you've decided which format you should use, move on to Chapter 4.

Chronological Resume

> **Warning**
> There is a mistaken impression among job seekers today that the chronological format is old-fashioned and should not be used. Don't fall for this faulty thinking! The chronological format is still the most widely accepted type of resume and should be used if you fit the criteria.

The chronological format is the most traditional resume. It highlights your dates and places of employment and your job titles by using them as headings for listing your achievements.

Use the chronological format if:

➤ You are staying in the same field.

➤ Your overall work history shows growth in the direction of your job objective.

➤ Your most recent (or current) position is one you are proud of.

➤ You have no major gaps in your work history.

> **Warning**
>
> The following chronological and functional templates are not boilerplates! (Boy, do I wish writing a resume could be that simple!) The bullet point statements in these templates are ideas that I might suggest if I were sitting next to you as you create your resume. Since not all of them will apply to your situation, use only the ones that give you the opportunity to support your job objective. If these prodders aren't enough, check out the brainstorming exercises in Chapters 6 and 9.

On the next page, you'll find a template for the chronological format, followed by six chronological resumes by real job seekers. On each resume I've noted why the applicant chose to use the chronological resume. Spend some time perusing the template and the examples to get a feel for the chronological format, then we'll examine the functional resume.

(Chronological Template)
Name
Street • City, State Zip • phone

JOB OBJECTIVE
> The job you want next

SUMMARY OF QUALIFICATIONS
> - How much experience you have in the field of your objective, in a related field, or using the skills required for your new position.
> - An overall career accomplishment that shows you'd be good at this job objective.
> - What someone would say about you as a recommendation.

PROFESSIONAL EXPERIENCE

19xx-pres. **Company Name,** City, State
> JOB TITLE
> - An accomplishment you are proud of that shows you're good at this profession.
> - A problem you solved and the results.
> - A time when you positively affected the organization, the bottom line, your boss, your co-workers, your clients.
> - Awards, commendations, publications, etc. you achieved that relate to your job objective.

19xx-xx **Company Name,** City, State
> JOB TITLE
> - A project you are proud of that supports your job objective.
> - Another accomplishment that shows you're good at this line of work.
> - Quantifiable results that point out your skill.

19xx-xx **Company Name,** City, State
> JOB TITLE
> - An accomplishment you are proud of that shows you will be valued by your next employer.
> - An occasion when someone "sat up and took notice" because of your skill.

EDUCATION
> Degree, Major (if relevant), 19xx (optional)
> University, City, State

Carolyn J. Kalmon

1208 Arlington Boulevard • San Leandro, CA 94511 • (510) 399-7805

JOB OBJECTIVE: Event Planner

Carolyn is the perfect candidate for a chronological resume since her career path is leading right toward her job objective: event planning.

SUMMARY OF QUALIFICATIONS

- 14 years' experience planning business and social events including conferences, celebrations, parties, dinners, and luncheons.
- Skilled at leading and working within a team to produce events that promote the organization's image, mission, and objective.

PROFESSIONAL EXPERIENCE

1992-present Logistics Coordinator/Administrative Assistant to Managing General Partner
ACCEL PARTNERS, San Francisco, CA

- Coordinated the company's 10th Anniversary Celebration at the de Young Museum for 185 top investors. This black tie event included dinner and dancing to Mike Carney's Band.
- Planned and produced an executive business retreat at Thomas Fogarty Winery.
- Orchestrated a 100-person private party in New York City. Arranged invitations, entertainment, accommodations, and transportation.
- Setup numerous live national and international video-conferences requiring special equipment, rooms, meals, and information packets.
- Handled multiple projects simultaneously using crisis management skills and resourcefulness to maintain smooth flow in a fast-paced office.

1989-1992 Administrative Assistant to President & CEO and to Vice President, Kingsford Products
THE CLOROX COMPANY, Oakland, CA

- Served on the United Way Campaign event planning committee that promoted and produced the 1500-person kickoff rally and closing party with celebrity speakers, entertainment, food, and contests.
- Organized 8 Board and 50 officers luncheons per year, working with caterer to plan menus and room layouts.
- Served as liaison to Board members, stockholders, staff, and general public on behalf of President & CEO.

1981-1988 Administrative Assistant to President & CEO and to Executive Vice President
SANTA FE PACIFIC REALTY CORPORATION, San Francisco, CA

- Planned annual Christmas parties at major San Francisco hotels for 250 employees and guests. Collaborated with hotel caterers on all aspects.
- Commended for producing the company's first outdoor employee events on very limited budgets, to boost morale during merger.
- Managed active schedule and travel arrangements for President & CEO who served on several national and international Boards.

1973-1981 Tour Escort and Sales Representative
UNRAVEL TRAVEL, San Francisco, CA

- Guided international groups such as:
  Stanford Alumni Group to the Yucatan Peninsula
  American Bar Association to San Francisco and Disneyland

EDUCATION

B.S., Education, Business, Wittenberg University, Springfield, OH
Independent Study: Catering, University of California Extension, San Francisco
Cooking, Weezie Mott Cooking School, Alameda

Resume written in 1995.

June C. Deltano

4700 Filmore Street • San Francisco, California 94223 • (415) 993-8812

JOB OBJECTIVE

Member of the Visual Merchandising Team

SUMMARY OF QUALIFICATIONS

- Experienced in merchandising for two of the nation's most successful retailers, as a sales associate for over 10 years.

- "Your sense of design is so good, you should be doing my job." — Visual Merchandiser for Pottery Barn nationwide.

- Knowledge of: Furniture   Clothing
                 Decorative pieces   Fashion accessories
                 Tabletop products   Gift items

RELEVANT PROFESSIONAL EXPERIENCE

The chronological resume works well for June since her job titles support her lateral career move into merchandising.

1992 to 1994   POTTERY BARN, San Francisco   Sales Associate

- Executed special holiday window and floor displays, using plan-a-grams and personal creativity.

- Maintained displays and floor stock, frequently changing presentations to accommodate inventory and seasonal trends.

- Demonstrated product enthusiasm that generated extremely high sales and numerous customer commendations. Achieved two district customer service awards.

- Monitored inventory and delivery systems to ensure timely in-store placement of products.

Notice how the chronological resume highlights June's stable employment history.

1979 to 1991   MERVYN'S, Sacramento   Sales Associate

- Merchandised clothing and accessories, following schematics and block plans for a department that generated 25% of store's sales.

- Tracked sales trends and collaborated with department manager to determine effectiveness of POPs and displays.

- Provided excellent service to a wide range of customers. Won several "Employee of the Month" awards.

- Conducted classroom and on-the-job training for new employees.

EDUCATION

Interior Design Program, University of California, Berkeley Extension

Resume written in 1994.

31

John Anderson, C.P.A.

3320 Chicago Avenue • Oakland, CA 94612 • (510) 440-2201

JOB OBJECTIVE

Audit Manager

> Since John wanted to make a step up the corporate ladder into management within his profession, the chronological resume is best for him.

SUMMARY OF QUALIFICATIONS

- More than seven years as an internal and external auditor with a strong financial and operational background in industries including manufacturing.
- Confident professional who facilitates cooperation and communication among parties.
- Knowledge of data processing and spreadsheet applications.
- Personal activity in futures and options trading.

PROFESSIONAL EXPERIENCE

1994
Operations Auditor
PMI MORTGAGE INSURANCE CO., San Francisco, CA

- Saved company $5,000 - $10,000 a month by analyzing project needs and recommending improved utilization of contractual and full-time staff.
- Audited management and employee expense reports to verify compliance with company policies and procedures.
- Originally contracted to perform field operation audits that led to CEO and CFO directed projects.

1989-1993
Senior Internal Auditor
AMERICAN BUILDING MAINTENANCE INDUSTRIES, San Francisco, CA

- Attained functional level of an audit manager, reporting to the Director of Internal Audit/Corporate Controller.
- Conducted extensive due diligence and auditing of more than 10 prospective company and customer contract acquisitions (up to $25 million).
- Made numerous productive recommendations to senior management, based on operational benefits and numerical findings.
- Coordinated participation of external auditors from KPMG Peat Marwick to complete timely audits according to professional standards.
- Co-wrote the management discussion and analysis sections of the SEC annual 10K and quarterly 10Q corporate reports.

1986-1989
Senior Accountant
ERNST & WHINNEY (now Ernst & Young), San Francisco, CA

- As CPA, provided auditing and financial consulting services for corporate clients including: U.S. Steel/Pohang Steel of Korea (joint venture)
  Sierra Pacific Industries (lumbering)
  Bank of America
  Transamerica Corporation

EDUCATION

B.S., Business Administration, Option in Accounting, *Magna Cum Laude*, 1986
Recipient of Chevron Accounting Scholarship Award
California State University, Hayward

> Resume written in 1994.

TRACY ANNE MILLER
15 Colusa Street • Trainwood, 2088 • N.S.W., Australia • (02) 531-7739

OBJECTIVE

Executive management position in Finance and Accounting for an Australian firm

SUMMARY OF QUALIFICATIONS

Tracy used a chronological resume because she is staying in finance and is applying to a conservative employer.

- Ten years as an accounting and audit professional with more than seven years in management.
- Extensive experience in international accounting and finance.
- Conversant in Australian and U.S. accounting and reporting requirements.
- Successful at designing, implementing, and completing projects to the satisfaction of senior management in a goal-oriented and deadline-driven profession.

PROFESSIONAL EXPERIENCE

1991-1994   G.T. CAPITAL MANAGEMENT, INC., San Francisco, California
Financial Controller
A high-growth company, which in the last three years has expanded from U.S. $5 billion to over U.S. $12 billion in retail, closed-end, and institutional funds under management.

- Oversaw all accounting and reporting for five subsidiaries: an investment management company, a transfer agency, a broker dealer, an insurance company, and a holding company.
- Significantly increased efficiency of accounting and reporting by computerizing manual processes and instituting accounting controls.
- Achieved high integrity in financial reporting with a three-day deadline for submission of final consolidated reporting packages to the U.K. parent company.
- Maintained a perfect record of zero proposed audit adjustments through three annual audits. Served as liaison to external auditors.
- Trained and directly supervised six accounting professionals and indirectly oversaw four additional staff.
- Designed and implemented accounting procedures for new products such as Contingent Deferred Sales Charges and Variable Annuity Funds.
- Supervised preparation of quarterly and annual regulatory reports including:
  - Focus reports for the National Association of Securities Dealers and The Securities and Exchange Commission.
  - Investment Management Regulatory Organisation reports for the British regulatory authorities.
- Controlled and supervised the department's development of computer systems, as the general ledger systems administrator.

1989-1990   SECURITY PACIFIC AUSTRALIA LTD., Sydney, Australia
Manager, Financial Markets Group Accounting
One of the largest merchant banks in Australia, which began closing operations in 1990.

- Reviewed monthly accounts and reconciliations for Corporate, Property, Leasing, and Securitisation divisions and Off-shore subsidiaries.
- Managed U.S. and Australian regulatory reporting to the U.S. Securities and Exchange Commission and the Reserve Bank of Australia.
- Prepared the annual financial statements and assisted in preparing tax returns for the Australian parent company, the main operating company, and seven subsidiaries.

— Continued —

Tracy Anne Miller
Page 2

1983-1989   PEAT MARWICK HUNGERFORDS AUSTRALIA LTD., Sydney, Australia, 1988-1989
Supervising Senior
PEAT MARWICK MAIN & COMPANY, San Francisco, California, 1983-1988
Audit Manager (last position)
A professional audit firm with locations worldwide.

- Promoted from Audit Assistant to Audit Manager in four years time.
- Managed multi-audit engagements for publicly and privately owned companies including financial services, oil and gas, real estate, and government agencies.
- Prepared financial statements, incorporating the requirements of U.S. Generally Accepted Accounting Principles and Australian Accounting Standards.
- Delivered presentations to audit staff as a trainer in the firm's national and local training programs. Topics included: technical accounting, auditing, and management training.
- Interviewed and assessed potential new-hires. Conducted annual performance evaluations for professional staff.

EDUCATION AND AFFILIATIONS

American Institute of Certified Public Accountants, Member since 1985

California State Board of Accountancy, Member since 1985

University of California at Santa Barbara, Santa Barbara, California
Bachelor of Science in Economics, 1983

Australian Securities Institute, Sydney, Australia
Money Market and Fixed Investment Securities and Financial Futures, 1990

Proficient in Lotus for Windows, Excel for Windows, and Sunsystems General Ledger Accounting packages

— Currently hold Permanent Resident Visa for Australia —

Resume written in 1994.

Terry Hummel

44 Divisadero Street • San Francisco, CA 94116 • (415) 331-8843

JOB OBJECTIVE: Program Coordinator in an educational environment

SUMMARY OF QUALIFICATIONS

- Eight years experience coordinating projects in academic environments.
- Excellent at generating new ideas and improving upon existing systems to further the administration of an organization.
- Success at motivating staff through clear communication and outstanding organizational skills.

RELEVANT EXPERIENCE

Although most of Terry's experience was unpaid, a chronological resume works for her since her unpaid "titles" support her job objective.

1994-pres. **The Tomlin School,** San Francisco, CA
Project Coordinator (volunteer)

- Currently creating a promotional multimedia presentation that reflects the high standard of this private elementary-middle school with a socioeconomically diverse student body.
- Promoted school allegiance and parent participation by:
  - Actively networking among parents, faculty, and students.
  - Organizing at least seven special events per year.
  - Re-evaluating current goals, strategies, and financial management to support extra-curricular activities.
- Assisted the Endowment Fund and Annual Fund Committees by serving as class representative.

1986-1993 **St. Luke's School,** Los Angeles, CA
Project Coordinator (volunteer)

- Played key role in restructuring volunteer activities. Collaborated with administration to prioritize need for volunteers, re-evaluate programs, and make improvements to optimize volunteer participation in light of today's family structure.
- Successfully initiated enhancements to academic programs by surveying needs and facilitating discussion between administration and parents.
- Started Class Art Projects which, for the first time, enabled students to gain recognition for their creativity while generating 10% of annual funds raised.
- As Head Parent Coordinator, directly supervised 8 parents and indirectly managed 50 volunteers, who organized educational, extracurricular, and fundraising activities.
- Drastically improved the school's promotional presentations by producing a creative slide show and contributing quality photographs for brochures and annual reports.

1979-1986 **Independent Property Reconstruction Coordinator,** Huntfield County, NV

- Supervised the reconstruction/remodeling of several residential properties that were resold at sizable profits.

1978 **EduFilmsAssociates,** Boston, MA
Research Associate

- Conducted research of subject matter to be used for educational films distributed to high schools nationwide.
- Compiled photographs for *Search for Solutions*, a hardback book to accompany films.

EDUCATION

B.A., Major: Economics, Minor: Urban Studies, 1976, University of Virginia, Charlotte, VA

Resume written in 1994.

Kelly A. Marlow

312 Mountain Street
Mill Valley, CA 94177
(415) 663-9742

JOB OBJECTIVE

Project Development Coordinator

HIGHLIGHTS OF QUALIFICATIONS

- Over two years experience marketing services for one of the Bay Area's most respected nonprofit career development centers.
- Skilled at resolving problems. Comfortable negotiating and enforcing policies.
- Enjoy building partnerships internal and external to the organization to promote a socially conscious mission.

PROFESSIONAL EXPERIENCE

1993-present **Alumnae Resources (AR)**, San Francisco, CA
CLIENT SERVICES ASSOCIATE

Kelly's chronological resume makes a good first impression since her current employer is well respected in her field.

- As a key member of the Client Services team, build and foster relations with job seekers and employers by educating them about career development in the non-profit and for-profit sectors.
- Market services by phone and in person, contributing to the growth of AR which now exceeds 80,000 client visits per year.
- Assess career development needs of clients and assist them in developing action plans.
- Manage member registration as well as scheduling and billing for 200+ workshops and 1000+ counseling sessions per quarter.
- Contribute to the development of administrative policies and public relations strategies.
- Enhanced AR's image as a supportive environment by recommending the increase of free services to members.
- Train and supervise volunteers.

1991-1992 **Palo Alto Weekly Newspaper**, Palo Alto, CA
ADVERTISING REPRESENTATIVE

- Developed a loyal client base of advertisers by:
  - Negotiating long- and short-term contracts.
  - Generating creative and effective ads.
  - Meeting strict deadlines.
  - Using interpersonal skills with a wide variety of clients.

VOLUNTEER SERVICE

Volunteer Coordinator, I Love A Clean San Diego County, Inc., San Diego, CA
Program Coordinator, Headstart Program, San Diego, CA
Patient Support Volunteer, Stanford Children's Hospital, Stanford, CA
Crisis Line Counselor, Boulder County Safehouse, Boulder, CO

EDUCATION

B.A., Business Administration, 1990
University of San Diego, San Diego, CA
Internship: Market Research Intern, Motivational Systems, Inc., National City, CA

Resume written in 1995.

Functional Resume

The functional format presents your accomplishments under skill headings, giving you the freedom to prioritize your accomplishments by impact rather than by chronology. In this format, your work history is listed very concisely in a section separate from your achievements.

Use the functional format if:

➤ You are changing careers.

➤ You are reentering the job market.

➤ You need to emphasize skills or experience from an early part of your work history.

➤ Your volunteer experience is relevant and needs to be highlighted.

➤ Your most recent position is not impressive.

Warning

A lot of job seekers think the functional format is the "resume of the 90s." Not so! The chronological resume is still the preferred version by most employers. However, if the chronological format doesn't work for your situation, the functional resume can be a very effective alternative.

If you're a career changer with a work history that makes the reader want to pigeonhole you into your previous line of work, use the functional format. The functional resume allows you to define yourself according to your skills instead of your former job titles.

Want to see what the functional resume looks like? The template for the functional format is on the next page, followed by six functional resumes from actual job seekers. On each resume, I've noted why the applicant decided on the functional format. After looking at the template and the examples, you'll understand the difference between the chronological and functional formats. Then you'll be ready to choose which one is right for you.

(Functional Template)

N a m e

Street • City, State Zip • phone

JOB OBJECTIVE

The job you want next

SUMMARY OF QUALIFICATIONS

- How much experience you have in the field of your objective, in a related field, or using the skills required for your new position.
- An overall career accomplishment that shows you'd be good at this job objective.
- What someone would say about you as a recommendation.

RELEVANT EXPERIENCE

MAJOR SKILL

- An accomplishment you are proud of that shows you're good at this skill.
- A problem you solved using this skill, and the results.
- A time when you used your skill to positively affectcd the organization, the bottom line, your boss, your clients.
- Awards, commendations, publications, etc. you achieved that relate to your job objective.

MAJOR SKILL

- A project you are proud of that supports your job objective.
- Another accomplishment that shows you're good at this line of work.
- Quantifiable results that point out your skill.
- An occasion when someone "sat up and took notice" because of your skill.

WORK HISTORY

19xx-present	Job Title	COMPANY NAME and city
19xx-xx	Job Title	COMPANY NAME and city
19xx-xx	Job Title	COMPANY NAME and city
19xx-xx	Job Title	COMPANY NAME and city

EDUCATION

Degree, Major (if relevant), 19xx (optional)
University, City, State

Trudy Philipp

522 Windsor Drive • San Anselmo, CA 95111 • (415) 328-7751

JOB OBJECTIVE

A position in video production with focus on editing, research, and writing.

SUMMARY OF QUALIFICATIONS

- 10 years as an editor in documentary film and television, including five years with ABC's 20/20.
- Ability to create interesting visuals to demonstrate concepts.
- Experienced researcher and interviewer for production projects.
- Continuing professional development in video and multimedia technology.

PROFESSIONAL EXPERIENCE

EDITING

- As Editor for 20/20, worked with producers and writers to meet deadlines for weekly shows. Two Emmy Award-winning segments: "Ray Charles" and "Mel Torme."
- Edited PBS documentaries on controversial topics such as the accident at Three-Mile Island and the arms race.
- Completed editing projects for corporate clients including Nabisco, IBM, and Coca-Cola.

RESEARCH AND WRITING

- For several documentary assignments, located archival footage, conducted historical research, interviewed subjects, and wrote evaluations.
- As Coordinating Editor for "20/20 Musical Album," an hour-long special, retrieved 20-30 hours of footage and coordinated distribution to editing teams.
- Performed library research, compiled relevant information, and wrote summaries as a paralegal in a corporate law firm.

WORK HISTORY

The functional resume works well for Trudy since she has a complicated work history.

1987-present	Paralegal	Thelen, Marrin, Johnson & Bridges, San Jose/San Francisco
1985-1987	Student	San Jose State University, San Jose
1985	Editor	HBO, Consumer Reports Documentary, New York City
1980-1984	Editor	ABC, 20/20, New York City
1979-1980	Asst. Editor	Bill Moyers' Journal and CBS Reports, New York City
1979-1980	Sound Editor	ABC Close-Up, New York City
1978-1979	Editor	WDR, German Television, Newsfilm, New York City
1977-1978	Editor	WGBH Documentary, New York City
1976-1977	Sound Editor	Frameworks (TV commercials), New York City

EDUCATION

B.F.A., New York University, Institute of Film and Television, New York City

Continuing Professional Development:
Non-Linear Editing/AVID, Bay Area Video Coalition, San Francisco
Video Editing and Interactive Multimedia, Film Arts Foundation, San Francisco

Resume written in 1994.

JULIE W. SCHWARTZ
644 Farmingdale Road   •   Kentfield, CA 94573   •   (415) 738-3312

OBJECTIVE: Position as a SENIOR MANAGER in a credit union with responsibilities in branch administration and lending.

HIGHLIGHTS OF QUALIFICATIONS

- 15 years experience in financial environments, including mortgage and consumer lending.
- Successfully turned around one credit union operation and two bank branches.
- Continuously achieved designated profitability and market share growth goals.
- "A strong community leader and team member" — Former Mayor of Santa Rosa.

Notice how Julie uses a quote from a local politician to enhance her image.

PROFESSIONAL ACHIEVEMENTS

MANAGEMENT
Sonya Bank
- Managed a new bank in Walnut Creek, turning a deficit of $113,000 to a profit of $650,000 and increasing loan base by $7.5M and deposits by $6.1M.
- Administered all aspects of daily credit union operations.
- Projected budgets for staffing, loan demands, and deposit growth.
- Developed a pipe line reporting system to keep senior management abreast of achievements.
- Motivated staff to extend their best effort in meeting customers' expectations.

LENDING
Federal Credit Union
- Managed loan portfolios of up to $70M.
- Hired, trained, and supervised staff of up to 30 in credit analysis, presentations, lending regulations, and product development and marketing.
- Utilized lending expertise in real estate (secondary market sales/servicing), consumer lending, and VISA credit and debit cards to achieve profitability and market share growth.

WORK HISTORY

1992-Present	**Branch Manager**	Federal Credit Union, Santa Rosa, CA
1989-91	**Vice President/Manager**	Sonya Bank, Orinda, CA
1986-89	**Business Development Lender**	Bank of the West, Orinda, CA
1984-85	**Business Development Lender**	First National Bank, Lafayette, CA
1981-84	**Commercial Loan Officer**	United Bank, San Francisco, CA
1979-81	**Commercial Loan Officer**	Glendale Federal Savings, Merced, CA

SPECIALIZED TRAINING AND EDUCATION

Certificates:	Sonya Bank: • Management Training Program • Consumer Lending • Credit Card Management Training
AIB Training:	• Beginning & Advanced Financial Statement Analysis • Tax Return Analysis • Business Development
Seminars:	• Negotiating Skills • Communication • Bank Management • Quality Control • Human Relations
B.A./A.B.	University of Vermont, Burlington, VT - 1978

Since Julie has had rather short-term jobs, the functional resume works best for her.

Resume written in 1994.

ALIXIA FELDMAN
644 Broadway, Skokie, IL 60721
(847) 934-6273

OBJECTIVE

Executive Director of a nonprofit organization

> Alixia used a functional format because she wanted to be defined by her skills. A chronological resume would have pigeon-holed her into her former job titles.

HIGHLIGHTS

- Seven years' management experience emphasizing a collaborative yet decisive style.
- Adept at building productive relationships to further the organization's goals.
- Persuasive skills, both written and verbal.
- Expertise in project management.
- Thrive under pressure, relying on a strong sense of organization and enjoyment of hard work.

PROFESSIONAL EXPERIENCE
As Partner and Associate at Sanders, Leroy, and Jones

MANAGEMENT
- Achieved a revenue growth from $500K to $1M per year within my area of management, while keeping overhead low.
- Planned and adhered to a budget of up to $500K.
- Supervised a staff of 17, involving training, work flow, quality control, conflict resolution, and review processes.
- Directed the planning, acquisition, installation, and maintenance of a 50-work station computer system.

SOLICITATION/MOTIVATION
- Built a large loyal client base through personal attention, quality service, and consistent follow through.
- Assisted clients in identifying their interests, and motivated them to act accordingly.
- Wrote persuasive letters and documents, frequently influencing decision makers.
- Motivated personnel by involving them in decision making and goal sharing, resulting in dramatically increased productivity.

WORK HISTORY

1987-1994	Law Offices of Sanders, Leroy & Jones, Chicago	Partner (1 year) Associate (6 years) Law Clerk (2 years)
1985-1987	MetLife Insurance Company, San Francisco	Claims Examiner

> The functional resume downplays the fact that Alixia was not employed at the time she wrote her resume.

EDUCATION

J.D., Hastings School of Law, San Francisco, CA, 1985
B.A., Finance, Brown University, Providence, RI, 1980

Relevant seminar work in fundraising

AFFILIATIONS

Board of Trustees, Evanston Hospital Foundation
Advisory Council to the Chicago AIDS Project

> Resume written in 1994.

The functional resume is ideal for Mary because she wants to change careers.

Mary E. Sibbitt

992 Leonard Place • San Francisco, CA 94104 • (415) 739-2245

JOB OBJECTIVE

Sales Service Administrator, Requisition #WH/AR-408

SUMMARY OF QUALIFICATIONS

- More than 10 years of administrative experience at the executive level.
- Keen understanding of business concepts in working with budgets and financial presentations.
- Able to manage a vast array of responsibilities including corporate meeting planning.
- Communicate clearly and persuasively; effective in contract negotiations.

RELEVANT ACCOMPLISHMENTS

Glenborough Corporation

Mary categorizes her achievements by organization, instead of by skills—an interesting twist to the typical functional resume.

- Coordinated events with up to $30K budgets. Negotiated contracts for catering, equipment, entertainment, and accommodations.
- Arranged luncheon for 150 journalists and politicians to introduce Oakland-San Francisco airport connection plan. Produced four-page accompanying booklet.
- Managed annual awards recognition program, determining awards and selection process.
- Improved speed and accuracy of president's financial reports, budget development and reconciliation, and expense tracking by computerizing his accounting system.
- Supervised work of administrative and customer service staff of four.

Largay Travel
- As sales agent, successfully persuaded airline representatives to clear space on overbooked flights and make special arrangements for clients.

KRON-TV
- Handled consumer relations and prioritized business matters for General Manager.
- Managed personnel administration including applicant processing and employment changes.

WORK HISTORY

1989-94	**Glenborough Corporation**, San Mateo, CA *Executive Assistant to the President*
1989	**Red Sail Sports/Red Sail Merchandising** (division of **Hyatt Corporation**), San Francisco, CA *Office Manager/Executive Assistant to the President*
1987-88	**LucasFilms, Mandarin Oriental Hotel, Northwest Airlines**, San Francisco, CA *Contractual Sales and Administrative positions*
1982-87	**KRON-TV**, San Francisco, CA *Assistant to the General Manager*
1980-82	**Natomas Company**, San Francisco, CA & Houston, TX *Expatriate Services Coordinator*
1979-80	**Largay Travel**, Waterbury, CT *Sales Agent*

EDUCATION

B.S., School of Business Administration, 1979
Central Connecticut State University, New Britain, CT

Resume written in 1994.

ANNE-MARIE HOLT
146 McAllister St., #217
San Francisco, CA 94102
(415) 626-4729

OBJECTIVE

Instructor — English as a Second Language

HIGHLIGHTS OF QUALIFICATIONS

- LIFE California Community College Instructor Credential in Basic Education.
- TESL Certificate with coursework in reading, writing, listening, and speaking.
- Strong practical and theoretical background in developing, selecting, and using ESL teaching methods and techniques.
- Proficient in Spanish and French.
- International experience: Two years as EFL teacher in Spain. Two years as Peace Corps volunteer.
- 11 years experience as an ESL teacher at the community college level.

PROFESSIONAL AND RELATED EXPERIENCE

CLASSROOM TEACHING

- Taught English language skills (listening, speaking, reading, writing) at all levels to non-native speakers:
    - Community college and university students
    - Spanish residents in Spain
- Approached classroom teaching as a facilitator of student learning, providing a wide range of learning activities in a warm, supportive environment.
- Integrated computer training (IBM and Macintosh) with English language instruction in the computer lab.
- Instructed adult students in basic education skills, required for their vocational training.
- Implemented an individual reading program for students, second grade through high school.

Anne-Marie used the same skills at all of her teaching positions. The functional resume makes it easy for her to present them concisely.

CURRICULA DEVELOPMENT AND COURSE EVALUATION

- Designed and implemented an ESP class in business English and marketing at Aspect ILS (International Language School).
    - Evaluated student needs through informal testing, discussion, and observation.
    - Formulated lessons to meet specific learning objectives.
- Developed two mini-courses for ESL students at Aspect ILS on ethnic art of San Francisco, and the culture of English language communication through music.
- Improved existing Basic Education Curricula at San Francisco Community College.
- As member of Mission Reading Clinic instructional team, participated in on-going course evaluation and curricula development of reading program.

(Continued)

MULTI-CULTURAL / MULTI-ETHNIC COMMUNICATIONS
- As an ESL teacher:
    - Lived in Spain for two years, teaching adolescents, university students, and adults.
    - Taught an extremely diverse student population in the San Francisco area for almost 12 years.
- As a Peace Corps Volunteer in West Africa for two years:
    - Taught physical education classes in French.
    - Participated in cross-cultural studies with five African teachers and six other volunteers.
- Worked as an au pair for one year in France.
- Proficient in Spanish and French.

WORK HISTORY

Teacher, ESL, 1983-present
San Francisco Community College, San Francisco, CA 1983-90, 1993-present
Lincoln University, San Francisco, CA 1989-90, 92-present
Aspect International Language School, San Francisco, CA 1991-present
ACHNA-American Language Program, Madrid & Badajoz, Spain, 1990-92

Teacher, Basic Ed, 1982
San Francisco Community College, San Francisco, CA

Reading Resource Teacher, 1980-83
Mission Reading Clinic, San Francisco, CA

EDUCATION

TESL Certificate, University of California, Berkeley, 1987
MA, Secondary Education, San Francisco State University, 1983
BA, Physical Education (minor: French), University of California, Berkeley, 1976
Education Abroad Program, Upsala, Sweden, Summer '70

CREDENTIALS

Lifetime California Community College Instructor Credential: Basic Education
Lifetime California Teaching Credentials: Standard Secondary, Reading Specialist

PROFESSIONAL AFFILIATIONS

Teachers of English to Speakers of Other Languages (TESOL)
California Teachers of English to Speakers of Other Languages (CATESOL)
Northern California Council of Returned Peace Corps Volunteers (NORCAL)

Resume written in 1995.

Notice how Kerry's functional resume highlights her skills while de-emphasizing her work history, which may not be as strong as her competition's.

Kerry S. Richards
1275 A Washington Street • San Francisco, CA 94104
(415) 648-0567

Objective	Graphic Designer/Photographer
Summary	• Experienced with design concepts for packaging, advertising, and corporate communications.
	• Photographer with skills in evaluating prints for reproduction.
	• Familiar with print preparation and production.
	• Understanding of video shooting and editing for television.

• Experienced in:

Quark Xpress	FreeHand
PageMaker	Persuasion
Photoshop	MSWord
Illustrator	FileMaker

Experience

GRAPHIC DESIGN

• Created consumer packaging using PMS and four-color processing; prepared designs for photo shoots.
• Produced advertising campaign strategies for a variety of products and services.
  - Designed thumbnails, roughs, and final comps for print advertising.
  - Wrote copy for television and print advertising.
• Communicated corporate identity through design of logo and collateral.
• Created mechanicals; proofed blue lines and color keys.
• Used a wide range of typography to appeal to specific audiences.

PHOTOGRAPHY

• Photographed fashion and food compositions in studio settings.
• Developed portfolio of color landscape prints from across the U.S.
• Exhibited photos in two San Francisco locations.
• Won award in black and white community photo contest.
• Black and white darkroom and other technical experience.

Relevant Work History
(Concurrent with Education)

1992-present	**Full-time Advertising Design Student** Academy of Art College, San Francisco, CA
1990-92	**Freelance Computer Graphic Designer/Writer** San Francisco, CA
1988-89	**Marketing Assistant** Dain Bosworth, Inc., Minneapolis, MN

Education

B.F.A., Advertising Design, anticipated Spring 1994
Academy of Art College, San Francisco, CA

Marketing Program
University of Minnesota, Minneapolis, MN

— Portfolio Available —

Resume written in 1994.

Tip
To develop a dynamite resume strategy, team up with a friend, fellow job hunter, counselor, or professional resume writer—someone who can ask you questions and be objective.

Decisions, Decisions!

At this point, you need to decide which resume format you are going to use. If you know which format is best for your situation, you're ready to charge ahead. If you're teetering on the fence between the two, try creating your resume in both formats, then see which one you think markets you best.

When you've made your choice, you're ready to move forward. Follow the directions in Chapter 4 for the type of resume you chose.

The Least You Need to Know

➤ Sell yourself with a good marketing strategy.

➤ Limit your resume to one page if possible, and no more than two pages.

➤ No paragraphs! Use bullet points to make your material look quick and easy to read.

➤ Use the resume format (functional or chronological) that markets you best.

Step Two—Look Who's Talking

In This Chapter

➤ Design a resume heading that makes your name stand out

➤ Use your address in your heading to create a stable image

➤ Putting contact numbers at the top of your resume

You've been putting your name at the top of papers since you learned how to write in the first grade. It's so automatic, you probably just write it there without thinking. Before you do that on your resume, consider how vital your name is to your marketing strategy.

When you introduce yourself at a social, business, or networking event, your name is frequently a springboard for conversation. Your name is the one thing you want people to remember, since it's the tool they will use to find you again. For that reason, clever folks say their name clearly and, if possible, say something to help the other person remember it. (I often say, "Susan Ireland, like the country.") On your resume, it's greatly to your advantage to use every trick you can to make your name noticeable and memorable (without being too obvious, of course).

As you might have guessed, this chapter is about creating the *heading* on your resume, which consists of your name, address, and phone number. Take a look at the following resume to see the area we'll be focusing on.

(Here's what I mean by the "Heading" on your resume.)

Name
Street • City, State Zip • phone

JOB OBJECTIVE
The job you want next

SUMMARY OF QUALIFICATIONS
- How much experience you have in the field of your objective, in a related field, or using the skills required for your new position.
- An overall career accomplishment that shows you'd be good at this job objective.
- What someone would say about you as a recommendation.

PROFESSIONAL EXPERIENCE

19xx-pres. **Company Name**, City, State
JOB TITLE
- An accomplishment you are proud of that shows you're good at this profession.
- A problem you solved and the results.
- A time when you positively affected the organization, the bottom line, your boss, your co-workers, your clients.
- Awards, commendations, publications, etc. you achieved that relate to your job objective.

19xx-xx **Company Name**, City, State
JOB TITLE
- A project you are proud of that supports your job objective.
- Another accomplishment that shows you're good at this line of work.
- Quantifiable results that point out your skill.

EDUCATION
Degree, Major (if relevant), 19xx (optional)
University, City, State

What's in a Name?

Contrary to what you might think, your resume is not a formal document—it's a marketing piece that introduces you. So refer to yourself the way you would like to be addressed. If your first name is Elizabeth but you want to be called Beth, then use "Beth" in your resume heading. Middle initials are optional.

If you think the reader might not be able to tell if you are male or female from your name, decide whether you want them to know. In some cases, it may be to your advantage if a reader *does* know your gender. For instance, Robin Harris (a man) knew that even though sex discrimination is illegal in the job placement process, the company for whom he wanted to work gives its most productive sales territories to men. Therefore, he wanted the employer to know right off that he was a man, knowing that would put him ahead of all the women candidates in the stack of resumes.

Tip
Although there is no prescribed size of type for your name on your resume, a good rule of thumb is that it should be no larger than 18 points and no smaller than 12 points. *Point size* is a measurement used by typographers to gauge the size of type. If you're using a computer to create your resume, your word processing program will indicate the size of type available to you.

Here are a few ways you can clarify your gender on paper:

➤ Use a gender-specific nickname instead of your given name (for example, "Rob Harris" instead of "Robin Harris").

➤ Include a middle name if it's clearly male or female (for example, "Robin Frank Harris").

➤ Start your name with Mr. or Ms. (for example, "Mr. Robin Harris").

If you're considering this last option, think twice. This technique is seldom used and looks somewhat awkward. However, if you are applying within the U.S. and have an unusual or non-American name that probably won't be recognized as male or female no matter *what* you do to it, this technique would work.

Now let's look at a situation where it might *not* be to the job hunter's advantage if her gender was known. Terry Hoover (a woman) was after the same job that Robin wanted. In order to be considered for the job, she chose not to add anything to her name—she simply put "Terry Hoover" on her resume, knowing the employer would have to guess whether she was a man or a woman until she met him in person. At that point, she'd be at the interview and able to sell herself as a fully qualified candidate.

> **Tip**
>
> Arrange the graphic layout of your heading so that your name appears either in the middle or on the right-hand side of the page. (It doesn't matter how you line up your address and contact numbers.) Here's why: once your resume is read, it will probably be filed (hopefully in a filing cabinet and not in a "circular file"). Because the left-hand side of the paper is usually placed in the spine of a file folder, your name will be seen more easily if you put it either at the top-middle or upper-right corner of the page.

Home Sweet Home

It's preferable to put your street address in your heading instead of a P.O. box number, since a home address conjures up a more stable image. If, however, you have a specific reason not to give out your street address, it's acceptable to use a post office address.

What's Your Number?

If you list only one phone number in your heading, it will be assumed that it's your home or personal line. If you give more than one phone number, you need to indicate the difference between them. For instance:

Home: 510-555-4238

Office: 510-555-1725

Fax and E-Mail

> **Warning**
>
> Don't list your work number on your resume unless you can talk freely from that phone and a message can be left without jeopardizing your present job. *Never assume that a caller will be discreet on your behalf.*

Fax numbers are not usually found on resumes since employers seldom fax a response to an applicant. Your e-mail address, on the other hand, may be useful. Providing your on-line address could do two things:

➤ Expedite the employer's response.

➤ Demonstrate that you're on-line savvy (a plus when applying for some positions).

On the next few pages, you'll find three resumes that have nice clear headings that include contact numbers.

Michael Left, P.E.

772 Alameda Avenue • Berkeley, California 947065 • (510) 221-9976

This straightforward heading has only the home phone number listed.

Civil Engineer
specializing in
Project Management • Construction Estimating

SUMMARY OF QUALIFICATIONS

- Wide variety of construction engineering experience ranging from heavy vessel transportation to commercial interior wall construction.
- Estimator and project manager for some of the most profitable specialty subcontracting jobs in the San Francisco Bay Area.
- Strong communication and analytical skills.

SELECTED ACCOMPLISHMENTS

- **Estimator and Exterior Wall Design Coordinator** for St. Francis Hospital, Fremont. Project consisted of 125,000 sq. ft. of EIFS material on built-in-place light-gauge metal framing. Coordinated structural analysis and shop drawing production for integration into project drawings by engineer-of-record.
- **Field Engineer, Scheduler, and Subcontract Administrator** for Shell Oil refinery modernization in Richmond, CA. Project involved transportation and erection of multiple refinery process vessels up to 500 tons.
- **Estimator and Project Manager** for highly profitable interior/exterior wall design and construction for the San Francisco Gift Center. Project included 12,000 sq. ft. of built-in-place EIFS wall and detailed interior atria.
- **Project Manager** for the $1 million structural fireproofing, load-bearing wall framing, and massive drywall and plaster ceiling construction for the redesign of San Francisco's Central Theatre. Maintained strict critical path schedule throughout project.

WORK HISTORY

1993-1994 **Estimator/Engineer**
                Jones Construction Management, Sausalito CA
1984-1993 **Estimator/Project Manager**
                Smith Specialty Co., Daly City, CA, 1992-1993
                Davis-Thompson Co., San Leandro, CA, 1990-1992
                Martin Davidson, Inc., San Francisco, CA, 1986-1990
                Price & Associates, Inc., Fog View, CA, 1984-1985
1983-1984 **Estimator/Project Engineer**
                J.P. Wright Construction, Inc., San Francisco, CA
1979-1982 **Project Manager/Project Engineer**
                Field Crane and Rigging, San Mateo, CA

EDUCATION AND CERTIFICATION

Registered Professional Civil Engineer, certified 1984, State of California

Bachelor of Science, Civil Engineering, 1978
University of California, Berkeley

Associate of Science, Electrical Engineering, 1976
Contra Costa College, San Pablo, CA

Resume written in 1994.

DON LORD
216 California Street #205, San Francisco, CA 94107
Home: 415-265-0937, Work: 415-274-4700

It's safe for a prospective employer to call Don at work, so he gave both his work and home phone numbers.

OBJECTIVE: Position in International Human Resources

SUMMARY OF QUALIFICATIONS
- Intercultural sensitivity, having lived abroad (Europe and Japan) for nine years.
- Ability to represent a company with professionalism and confidence.
- Highly developed communication skills: written, verbal and presentational.
- Word-processing, database entry and office administrative experience.

INTERNATIONAL EXPERIENCE
- As official translator, facilitated communications between Americans living in Germany and local government and community officials.
- Developed curriculum on "survival" techniques for Americans living abroad, which was incorporated into teaching program at the U.S. Department of Defense School.
- Taught English Conversation to Japanese businessmen, spouses and children, while living in Osaka, Japan for three months.
- Recognized by International Studies Academy for outstanding research project and written report on the European Economic Community, involving multiple markets and business issues.
- Traveled extensively throughout Europe as a citizen abroad, age 12-21. Fluent in German.

PROJECT MANAGEMENT
- Assisted Alumnae Resources' clients in career transition regarding educational steps needed to achieve professional goals.
- Recruited and interviewed Hispanic high school students for San Francisco State University.
- Trained new Macy's sales employees from diverse cultural backgrounds.
- Ranked one of top recruiter for the American Red Cross "CPR Saturday" event.
- Organized international and national projects for senior stock broker at Merrill Lynch.
- Maximized operations in San Francisco State University department, as sole office administrator for eight professors and their students.

WORK HISTORY
Alumnae Resources Career Center, San Francisco, CA, Client Services Associate, 1995-present
Aeon Corporation, Osaka, Japan, Teacher of English Conversation to Japanese, 1995
American Red Cross, San Francisco, CA, Intern/Special Events Coordinator, 1995

Mostly Concurrent with Education
Macy's, San Francisco, CA, Sales Associate, 1989-1994
International Studies Academy, San Francisco, CA, Researcher, 1988
Merrill Lynch, San Francisco, California, Stockbroker Assistant, 1987
San Francisco State University, San Francisco, CA, Humanity Dept. Resources Technician, 1987
U.S. Department of Defense Schools, Munich, Germany, Translator/Teacher, 1984

EDUCATION
San Francisco State University, San Francisco, CA
Bachelor of Arts, International Relations/Business, 1991

University of Maryland, Munich Campus, Munich, Germany
Associate of Arts, 1987

Helm Holz Gymnasium, Mannheim, Germany
German Language Award, 1984

Resume written in 1996.

Cathy put her e-mail address in her heading because she wants her potential nonprofit employer to know that she is on-line savvy.

Cathy Barret

33 Paris Ave., #1 • San Francisco, CA 94133
Tel/Fax: (415) 211-5549 • E-Mail: cbgfc@prodigy.com

JOB OBJECTIVE

Position in Development

SUMMARY OF QUALIFICATIONS

- More than three years professional experience developing strategies and proposals for generating revenue.
- Comfortable initiating and building rapport with affluent individuals.
- Excellent research and writing capabilities. Articulate ideas clearly and concisely.

RELEVANT EXPERIENCE

DEVELOPMENT

- As liaison to individual donors, cultivated ongoing relationships and encouraged donor involvement in fundraising activities. (The Wilderness Society)
- Collaborated in grant proposal formulation by compiling and summarizing supporting data. (The Wilderness Society)
- As campaign fundraiser, produced promotional events at celebrity homes that raised funds and generated public support. (U.S. Congressional campaign)

COMMUNICATION

- Used strong listening and verbal skills to resolve countless technical, political, and inter-personal problems among individuals from diverse backgrounds. (Pantell Investment Co.)
- Persuaded decision makers within the government and business sectors through proposals, reports, and correspondence. (Pantell Investment Co.)
- Increased revenue 12% by drafting mutually beneficial contracts that frequently led to renewals. (Pantell Investment Co.)
- Handled media relations providing an accurate and concise portrayal of the organization's positions on current issues. (The Wilderness Society)

WORK HISTORY

1995-present	The Women's Foundation, San Francisco, CA
	Volunteer, Assistant to Development Database Manager
	Alumnae Resources, San Francisco, CA
	Volunteer, Client Services
1989-1994	Pantell Investment Co., New York, NY
	Portfolio Manager
1988-1989	The Wilderness Society, Boise, ID
	Regional Associate
1988	The Trust For Public Land, Boston, MA
	Research Intern

PROFESSIONAL DEVELOPMENT AND EDUCATION

Support Center for Nonprofit Management, San Francisco, CA
Successful Fundraising Strategies
Writing Successful Grant Proposals

University of Vermont, Burlington, VT
B.S., *cum laude*

Resume written in 1995.

The Least You Need to Know

➤ When creating your resume heading, place your name in the center or on the right-hand side of the page.

➤ Use the name you would like the interviewer to use when addressing you in conversation.

➤ Create a stable image by providing a street address instead of a P.O. box number.

➤ Include only those phone numbers where employers can leave messages and where you can speak freely.

➤ Include your e-mail address if you think it will impress your potential employer or be relevant to the job.

Chapter 5

Step Three—Be Careful What You Ask For...You Might Get It

In This Chapter

➤ How a concise job objective statement helps you get the job you want

➤ When to use a professional title instead of a job objective

➤ Including your degree or credential in the heading

➤ A strong profile statement sends the message home

➤ Is a job objective always necessary?

Whether you're a world traveler or a job seeker, it's important to know where you are going in order to get there. (At least Columbus *thought* he knew where he was going when he set sail.) And when asking for help in getting there, you need to tell the guide where you're headed.

On your resume, this directive is given through the *job objective statement* that appears just below your heading. The highlighted section of the following resume template shows where your job objective should be placed. (To learn about alternatives to having a Job Objective section on your resume, see "Breaking the Rules" later in this chapter.)

(Here's where the "job objective" appears on the resume.)

Name
Street • City, State Zip • phone

JOB OBJECTIVE
The job you want next

SUMMARY OF QUALIFICATIONS
- How much experience you have in the field of your objective, in a related field, or using the skills required for your new position.
- An overall career accomplishment that shows you'd be good at this job objective.
- What someone would say about you as a recommendation.

PROFESSIONAL EXPERIENCE
19xx-pres. **Company Name**, City, State
JOB TITLE
- An accomplishment you are proud of that shows you're good at this profession.
- A problem you solved and the results.
- A time when you positively affected the organization, the bottom line, your boss, your co-workers, your clients.
- Awards, commendations, publications, etc. you achieved that relate to your job objective.

19xx-xx **Company Name**, City, State
JOB TITLE
- A project you are proud of that supports your job objective.
- Another accomplishment that shows you're good at this line of work.
- Quantifiable results that point out your skill.

EDUCATION
Degree, Major (if relevant), 19xx (optional)
University, City, State

Why You Need a Job Objective Statement

By starting your resume with a job objective statement, you immediately tell the reader:

➤ *What position you're looking for.* A resume without a job objective statement effectively says, "This is what I've done. Could you figure out what I should do next?" That's a weak approach. By having an objective, you give your resume focus and strength—a powerful first move toward job title and salary negotiations.

➤ *Who needs to get your resume.* It's very likely your envelope will be opened by a human resources clerk. Your job objective statement indicates which hiring person should receive your resume. Without that statement, you leave it up to the clerk to decide which department you belong in.

Tip
Providing your job objective statement near the top of your resume is the clearest way to tell the reader what you want for your immediate future.

➤ *How to interpret your resume.* Your job objective statement tells the reader, "Everything that follows is relevant to this position." That's an important point to make. This is a marketing piece, not your life history!

Wording Your Job Objective Statement

I've said it before and I'll say it again—Less is more! You need to say everything as concisely as possible, starting with your job objective statement.

Some resumes have flowery opening statements with the job objectives buried deep inside them. They use phrases like "challenging position," "room for advancement," and "opportunity to grow." Give the reader a break and cut out all the "fluff" since it doesn't really say much anyway. Stick to the important stuff, such as:

➤ The job title you'd like next, if you know it (for example, "Manager" or "Sales Representative").

➤ The area of work you want to be in (for example, "Marketing" or "Sales"). On rare occasions, this might include an area of specialization (for example, "with an emphasis on new business development" or "focusing on graphic design").

Take a look at the following examples.

Instead of:

A challenging position that will utilize my skills and experience as Director of Marketing.

(Yawn! Everyone wants to be challenged; and of course you'll be using your skills and experience.)

Say:

Director of Marketing

Instead of:

An administrative position in a growth-oriented company where I can use my background in finance to promote the firm.

(Come on! It doesn't take a rocket scientist to figure out that you want to work for a company that's going to be around long enough to write you a few paychecks.)

Say:

Administrative position with a focus on finance

Instead of:

A position as Associate Field Producer in TV Programming that offers room for advancement and high rewards.

(Bad idea! It sounds like you want the job of the person reading the resume!)

Say:

Associate Field Producer, TV Programming

Want to see this concept at work? Review the concise job objective statements in the following four resumes.

YOU'RE HIRED.

Tip

Don't include "entry-level" in your job objective statement. Why tell the reader you want the lowest job? Leave it out, and you may be given a position that's a little higher up the food chain.

Elizabeth J. Euser

9931 Berkeley Park Street • El Cerrito, CA 94809 • (510) 651-8840

JOB OBJECTIVE

A position in Public Relations with an emphasis on Event Planning.

(Elizabeth qualified her job objective by saying that her strength is in event planning.)

SUMMARY OF QUALIFICATIONS

- Experienced at public relations for a provider of promotional merchandise for national and international concert tours.
- Success in producing events for up to 7,000 people.
- Reputation for achieving goals using a professional yet personable approach.

EDUCATION

MBA, International Marketing, Clemson University, Clemson, SC, 1991
     Exchange Program (50% of MBA credit), École Superièure de Commerce de Pau, France
BA, Marketing and French, Clemson University, Clemson, SC, 1989

RELEVANT ACCOMPLISHMENTS

PUBLIC RELATIONS

The Brockum Group and AGF Entertainment, promotional merchandise providers for concerts

- Represented promotional merchandise providers to concert hall managements, bands, and the public. Tours included:

Prince	Dolly Parton	Shawn Colvin
Lollapalooza	The Lemonheads	Michael Franks

- Saved as much as 5% of revenues when negotiating venue contracts for promotional merchandise sales of up to $20,000 per night.
- Developed positive rapport between band and merchandise company by creating a team atmosphere rather than a strictly business relationship.
- Commended for establishing strong working relationships with bands and management companies. Consistently requested by bands for repeat and new tours.
- Acted as tour public relations person, handling questions and comments from fans.

EVENT PLANNING

Clemson University

- As event planner on the Cultural Arts Committee, produced sell-out musical and theatrical programs for up to 7,000 attendees.
- As hospitality director for Central Dance and Concert Committee, negotiated contracts, supervised catering, and managed backstage accommodations for concerts including:

Rolling Stones	Beach Boys/Chicago	B-52's
REM	Jimmy Buffet	Hank Williams, Jr.

- Team-planned all extra-curricular activities (lectures, outdoor recreation, social, and performing arts) for student body of 15,000.

WORK HISTORY

1993-present	**Tour Manager for Merchandise**	THE BROCKUM GROUP, nationwide, 1993-present AGF ENTERTAINMENT, nationwide, 1994 tour
1994	**Executive Assistant** (contractual)	THE ADGAP GROUP (advertising/promotions), San Francisco, CA
1991-1993	**Department Manager**	FAMOUS FOOTWEAR, Atlanta, GA

(Resume written in 1995.)

Sheila Todd

84 Maryland Drive • San Francisco, CA 94141 • **(415) 558-3124**

OBJECTIVE: Sales Trainer in the areas of:
- Interpersonal Communication
- Sales Techniques
- Product Knowledge

Sheila highlighted her areas of expertise in her job objective statement by putting them in a column.

SUMMARY OF QUALIFICATIONS
- 15 years as a successful sales professional.
- Experienced at teaching others how to improve interpersonal communication.
- Skilled at training sales associates in proven sales techniques.
- Ability to develop presentation and training materials.

PROFESSIONAL ACCOMPLISHMENTS

TRAINING

American Fashion Jewelry (Impostors)
- Trained 30+ new franchisees regarding:

Product knowledge	Projected trends
Merchandising	Proven selling techniques
Company philosophy	

- Trained Union Square sales staff including 15 associates and one assistant manager.
- Led regular staff meetings to introduce new products and instill respect and enthusiasm for merchandise.
- Served on the product development committee charged with determining seasonal merchandise and promotions.
- Diffused numerous conflicts among sales staff through group and individual counseling.
- Designed employee incentive program that rewarded improved performance.

Arrowhead, Inc.
- Trained sales staff in numerous department stores nationwide for short-term promotional sales of Arrowhead accessories.

Dillards
- Conducted product demonstrations for clients by appointment.

SALES
- Consistently ranked among the highest in sales at **American Fashion Jewelry**, using strong presentation skills to sell luxury items in a slow economy.
- Commended for achieving above average sales and for developing strong rapport with customers at **Jefco Jewelry Distributors**.
- Exceeded sales record 12% in a six-states, 14-store region of **Arrowhead, Inc.**
- Recognized for meeting/exceeding quotas in a commission-based **I. Magnin** position.

WORK HISTORY

1990-present	**Merchandising Manager**, American Fashion Jewelry (Impostors), San Francisco
1988-1989	**Customer Service/Sales Associate**, Jefco Jewelry Distributors, San Francisco
1985-1987	**Sales Associate**, Dillards (department store), Phoenix, AZ
1984	**Promotional Representative**, Arrowhead, Inc., San Rafael
1980-1983	**Sales Representative**, I. Magnin, San Francisco

EDUCATION

Liberal Arts, Long Beach College, Long Beach, CA
Professional development coursework: • Interpersonal Communications
• Sales Training • Product Knowledge and Presentation

Resume written in 1994.

Clair Brooks

2728 Loren Street, Redding, CA 94733   (707) 332-1185

Clair's job objective statement is the exact title she was applying for at a university. Good way to handle it!

JOB OBJECTIVE
Student Affairs Officer II, Housing & Dining Services: Residential Programs

SUMMARY OF QUALIFICATIONS
- 19 years as a professional educator with strengths in program development and administration.
- Enthusiastic team leader and outstanding communicator, both one-to-one and before groups.
- Creative in solving problems and maximizing resources. Computer literate.

EDUCATION
M.A., Educational Administration, St. Mary's College, Moraga, CA, 1985
B.A., Psychology, California State University at Hayward, CA, 1975

RELEVANT ACCOMPLISHMENTS
PROGRAM ADMINISTRATION
Redding Unified School District
- Developed new educational programs including:
    - Tutoring program for ESL students that achieved highest recommendations.
    - "Future System" curricula, a hands-on approach that included a computer lab.
    - $10,000 ham radio station project for high-achieving students.
    - A drivers training program for students with disabilities.
- As Teacher-in-Charge, supervised 30 teachers in principal's absence and assisted in administrative decision-making and program development.
- Chaired ESL Advisory Committee comprised of parents, administrators, and teachers, that served as a forum for student issues.

American Field Service
- Coordinated one-year placements of international students participating in the foreign exchange program.

Navy League
- As a program director for five years, assisted in organization of Fleet Week, including a 500-person ball, ship visitations, and VIP protocol.

TEACHING
Computer Institute of Technology
- Currently teach basic college courses (English, psychology, and writing) to students, ages 18-50 and from diverse educational and cultural backgrounds.
- Tutor and advise students regarding study skills and career development.

Redding Unified School District
- Instructed adults in basic education skills, GED preparation, and ESL, in addition to holding a full-time elementary teaching position.

CNN Newsroom Guest Speaker
- Delivered presentations to school groups, cable companies, and civic groups on the new technology of television in the classroom.

WORK HISTORY
1993-present	Instructor	Computer Institute of Technology, Redding, CA
1991-1993	Guest Speaker	CNN Newsroom, San Francisco, CA
1975-1993	Educator	Redding Unified School District, Redding, CA
1984-1987	Manager	Brooks Group Travel Service, Redding, CA

COMMUNITY LEADERSHIP
Program Director, Navy League, San Francisco Council
Host Parent and Western Troubleshooter, American Field Service

Resume written in 1994.

61

Kathleen Quaro

615 San Antonio Rd. • Fairfield, CA 94516 • (415) 662-9457

JOB OBJECTIVE: ESL Teacher

Just the facts, ma'am! This job objective statement couldn't be more to the point.

SUMMARY OF QUALIFICATIONS

- More than 15 years as a teacher in Bay Area communities rich in cultural diversity.
- Extensive experience living and traveling abroad in Asia, South America, Central America, and Europe.
- Ability to integrate theoretical concepts and practical ideas, and apply them to actual classroom situations.
- View teaching and learning as a dynamic and interactive process.

EDUCATION & CREDENTIAL

ESL Certificate, anticipated Winter 1994
    Coursework to date: Strategies for Teaching Beginning ESL Students, K-Adult
                            Methods and Materials for Teaching ESL
                            Cross-Cultural Communication
                            Fundamentals of Linguistics for ESL Teachers

University of California, Berkeley
    M.A., Education, 1991
    B.A., Social Science, emphasis: Psychology, 1970

California Early Childhood Teaching Credential, 1973

Universidad Nacional Autonoma de Mexico, Mexico City
    Spanish, Mexican Archaeology coursework, Summer 1968

RELEVANT EXPERIENCE

TEACHING

- As classroom teacher, built personal rapport with students and families from a wide range of cultural backgrounds.
- Created trusting atmosphere through sensitivity to students' strengths, weaknesses, and personal learning styles.
- Engaged students through humor and activities designed for maximum interaction in large and small groups.
- Developed curriculum that was appropriate to students' learning abilities and reflected their needs and interests.
- Achieved maximum results by breaking down seemingly large learning tasks into meaningful and manageable segments.

MULTICULTURAL / INTERNATIONAL

- As an American Field Service Exchange Student, lived with a non-English speaking Brazilian family as their "adopted daughter" in Fortaleza and Rio de Janeiro.
- Married into an Indian family and participated in cultural ceremonies while living within my extended family in New Delhi and traveling throughout the country.
- While studying Spanish at the Marroquin Institute in Antigua, Guatemala, stayed with a non-English speaking family.

— Continued —

Kathleen Quaro
Page 2

MULTICULTURAL / INTERNATIONAL (continued)
- Lived with a Mexican family while studying Spanish and Archaeology at Universidad Nacional Autonoma de Mexico.
- Boarded with a Costa Rican family while studying at the Forrester Language Institute in San Jose, Costa Rica.
- Hosted exchange students from Sweden, Switzerland, and France for periods of six months to a year each.
- Accompanied electronics firm CEO on business trip to Taiwan, Hong Kong, and Japan.
- Toured the French Dordogne by bicycle. Traveled extensively throughout France and England.

WORK HISTORY

1983-1985, 1988-present	TEACHER / SUBSTITUTE TEACHER, Prospect School, Richmond, CA
1985-1986	TEACHER, Berkeley Hills Nursery School, Berkeley, CA
1980-1983	Full-time parent, Part-time student - M.A. Education Program
1978-1980	TEACHER, Skytown Nursery School, Kensington, CA
1973-1977	TEACHER, Lafayette Public School District, Lafayette, CA
Previous experience:	
1/2 year	ESL TEACHER, Instituto Norteamericano de Ingles, Mexico City, Mexico

Resume written in 1994.

Breaking the Rules

Now that you've bought the rule of having a job objective statement, I'm going to tell you when to break, or at least bend, that rule.

If you're continuing in a profession in which you have substantial experience, consider using one of the following alternatives to the job objective statement. These options give you an edge on your competition by presenting you as an established professional in your field. Here are four such scenarios and advice on how to handle them.

Use a Professional Title in the Heading

Putting a title next to your name or near the top of your resume can be a stronger approach than using a job objective statement. A title effectively says, "This is what my profession is." A job objective statement says, "This is what I want to be." If you have enough experience to give yourself a title, it can be a more forceful introduction. For example:

Sally Johnson, Public Relations Specialist

Frank Smith, Insurance Underwriter

Look at Nancy, Kirk, and Roch's resumes that follow. Do you see how this technique makes them look accomplished in their careers?

> Since Nancy is well established in her field, she used a professional title in her heading instead of a job objective statement.

Nancy Larsen
International Sales Representative / Sales Manager

447 41st Street • San Francisco, California 94133 • (415) 278-9982

SUMMARY OF QUALIFICATIONS

- 12 years successful direct sales and sales management career in corporate culture.
- Courageous selling style that results in:
    - Win-win gains for client and company
    - Achievement of unlikely sales
    - Reversal of lost sales
- Skilled at closing sales through ingenious and spontaneous "packaging" of products/services.
- Bilingual: Italian/English.

PROFESSIONAL ACCOMPLISHMENTS
Dictaphone Corporation

Personal Quota Attainment
- Consistently attained top national rankings out of 110 managers:
    - 110-125% of quota, five out of six years   - #2 Sales Manager
    - #1 Female Sales Manager   - #3 Sales Manager
- Won annual awards including "Top Systems Sales Performer."
- Ranked #3 out of 625 sales representatives.
- Exceeded annual quota 110% the first year, with no previous sales experience.

Selected Achievements
- As an outsider in an established market, closed a $100,000 sale of a newly launched product.
- Increased business substantially with a major client and exceeded average monthly sales quotas by 34%.
    - Secured an exclusive vendor agreement.
    - Established an accelerated ordering process.
- As District Manager, increased sales force productivity by 20%.
- Introduced a successful training program that developed each salesperson's abilities in proven sales techniques.

Promotions
- One of six women nation-wide promoted to District Manager.
- Promoted to Sales Manager out of field of 21 candidates.
- Advanced to Manager, Key Accounts due to mastery of technical system selling.
- Mentored and promoted sales representatives who became successful sales managers.
- Out of 625 Sales Representatives, chosen as coach for training center.

WORK HISTORY

1993	NOVAL ENTERPRISES, Mill Valley, CA	Organizational Consultant
1992	ACCELERATED VOICE, San Francisco, CA	Sales & Marketing Consultant
1980-91	DICTAPHONE CORP., San Francisco, CA	District Manager, 1989-91
		Sales Manager, 1983-89
		Manager, Key Accounts, 1981-83
		Sales Representative, 1980

EDUCATION

B.S., Psychology (Minor: Italian), 1978
University of Massachusetts, Amherst, MA

> Resume written in 1993.

Kirk Pietro

681 Filmhurst Avenue • Emeryville, CA 94707 • (510) 523-1644

Construction Dispute Consultant

> Kirk's title is very pronounced, making it quick and easy for an employer to know who he is and what he wants. This approach shows confidence!

HIGHLIGHTS OF QUALIFICATIONS

- 16 years as construction consultant and owner of mid-sized construction firm.
- Extensive experience in woodframe construction.
- Skilled at resolving contract disputes.

RELEVANT EXPERIENCE

CONSTRUCTION BUSINESS MANAGEMENT

- Built a prominent construction business that grew from 0 to 250 employees and from annual gross of $50K to $17M in six years.
- Managed approximately 600 construction projects including:
  New commercial buildings
  Commercial tenant improvement
  New and remodel residential work
  Seismic upgrades
  Structural rehabs
- Oversaw one million sq. ft. per year wood framing operation.

PROBLEM RESOLUTION

- Successfully negotiated numerous contract and labor disputes, initiating compromises that led to resolutions of up to $250K.
- Collaborated with architects and owners to create most cost effective designs on projects up to $5M in value, frequently requiring resolution of competing interests.
- Continually generated technical and interpersonal solutions that met tight budget and time constraints.

PRESENTATIONS

- Wrote hundreds of analyses for construction projects, focusing on financial, safety, and time issues.
- As guest lecturer at local community college, spoke on resource efficient construction.

WORK HISTORY

1994-present	Construction Consultant /General Contractor	WAHB. Corp., Berkeley, CA
1984-1994	President/Operations Manager	Stokes, Russell, and Hayden, Inc., Berkeley, CA
1978-1984	General Contractor	Peitro Construction, Berkeley, CA
	Freelance Writer for specialized magazines	

EDUCATION

B.A., Rhetoric, University of California, Berkeley, 1978

> Resume written in 1995.

Roch noted his profession just under his name and backed it up with a strong first statement under "Qualifications."

Roch Colgate
Security Professional

2534 35th Avenue, San Francisco, CA 94116   (415) 458-0821

QUALIFICATIONS

- 20 years as a Security Professional who has demonstrated the ability to research, evaluate, and implement procedures that encompass all levels of security.
- Committed to the delivery of high quality, complex assignments of local, national, international importance.
- Track record of handling privileged and sensitive situations discreetly, maintaining a level of respect and dignity for all involved.
- Extensive network of professional contacts in all areas of public and private security.
- Superior interpersonal skills with the ability to work with all levels of personnel.

PROFESSIONAL SECURITY EXPERIENCE

- Provided executive protection to a wide range of clients from corporate executives to international celebrities, remaining prudent and discreet in both formal and informal settings.
- Designed corporate and estate security programs, utilizing CCTV, physical security, and access control systems.
- Developed and implemented security programs ($1.6M annual budget) for five luxury hotels in the Union Square area of downtown San Francisco.
- Served as team leader for many foreign and domestic assignments, handling all travel assignments.
- Successfully discharged potentially explosive workplace violence through crisis intervention.
- Infiltrated and broke a large criminal team accounting for the sabotage, theft, and embezzlement within a major corporation.
- Assisted in personal matters including shopping, errands, and domestic assignments, frequently managing large amounts of cash.
- Directed the maintenance and management of a private auto collection to uphold full functionality and optimum market value ($2.2M).

SELECTED CLIENTS

Sony Corp., Office of the Chairman	Driehouse Securities
Ford Motor Corp., Office of the Chairman	Danielle Steel Traina
US Surgical Corp., Office of the Chairman	Pepsico
Oliver North	Limited Clothing Corporation
Casper Weinburg	San Francisco Jewelry Mart

WORK HISTORY

1991-present	Executive Protection Specialist	R.W. Kobetz & Assoc., Berryville, VA
		Factor One, San Leandro, CA
		Barbary Coast Corp. Security, San Francisco, CA
		Protective Solutions, Inc., Los Angeles, CA
1988-1991	Investigator	Woodland Management, San Rafael, CA
1982-1988	Director of Security Operations	Hotel Group of America, San Francisco, CA
1980-1988	General Manager	Roche Security Consultants, Inc., San Francisco, CA
1979-1980	Retail Loss Investigator	Western Intelligence, Sacramento, CA
1976-1979	Area Supervisor, UAL	The Wackenhut Corporation, Burlingame, CA

— Continued —

Roch Colgate
Page 2

EDUCATION

San Francisco City College: Hotel and Restaurant Management
High-Rise Fire and Life Safety Certified
Solano Community College: Criminal Justice, Correctional Sciences

TRAINING

POST Certified #42279, San Francisco Police Academy
American Red Cross Certified, CPR, Emergency First Aid
Executive Protection, MM #133, J. Mattman Protective Training Center
Defensive Driving Skills, The Boundurant School
Evasive, Anti-Kidnapping Driving, Tony Scotti Executive Driving School
Terrorism, California Specialized Training Institute
Executive Protection Training Institute, NLA#418

LICENSES

California Concealed Weapons Permit, LN #94-01 CIIN #10456405 "ORI" N #CA0349400
Certified Protection Specialist, MM133 & NLA418
California Consumers Affairs Registered, PPO #PQ 009291 - Weapons #009291

PROFESSIONAL ACHIEVEMENTS

Qualified Expert in Security, United States Supreme Courts
Co-author, *Providing Executive Protection Book II*, Executive Protection Institute

Resume written in 1994.

Use a Degree or Credential in the Heading

If you have a degree or credential that indicates your profession, you could put the initials of your degree or credential next to your name in the heading instead of writing an objective statement. For example:

Linda Harmon, CPA

Warren Samuels, M.D.

Take a look at Ami and Sandra's resumes that follow. Notice how their credentials indicate the role they want to play for their next employer.

Ami's MPH (Master's in Public Health) degree implies that she's interested in a job in health-care management.

Ami Ann Sparks, MPH

2606 Filmore Street • San Francisco, CA 94132 • (415) 882-1254

PROFILE

- Success at developing and managing programs recognized internationally for raising awareness of women's health issues.

- Skilled at generating media and public attention through social marketing campaigns, public speaking, and educational materials.

- Special interest in producing events to promote women's health education.

EDUCATION

Master's in Public Health, 1991
Hadassah Hebrew University
School of Community Medicine and Public Health, Jerusalem, Israel
Thesis: The knowledge, attitudes, and practices of sexual behavior and contraceptive use of recently arrived young Soviet immigrants to Israel.

Bachelor of Arts, Anthropology, 1990
University of California, Santa Cruz

PROFESSIONAL ACCOMPLISHMENTS

PROGRAM DEVELOPMENT AND MANAGEMENT

- Drastically improved efficiency of the Women's AIDS Network by streamlining operations and improving communications among Board members, staff, and the community.
  Results:
  - 400% increase in membership.
  - Volunteer recruitment has grown five-fold.
  - Attendance of monthly public lectures tripled.
  - Improved quality and promptness of response to inquiries (50 per day).

- Wrote successful $30,000 AmFAR grant, and developed and implemented The AIDS Education and Prevention Program in Nepal. Designed this sustainable program based on cultural assessment, ongoing evaluation, and community involvement.

- Developed curriculum and co-led training workshops for participants of Project Ahead, the only speakers' bureau in the world comprised of youth with HIV.

SOCIAL MARKETING

- Initiated and directed the production of a 20'x70' mural in inner-city San Francisco that promoted education about women and HIV. Project generated media coverage, public response, and community group collaboration. Artwork was reproduced in several publications.

- As a spokesperson for the women's health community, interviewed by national and international TV, radio, and print media.

- As Health Educator for Save the Children, developed culturally sensitive visual aid materials for refugee women from Laos, Vietnam, and Cambodia.

- Enhanced image of Women's AIDS Network by redesigning its newsletter, providing higher quality content, design, and distribution.

- Conducted hour-long interviews with women at risk for STDs to collect epidemiological data for PHREDA (Perinatal HIV Reduction Education Demonstration Activities).

— Continued —

EVENT PLANNING

- Produced a block party and mural dedication to honor women living HIV, which was featured in the *San Francisco Chronicle*, as well a number of radio and TV stations.
  - Speakers included Roberta Achtenberg (mayoral candidate), Patti Chang (president, Commission on the Status of Women), and women with HIV.
- Designed and organized a two-day AIDS seminar in Nepal, attended by representatives from 20 local and international organizations.

EMPLOYMENT HISTORY

1994-95	Administrator	Women's AIDS Network, San Francisco, CA
1994	Training Coordinator	Project Ahead, Dept. of Public Health, San Francisco, CA
1993	Program Coordinator	Institute of Community Health, Kathmandu, Nepal
1992	Health Educator	Save the Children, Chonburi, Thailand

COMMUNITY SERVICE

1995	Community Organizer	Mural: Woman and HIV, San Francisco, CA
1993	Interviewer	PHREDA Project, San Francisco, CA
1993	Outreach Educator	STOP AIDS Project, San Francisco, CA
1988-90	Educator	Santa Cruz Women's Health Center, Santa Cruz, CA
1988	Midwife Assistant	San Francisco General Hospital, San Francisco, CA

Resume written in 1995.

Sandra Fleming, M.A., M.F.C.C.

224 Hearst Ave. • Berkeley, CA 94706 • (510) 215-8753

> M.F.C.C. stands for Marriage Family Child Counselor, which is Sandra's professional title and her desired area of employment.

EDUCATION

M.A., Counseling Psychology, John F. Kennedy University, Orinda, CA, 1990
Four Fold Way Training with Angeles Arrien, Ph.D., 1988-present
B.A., Psychology, State University of New York, Albany, NY, 1972

CERTIFICATION

M.F.C.C. License # MFC 32420
Certification, Imagery-In-Movement Expressive Art Therapy

PROFESSIONAL EXPERIENCE

1988-pres.   THERAPIST INTERN

Group Therapy Intern, 1995-present
Berkeley Group Psychotherapy Institute, Berkeley, CA

- As co-therapist, facilitate sessions for 16 single men and women from diverse cultural backgrounds, working on intrapsychic and interpersonal relationship issues.

National Expressive Art Therapy Intern, 1994-present
Francine Pendleton, C.E.A.T., Berkeley, CA

- Built a private client base of individuals, couples, and groups.
- Focus on the Imagery-In-Movement method, which integrates artistic expression, psychodrama, journaling, and dream work.

Marriage & Family Child Counselor Intern, 1991-1994
Expressive Arts Training & Counseling Center, Berkeley, CA

- Provided therapy for a client base of individuals, couples, and groups.
- Designed and delivered public lectures and workshops, introducing expressive art as a means of addressing:

Depression	Illness	Adoption
Eating disorders	Death	Job transition
Sexual abuse	Trauma	Personal growth
Substance abuse	Divorce	Spiritual emergence

M.F.C.C. Intern, 1988-1989
John F. Kennedy University Counseling Center, Oakland, CA

- Worked with individuals and couples, drawing upon:

Psychodynamic theory (Jungian)	Process psychology (Mindell)
Family systems theory	Hypnotherapy
Imagery-In-Movement psychology	

— Continued —

1988-pres. ADMINISTRATOR
Softech, Inc., Emeryville, CA
- Managed the administrative operations of this firm that grew from a start-up to a $6M business in seven years.
- Resolved personnel issues (interpersonal and performance); handled customer relations.

1980-1987 CUSTOMER SERVICE REPRESENTATIVE, Food and Beverage
St. Francis Hotel, San Francisco, CA, 1985-1987
Hilton Union Square Hotel, San Francisco, CA, 1980-1985

PROFESSIONAL AFFILIATIONS
California Association of Marriage and Family Therapists (CAMFT)
National Expressive Art Therapy Association

Resume written in 1995.

Use a Professional Profile Section

A third option is to substitute your Job Objective and Summary of Qualifications sections with a Profile section. This section should be made up of three or four strong qualification statements, the first of which makes it immediately clear what your line of work is. To understand how to write profile statements, jump ahead to Chapter 6 and follow the instructions for creating the Summary of Qualifications section. Following are two resumes that show the effectiveness of the profile technique.

Linda Geiber
815 N. Monterey Way
Lafayette, CA 94595
(510) 832-9412

> Linda used a strong opening profile statement to declare her career objective.

PROFILE

- Aspiring Interior Designer with experience in design development and drafting.
- Produced preliminary drawings and construction documents for commercial and residential projects.
- Creative approach to problem solving.

EDUCATION

BS, Interior Design, San Jose State University, San Jose, CA

> Conceptual Design
> Creative Problem Solving
> Space Planning
> Architectural Lighting Design
> Model Making
> Computer Design: MiniCAD, Adobe Illustrator

RELEVANT ACCOMPLISHMENTS

INTERIOR DESIGN

- Designed residential addition. Drafted preliminary drawings and construction documents. Worked with architect who followed plans through to completion.
- Completed drafting for projects including: water treatment plant
  housing developments
  apartment complexes
- Developed floor plans and elevations for commercial and residential projects.
- Conceptualized and created design for a delicatessen. Completed a specification book and made material selections for presentation boards.

CLIENT RELATIONS

- As part of space planning class, met with business owners to discuss their ideas and needs for developing conceptual plans.
- Built a clientele at Nordstrom by providing personal attention to customer needs and comprehensive product knowledge.

WORK HISTORY

1991-present	Salesperson	Nordstrom, Walnut Creek, CA
1988-1991	Junior Designer	Craig and Wood Architects, Danville, CA
1987-1988	Assistant to Interior Designer	Nina & Associates, Alamo, CA

— Portfolio available —

> Resume written in 1994.

Elisa K. Goloff

4252 Isle Street • Oakland, California 94641 • (510) 634-5536

PROFILE

> The first line of Elisa's profile is clear, concise, and identifies her profession.

- Elementary School Teacher with experience working with culturally and linguistically diverse students.
- Expert at designing and implementing Whole Language programs.
- Competent working knowledge of written and spoken Spanish gained through extensive travel and study in Mexico and Central America.
- Currently applying for Language Development Specialist Certificate.

EDUCATION AND CREDENTIAL

California State Multiple Subject (Elementary) Teaching Credential, 1991

M.A., Educational Psychology, 1991
Developmental Teacher Education Program
UNIVERSITY OF CALIFORNIA, Berkeley, CA

B.A., Psychology, 1988
CARNEGIE MELLON UNIVERSITY, Pittsburgh, PA

TEACHING EXPERIENCE

1991-present **Elementary School Teacher**
GRACE PATTERSON ELEMENTARY SCHOOL, Vallejo, CA

- Taught primary grade classes in this State Compensatory Education School with diverse student populations including:

Latino	European American	Pacific Islander
African American	Filipino	East Indian

- Designed and implemented developmental, student-centered, integrated curriculum covering all subject areas.
- Created and taught Whole Language program, including Writers' Workshop.
- Used Sheltered English and bilingual (Spanish) instructional techniques to help students of diverse linguistic backgrounds build content knowledge.
- Conducted parent conferences in both Spanish and English.
- Served as Master Teacher for four University of California student teachers.
- As a member of Patterson's Leadership Team, helped write three-year improvement plan and conducted staff inservices.
- Played active role in developing and writing Patterson's Achieving Schools proposal which was chosen one of ten in California for review in national competition.
- Planned and conducted staff inservice on teaching the concept of multiplication throughout the grade levels.
- Acted as Co-Chairperson for school-wide Multicultural Festival.
- Served as unofficial school photographer.

— Continued —

Elisa K. Goloff
Page 2

1991   **Student Teacher, five months**
GARFIELD ELEMENTARY SCHOOL, Oakland, CA
- Participated in an innovative university/public school liaison project.
- Worked extensively with Spanish and Mien speaking students, grades 1-6, using Sheltered English as an instructional technique.
- Implemented on-going dialogue journal writing for first grade Mien speaking students to increase English literacy.
- Conducted research and wrote Master's Project on the use of games to facilitate mathematical concept and language development.

1990   **Student Teacher, four months**
CRAGMONT ELEMENTARY SCHOOL, Berkeley, CA

1990   **Student Teacher, five months**
CORNELL ELEMENTARY SCHOOL, Albany, CA

1989   **Student Teacher, two months**
SCHAFER PARK ELEMENTARY SCHOOL, Hayward, CA

1989   **Student Teacher, two months**
GRASS VALLEY ELEMENTARY SCHOOL, Oakland, CA

1988-1989   **Teacher, ten months**
CARNEGIE MELLON UNIVERSITY CHILDREN'S SCHOOL, Pittsburgh, PA
- Participated in team instruction of children, ages 3-5.
- Planned and executed activities in the areas of language arts, math, science, computers, art, and dramatic play.
- Adapted and tested a developmental science curriculum for young children.

ADDITIONAL EXPERIENCE

1990   **Instructional Assistant**
ACADEMIC TALENT DEVELOPMENT PROGRAM, Berkeley, CA
- Co-taught a hands-on physical science class for gifted and talented primary students.

1990   **Research Assistant**
UNIVERSITY OF CALIFORNIA, Berkeley, CA
- Assisted in educational research by conducting experimental sessions and coding data.

1989   **Teaching Assistant**
UNIVERSITY OF CALIFORNIA, Berkeley, CA
- Taught section of undergraduate developmental psychology course. Supervised students and conducted review and study sessions.

Resume written in 1994.

When a Job Objective Statement Is Not Necessary

If you're well established in your profession and plan to stay in your line of work, your resume could work even if it doesn't have a job objective statement of any kind. The contents must so strongly paint the picture of your profession that no one could possibly think that you want to do anything else. This strategy is especially effective if you use a chronological resume (this format is discussed in Chapter 3) and if your most recent job title is the same as the one you're seeking.

The following two resumes don't include job objective statements. In each case, the reader will rightly assume that the job seeker wants to continue in his or her current profession.

Mary Hart
1980 Wawona Street, #221 • San Francisco, CA 94123 • (415) 331-8832

> Even without a job objective statement, it's evident from Mary's current and former job titles that she's a marketing professional.

Professional Experience

1992-present **ABC Asset Management Partners, Inc.**
VICE PRESIDENT, MARKETING, Hartford, CT (1992-1994), San Francisco, CA (1994-pres.)
- Led national marketing effort during the first three years of this young investment management firm which grew from $500 million to $1.8 billion.
- Targeted public, Taft Hartley, and corporate pension funds of $100+ million in assets.
- Contributed 35% of firm's asset growth and secured 45% of total client base. Provided ongoing client service.
- Increased assets by maintaining strong relationships with consultants.
- Opened the San Francisco office to increase business in the western region.

1988-1992 **Forcasters, Inc.,** New York, NY
MANAGER, MARKETING AND CLIENT SERVICES
- Cold called and developed relationships with corporate and public plan sponsors during the firm's growth in fixed income assets from $1.7 billion to $5 billion.
- As liaison to consultants, responded to RFPs for fixed income products.
- Involved in client service and portfolio review meetings. Managed monthly reporting to 72 clients.

1987-1988 **Smith, Franklin & Jones Securities Corporation,** New York, NY
ASSISTANT TO SENIOR VICE PRESIDENT, Fixed Income Department
- Gained fixed income experience through projects related to government, mortgage-backed, and money market securities.
- Trained and supervised department staff.

1986-1987 **Pekingwood & Company,** New York, NY
MANAGER, SHAREHOLDER SERVICES
- Produced financial projections and proposals for this investment banking boutique.
- Invested money won through legal settlement until disbursed to shareholders.

1984-1985 **AT&T Communications,** Basking Ridge, NJ
MARKETING CONSULTANT
- Developed and managed information centers at three locations that tracked 50 million customers for national marketing project resulting from AT&T's divestiture.

Education

B.A., University of Colorado, Denver, CO, 1984
Phi Kappa Phi, National Honors Society, Deans List

Candidate, second level, Chartered Financial Analyst designation
Registered Representative (Series 7)

Professional Affiliations

Association for Investment Management Research
San Francisco Society of Security Analysts

> Resume written in 1995.

(707) 339-5647

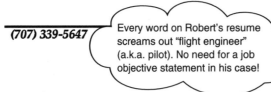

Every word on Robert's resume screams out "flight engineer" (a.k.a. pilot). No need for a job objective statement in his case!

Robert   Freeman

631 Lucerne Avenue
Lodi, CA 95687

PROFESSIONAL EXPERIENCE

FLIGHT ENGINEER
- 10 years flying and working on the L-1011 aircraft.
- 3 years instructing new L-1011 flight engineers during ground, simulator, and flying phases.
- 15 years flying and working on the C-5A/B military cargo aircraft.
- Extensive experience in Operations and Maintenance, transporting passengers and cargo worldwide.
- Over 12,000 hours flying and simulator time.
- Performed functional check flights after heavy maintenance.

CHIEF FLIGHT ENGINEER
- Wrote annual performance reports on aircrew members.
- Developed a new airman performance report system that was adopted by the unit.
- Oversaw interviewing and hiring process to ensure that new engineers have adequate experience and good working attitude.
- Created an orientation package to welcome new personnel.
- Held monthly meetings to keep flight engineers fully informed of changes in policies and job responsibilities.
- Developed work organizational chart that clarified responsibilities.

CERTIFICATES
FAA Flight Engineer Turbojet
FAA Airframe and Powerplant Mechanic
FCC Radio Operator
FAA Medical Class II
Former RII Inspector

EMPLOYMENT HISTORY
1983-present	Chief Flight Engineer C-5A/B	USAF RESERVES, Travis AFB, CA
1991	Flight Engineer L-1011	AIR ATLANTA, Iceland
1984-1990	Instructor Flight Engineer L-1011	AIR AMERICA, Los Angeles, CA
1980-1983	Flight Engineer L-1011	SAUDI ARABIAN AIRLINES, Jeddah, SA
1975-1980	Flight Engineer C-5A	U. S. AIR FORCE, Travis AFB, CA

EDUCATION AND TRAINING
B.S.,   Industrial Technology, Southern Illinois University
A.S.,   Flight Engineering, Community College of the Air Force
A.S.,   Aircraft Maintenance Technology, Community College of the Air Force
Flight Engineer Courses: Air National Guard
U.S. Air Force Reserves
Saudi Arabian Airlines
Lockheed Aircraft Corporation

LANGUAGE
Fluent in Spanish

Resume written in 1993.

Go For It

Ready to commit your thoughts to paper? Good. If you've decided you need a job objective, write it as concisely as possible, using the creative approaches discussed in this chapter. If you've decided to go with a Professional Profile section instead, write one now.

The Least You Need to Know

➤ Keep your job objective concise and to the point.

➤ Consider one of the following alternatives to the job objective statement: a professional title, a degree or credential after your name, or a Professional Profile.

➤ If you want your next position to be the same as your last (or current) one, and your career path strongly (and I mean *strongly*) supports that job objective, consider not using a job objective statement on your resume.

Step Four— Knock 'Em Off Their Feet... in the First Few Lines

In This Chapter

➤ Strong summary statements make a good first impression

➤ Avoiding resume clichés

➤ Your heading and summary statements as a mini-resume

Experienced players in the marketing game know it's important to create a splash right away in a promotional piece. The way to do that on your resume is to give top billing to claims that knock the employer off his or her feet. For example, the opening section of Christopher Columbus's resume might have read:

Summary of Qualifications

➤ First European to make verified contact with Americans since the Vikings five centuries before.

➤ Christened six Caribbean islands, whose names now signify choice vacation spots.

➤ Noted captain and navigator of four Atlantic crossings who set world sailing records for his time.

What do you think? Wouldn't you want this guy to captain your next trans-oceanic sailing trip?

Highlight Your Qualifications

Kick off your resume with a Summary of Qualifications section (also called "Highlights of Qualifications" or just plain "Highlights") near the top of your resume. You may not be able to tout mind-blowing achievements like Columbus, but you can look pretty terrific with three or four smashing statements that set you apart from the crowd. Talk about your experience, credentials, expertise, personal values, work ethics, background, or anything that makes you outstanding in your field. You're free to make claims, drop names, and do your best to entice the employer to call you for an interview. Remember, all claims must be substantiated later when you write the body of your resume, so be *honest* while giving yourself *full credit*.

The resume template on the following page shows you where the Summary of Qualifications section appears on the resume.

Say It With Style

Whatever you do, don't use hackneyed phrases such as "Excellent written and oral communication skills," "Outstanding organizational abilities," "Goal-oriented individual," and countless other overused, vague lines. Columbus's resume would have gotten lost in the pack if it had read:

Summary of Qualifications

➤ Exceptional organizational and people skills

➤ Goal-oriented, self-motivated individual

➤ Excellent written and communication skills

Don't get me wrong, the meanings behind most of those phrases are wonderful and may be exactly true for you. But since these clichés appear on almost everyone's resume, they don't have punch and, frankly, are not taken seriously.

Before you put a sentence in your Summary of Qualifications, ask yourself: Is it a "grabber"? Is it news to the reader? If it's what everyone else says, it's not news and it won't grab the reader. It has to be said in a way that's unique, remarkable, and memorable.

(Here's where the "Summary of Qualifications" goes on your resume.)

Name
Street • City, State Zip • phone

JOB OBJECTIVE
The job you want next

SUMMARY OF QUALIFICATIONS
- How much experience you have in the field of your objective, in a related field, or using the skills required for your new position.
- An overall career accomplishment that shows you'd be good at this job objective.
- What someone would say about you as a recommendation.

PROFESSIONAL EXPERIENCE

19xx-pres. **Company Name,** City, State
JOB TITLE
- An accomplishment you are proud of that shows you're good at this profession.
- A problem you solved and the results.
- A time when you positively affected the organization, the bottom line, your boss, your co-workers, your clients.
- Awards, commendations, publications, etc. you achieved that relate to your job objective.

19xx-xx **Company Name,** City, State
JOB TITLE
- A project you are proud of that supports your job objective.
- Another accomplishment that shows you're good at this line of work.
- Quantifiable results that point out your skill.

EDUCATION
Degree, Major (if relevant), 19xx (optional)
University, City, State

My motto: no mushy statements. Always make the point as concretely as possible. Use facts to create credibility and to instill a sense that you are unlike any other candidate applying for the job. Ask yourself: What specifically have I done that demonstrates that I have the desired quality? How does my skill translate into success at my next job? Here are some examples of what I mean:

➤ Fred was applying for a pizza delivery position. Since there's a high turn-over rate in this type of employment, he felt his reliability was a marketable asset. So instead of "Excellent record of attendance," he wrote, "Never missed a day of work in 11 months."

➤ When Sandy was going for a customer service position, she knew the potential employer was looking for someone with "Excellent communication skills." She wrote, "Deemed 'Customer Service Rep of the Month' for resolving problems diplomatically."

➤ Instead of "Goal-oriented professional," Frank wrote, "Exceeded quotas four consecutive years" on his resume for a sales position.

Commandments

Commandment I: Thou shalt not write about your past; thou shalt write about your future! Your summary statements should so strongly paint the picture of you at your next job that there appears to be little or no transition into your new job—even if you're making a big career change.

Commandments

Commandment IV: Thou shalt not write about stuff you don't want to do again. Be careful to avoid including tasks that you don't like to perform. Mentioning them is a sure way of having them in your next job description.

Throughout the resume, write in the first person without using pronouns. In other words, phrase your statements as if you are talking about yourself without saying "I." For example, write "Understand the art of conflict resolution" instead of "I understand the art of conflict resolution."

For ideas on summary statements, browse through the following four resumes.

William I. Jansen

44 Windor Court • Vacaville, CA 94661 • (916) 882-0032

JOB OBJECTIVE
Technical Sales Account Manager

SUMMARY OF QUALIFICATIONS

Strong summary of qualification statements. No hackneyed phrases here!

- 13 years as an engineer collaborating on key marketing/sales strategies for one of the nation's largest corporations.
- Thoroughly enjoy making sales presentations that motivate audiences to "buy into" new products.
- Technical versatility: construction, computer systems, telecommunications, safety, and environmental.

PROFESSIONAL ACCOMPLISHMENTS

SALES / MARKETING

- Increased premium product sales 10% ($3.5 million) by designing a $2 million advertising and point-of-sale strategy. Led team of sales experts, merchandising specialists, market researchers, P.O.S. vendors, and product engineers.
- Made winning "sales" presentation regarding a $25 million retail automation project. Built consensus among company divisions with competing interests by facilitating needs assessment, goal setting, and cooperative strategy planning.
- Increased revenue $10 million annually by convincing 7,000 retailers to use electronic funds transfer system.
- Led several testimonial and training presentations that "sold" new technologies to audiences with resistance to change.

TECHNICAL PROJECT MANAGEMENT

- Led the technical development of customer activated credit/debit card payment system implemented at Shell stations nationwide. Increased corporate annual sales $127 million.
- Designed and led development of a computerized maintenance dispatch system for 7,000 retail outlets and 50 bulk facilities nationwide that eliminated service station down-time, increasing corporate sales $7.7 million per year.
- Directed the $70 million construction of 60 service stations in California, designing architectural plans that met regional public appeal, environmental regulations, and local government demands.

WORK HISTORY

1981-present Shell Oil Corporation, Sacramento, CA
        Environmental Safety Fire and Health Specialist, 1993-present
        Trading Analyst, 1991-1993
        Project Manager, Market Place Development, 1990-1991
        Project Manager, Electronics Systems - Service Stations, 1987-1990
        Analyst for Product Order and Delivery, 1986-1987
        Project Manager, Service Station Construction, 1983-1986
        Staff Engineer, 1981-1983

EDUCATION

B.E., Chemical Engineering, Massachusetts Institute of Technology, Cambridge, MA, 1981
Professional Development: American Demographics Annual Marketing Conference
Sales and negotiations seminars

Resume written in 1994.

Alon Hunt
3-D Modeler and Animator

1915 Appian Drive
Crofford, CA 94411
(510) 565-7764

SUMMARY OF QUALIFICATIONS

Alon's summary statements build a nice bridge between his professional and personal achievements.

- Skilled at generating organic models and character animation.
- Creative interest in surreal productions.
- Proficient in:
  SGI: Alias Power Animator with all advanced modules
  Macintosh: MacroModel, StradaVision, Sketch, Illustrator, and FreeHand
- Lifelong pursuit of drawing, painting, modeling, music, and acting.

RELEVANT ACCOMPLISHMENTS

3-D MODELING, RENDERING, AND ANIMATION

- Contracted by Atari as 3-D animator for Virtual Racing video game for the new 32-bit Saturn by Sega (to be released by December 1994):
  - Generated all animation.
  - Created human and object models.
  - Produced a realistic feel despite restricted resolution.
  - Completed project prior to deadline.
- Modeled and animated pyrotechnical effects for Rocket Science's new CD Rom game.
- Applications engineer for Vastec, one of the largest Alias retailers in the U.S.
- Generated models and flying logos for Channel 1, TV Broadcast of Israel.

FINE ARTS AND MUSIC

- Achieved scholarship to attend Bezalel Academy of Art.
- Contracted by the Tel Aviv Museum to use recently discovered plans to construct a wooden model of a ship from Biblical times.
- Won the Charat Foundation Scholarship for gifted musicians.

PROJECT MANAGEMENT

- Started and built the largest AT&T security system dealership in California.
- Opened and managed two branch offices of Knight Protective Industry, which led the company in a nationwide expansion.

WORK HISTORY

1989-present Marketing Director/President, Global Security, Inc.
1986-1989 Marketing/Sales Manager, Knight Protective Industry, Inc.

PROFESSIONAL DEVELOPMENT

Computer: SGI System Administration Course
Advanced Animation Course by Alias
Fine Arts: Drawing Classes, Bezalel Academy of Art, Jerusalem, Israel
Ship Modeling Workshop
Music: Classical Guitar, Harmony, and Composition with Larry Ferrara of the San Francisco Conservatory of Music
Classical Guitar with Joseph Yerusalemi (renowned concert guitarist)

Resume written in 1994.

Frances Morgan

77 Fairmont Road • Oakland, CA 94611 • (510) 883-0042

OBJECTIVE

Employee Relations Specialist

SUMMARY OF QUALIFICATIONS

In her summary statements, Frances used a quote from a former client to gain credibility.

- More than 10 years as an expert in:
  Psychology of Change in the Workplace
  The Psychology of Work
- Skilled at assisting people from all levels of employment and cultural backgrounds.
- "You've changed my understanding of work. I now find it a dynamic and energizing principle." — Manufacturing Manager

TRAINING AND DEVELOPMENT ACCOMPLISHMENTS

1991-present Hingchi Institute, Berkeley, CA
Instructor, The Skillful Means of Work, 1992-present
Chef, 1991-1992

- Taught professionals, managers, office workers, and tradespeople from multicultural backgrounds. Topics include:

  Dealing with Stress   Concentration
  Responsibility and Commitment   Organizational Skills
  Dynamics of Teamwork   Dealing with Difficult People

- Turned around a failing institutional kitchen and, with no previous professional culinary experience, produced a sparkling, efficient system within four weeks.
  - Trained staff.
  - Organized inventory and standardized procedures.

- Managed a building renovation project, training and supervising a crew of student volunteers with no experience in construction. Finished project at professional standards within time constraints.

1983-1990 Human Development Training Company, Miami, FL
Trainer/Manager

- Trained professionals, artists, tradespeople, and students in productive work habits that increased proficiency, work satisfaction, and income.

- Created a "work laboratory" that provided hands-on experience in development of:
  Teamwork   Self-Esteem
  Conflict Management Skills Client Relations
  Dynamic Work Style   Time Management Skills

1979-1983 Fellowship of Light: School of Daoist Skills, Miami, FL
Full-time Student, Human Development

1975-1978 San Clemente Real Estate, San Clemente, CA
Co-manager

- Trained and supervised renovation staff working on residential projects.

EDUCATION

M.A. equivalent, Training and Development:
University of California Extension, Berkeley, CA
California Institute of Integral Studies, San Francisco, CA
Nyingma Institute, Berkeley, CA
Fellowship of Light: School of Daoist Skills, Miami, FL

Resume written in 1994.

Eric C. Greenwood
735 Idleton Drive, Apt. 12 • Santa Clara, California 94404 • (408) 322-9713

JOB OBJECTIVE

Communications Manager/Writer/Editor

SUMMARY OF QUALIFICATIONS

- Six years as a professional communications specialist, writer and editor for high-profile organizations and individuals.
- Experience in front-line positions requiring maturity and sound judgment to handle sensitive and volatile communications.
- Skilled at becoming an "expert" in complicated subjects and translating them into lay terms for the media, government bodies and the public.
- Proficient at:

Press releases	News reporting	Column writing
PR material	Speeches	Letters to the editor
Op-ed pieces	Legislation	Humor pieces
Editorials	Sports reporting	Reviews

Eric used a good graphic technique—multiple columns—to make his assets visible at a glance.

PROFESSIONAL EXPERIENCE

1992-present Media Specialist/Senior Account Executive
DELACORTE/SHINOFF ADVOCACY COMMUNICATIONS, San Francisco, CA
Assist clients in developing their messages and presenting them effectively to the media.

- Managed a western U.S. department store campaign that won "Best Communications Package," an annual public relations award presented by the Bay Area Publicity Club.
- Instigated a public demand for local representation on a regional governmental body. Wrote press releases that led to newspaper coverage and supporting editorials. Authored resolutions passed by two city councils.
- Played a significant role in managing a unique public relations program that saved the jobs of 800 workers facing termination. Wrote releases, arranged press conferences and served as media spokesperson.
- Edited material for the Bay Area's only successful pro-development election campaign in 1993.
- Help clients prepare for press conferences, governmental hearings, council meetings and other forums where effective presentation is crucial.

1990-present Editor in Chief
NORTHERN CALIFORNIA TEAMSTER NEWSPAPER, San Francisco, CA
Produce a quality bi-monthly newspaper with circulation of 70,000.

- Manage the writing, photography, layout and on-time production of the publication in a highly-charged political environment.
- Upgraded quality by computerizing production and widening the scope of coverage.
- Serve as media spokesperson. Write news releases, speeches and PR pieces.
- Reported on first open election in the history of the Teamsters. Served as liaison among lawyers, election overseers and local unions in the publication of critical election notices.

— Continued —

Eric C. Greenwood
Page 2

1990-1993   **Assignment Editor/Reporter**
1988-1989   BAY CITY NEWS SERVICE, San Francisco, CA
Managed news reporting, editing and client relations for this regional wire service with 80 clients including top print and broadcast news outlets.

- Supervised staff of 12 reporters. Selected stories for assignment. Edited up to 40 stories a day.
- Scooped Bay Area media with major developments in the case of mass murderer Ramon Salcido and the arrest of sport celebrity Jose Canseco on felony charges.

1989-1990   **Administrative Aide to Supervisor Wendy Nelder**
CITY AND COUNTY OF SAN FRANCISCO, BOARD OF SUPERVISORS
Managed this high-profile office under constant media scrutiny.

- Authored legislation, summarized Board agendas, and wrote news releases and letters on behalf of Supervisor Nelder.
- Represented the supervisor before committees to present legislation.

EDUCATION

B.A., Journalism, 1988
Golden Key National Honor Society, Dean's List
San Francisco State University, San Francisco, CA

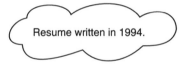

Resume written in 1994.

Go For It

Now it's time to write your summary statements. To help you come up with three or four strong statements, answer the following questions:

How much experience do you have in this profession, in this field, or using the required skills?

Example: Someone staying in the field of financial management might say: "I have 14 years of experience as the financial manager of a company with current sales of $75 million."

Summary statement: Fourteen years as the financial manager of a company with current sales of $75 million.

Example: A job seeker transitioning from teaching to corporate training might say: "I have seven years of professional experience using strong communication skills to enhance learning of individuals from diverse backgrounds."

Summary statement: Seven years of professional experience using strong communication skills to enhance learning of individuals from diverse backgrounds.

Imagine your best friend is talking to the hiring person for the job you want. What would your best friend say about you that would make the employer want to call you for an interview?

Example: The best friend of a job hunter desiring an editorial position with a newspaper might say: "He's the first syndicated journalist from the *Examiner* to receive the Pulitzer Prize."

Summary statement: First syndicated journalist from the *Examiner* to receive the Pulitzer Prize.

Example: The colleague of a CEO seeking a membership on the Board of Directors of a crisis prevention nonprofit organization might write: "He's known for leading a committee that took the first step toward community rehabilitation after the 1989 earthquake."

Summary statement: Known for leading a committee that took the first step toward community rehabilitation after the 1989 earthquake.

How is success measured in the position mentioned in your objective? How do you measure up?

Example: A salesperson reaching for a sales management job might write: "I consistently exceeded personal quotas and inspired sales team members to meet group goals."

Summary statement: Consistently exceeded personal quotas and inspired sales team members to meet group goals.

Example: A software developer wishing to make a move into technical writing might say: "I have a reputation for writing clear and concise explanations for technical and non-technical users."

Summary statement: Reputation for writing clear and concise explanations for technical and non-technical users.

What credentials do you have that are important for this job?

Example: A fashion buyer looking for a position as a graphic designer might say: "I have a Bachelor of Fine Arts with an emphasis on design."

Summary statement: Bachelor of Fine Arts with an emphasis on design.

Example: A geology teacher seeking a position at a community college in California might write: "I got my Lifetime California Community College Teaching Credential in Earth Science."

Summary statement: California Community College Teaching Credential, Earth Science, Lifetime.

What is it about your personality that makes this job a good fit for you?

Example: A customer service representative staying in the same field might write: "I have outstanding diplomacy that consistently produces win-win results for customers and the company."

Summary statement: Outstanding diplomacy that consistently produces win-win results for customers and the company.

Example: An architect applying for a post in a professional organization could say: "I have natural problem-solving skills that create both practical and agreeable solutions."

Summary statement: Natural problem-solving skills that create both practical and agreeable solutions.

What personal commitments or passions do you have that would be valued by the employer?

Example: Someone wanting to lead an environmental organization could write: "I have a strong commitment to preserving nature through education about environmental hazards."

Summary statement: Strong commitment to preserving nature through education about environmental hazards.

Example: A psychologist going for a job in human resources might say: "I'm dedicated to maximizing others' potential through careful assessment and acknowledgment of their personal skills."

Summary statement: Dedicated to maximizing others' potential through careful assessment and acknowledgment of their personal skills.

What other experience do you have that will be a bonus to the employer?

Example: A new graduate seeking her first job as a nurse could say: "I have volunteer experience in a clinic with an interdisciplinary staff of 12."

Summary statement: Volunteer experience in a clinic with an interdisciplinary staff of 12.

Example: Someone trying for a position on the mayor's administrative staff might mention: "I have developed a talent for debating controversial issues, as a member of a family with three generations of political professionals."

Summary statement: Developed talent for debating controversial issues, as a member of a family with three generations of political professionals.

Do you have any technical, linguistic, or artistic talents that would be useful on the job?

Example: Someone applying to be a teacher in a multilingual school might write: "I am multilingual: Spanish/English/Italian/Russian."

Summary statement: Multilingual: Spanish/English/Italian/Russian.

Example: An artist seeking a commission from the city's museum could say: "I'm adept at working in a range of mediums, including paint, pen and ink, clay, metal, collage, and wood."

Summary statement: Adept at working in a range of mediums, including paint, pen and ink, clay, metal, collage, and wood.

Tip

YOU'RE HIRED.

Put your best foot forward! After you've listed your Summary of Qualifications statements, prioritize them so that the most relevant and most impressive one comes first.

Your Mini-Resume

Now that you've written the Job Objective (see Chapter 5) and Summary of Qualifications sections, notice how the top of your resume is sort of a mini-resume. It tells the employer:

➤ Who you are

➤ What you want

➤ Why you should have it

If you've done a good job, it should be enough to convince the employer to consider you for the position.

The Least You Need to Know

➤ A strong Summary of Qualifications section will grab the employer's attention and make him think, "Here's the person for the job."

➤ Don't use overused phrases such as "Excellent communication skills."

➤ Prioritize your summary statements so that the strongest one comes first.

Chapter 7

Step Five—Been There, Done That

In This Chapter

➤ Creating a work history that shows off your strengths

➤ Using dates on your resume to fight age discrimination

➤ How to disguise gaps in your employment history

➤ Adding volunteer experience to your Work History section

➤ How to make your promotions noticeable at a glance

Employers give a lot of attention to a job seeker's work history. It's one of the first things they look for after they see what your job objective is. They want to know about your track record—where you've been and how long you stayed there. Of course, what they're trying to figure out is: Are you a stable person? What are your talents? And most importantly, would you be a good fit for the job opening they have?

A healthy work history presentation is clearly important. Building one that maximizes your experience is what this chapter is all about.

Work History

To start, I want to be sure you understand what I'm referring to when I say "work history." If you're a chronological resume writer (remember that lesson in Chapter 3?), your history will be distributed throughout the midsection of your resume. If you're a functional resume writer, your work history will be listed in one section at the bottom of your resume. The resumes templates on the following pages show you which areas I mean.

> **Tip**
>
> If you're running short on space, be creative in how you present your work history information. Check out the sample resumes in this book to find clever techniques that save a line here and there.

The next step is to insert your work history into your resume. Sounds easy enough, doesn't it? But what if you have a situation that's tricky to present in your employment history, such as:

➤ Dates that go back so far that they trigger age discrimination

➤ So little employment history that you appear too young for the job

➤ Gaps in your work history

➤ Multiple positions at the same company

Remember Commandment II: *Thou shalt not confess.* In other words, you don't have to "tell all." Stick to what's relevant and marketable.

> **Tip**
>
> Here's a rule of thumb: If you've owned a business, don't say so on your resume. In the hiring world, it's often thought that once someone has worked for himself, he'll never make a good employee again. Of course, that statement isn't necessarily true, but it is an assumption frequently made by employers since the self-employed person usually likes being the boss and is driven by profit. A way around revealing your self-employment is to give yourself a job title in your business, choosing a title that supports your current job objective, if possible.

Let's take a closer look at these issues and figure out ways you can resolve them.

(Here's where the "Work History" appears in the choronological resume.)

Name
Street • City, State Zip • phone

JOB OBJECTIVE
The job you want next

SUMMARY OF QUALIFICATIONS
- How much experience you have in the field of your objective, in a related field, or using the skills required for your new position.
- An overall career accomplishment that shows you'd be good at this job objective.
- What someone would say about you as a recommendation.

PROFESSIONAL EXPERIENCE

19xx-pres. **Company Name,** City, State
JOB TITLE
- An accomplishment you are proud of that shows you're good at this profession.
- A problem you solved and the results.
- A time when you positively affected the organization, the bottom line, your boss, your co-workers, your clients.
- Awards, commendations, publications, etc. you achieved that relate to your job objective.

19xx-xx **Company Name,** City, State
JOB TITLE
- A project you are proud of that supports your job objective.
- Another accomplishment that shows you're good at this line of work.
- Quantifiable results that point out your skill.

EDUCATION
Degree, Major (if relevant), 19xx (optional)
University, City, State

(Here's where the "Work History" appears in the functional resume.)

Name
Street • City, State Zip • phone

JOB OBJECTIVE
> The job you want next

SUMMARY OF QUALIFICATIONS
- How much experience you have in the field of your objective, in a related field, or using the skills required for your new position.
- An overall career accomplishment that shows you'd be good at this job objective.
- What someone would say about you as a recommendation.

RELEVANT EXPERIENCE

MAJOR SKILL
- An accomplishment you are proud of that shows you're good at this skill.
- A problem you solved using this skill, and the results.
- A time when you used your skill to positively affected the organization, the bottom line, your boss, your clients.
- Awards, commendations, publications, etc. you achieved that relate to your job objective.

MAJOR SKILL
- A project you are proud of that supports your job objective.
- Another accomplishment that shows you're good at this line of work.
- Quantifiable results that point out your skill.

WORK HISTORY

19xx-present	Job Title	COMPANY NAME and city
19xx-xx	Job Title	COMPANY NAME and city
19xx-xx	Job Title	COMPANY NAME and city
19xx-xx	Job Title	COMPANY NAME and city

EDUCATION
> Degree, Major (if relevant), 19xx (optional)
> University, City, State

Fighting Age Discrimination

"How far back should I go in my work history?" is a good question to ask yourself as you set out to document your history. In general, you're not expected to go back more than ten years, but you can if it's to your benefit. To help you figure out how far back to go in your work history, consider the following:

➤ How relevant your earliest positions are to your job objective

➤ How old you want to appear on your resume

Age discrimination is illegal, but like it or not, employers usually try to figure out your age using the dates you give. Most employers have an age range they consider to be ideal for a particular job, based on salary expectations, skill level, ability to supervise or be supervised, and amount of life experience needed (age discrimination works both ways—too old *and* too young). A well-written resume uses dates to lead the employer to deduce that you are *at least* the ideal age for the job you're after, regardless of your actual age.

The following two sections show you how to work with dates on your resume to create the ideal image.

How to Create a Younger "Look" on Your Resume

Sally, 43 years old, is applying for a job as a sales clerk in a clothing store that caters to young professional women. She thinks the employer is probably looking for a woman in her early 30s since the employer wants someone who fits the image of the store and won't expect as high wages as someone who has been in the field for many years.

To present herself in her resume as the ideal candidate, Sally decides to go back only ten years in her work history, since the employer will most likely take 20 years old as a starting point, add the ten years of work experience shown in her work history, and conclude that Sally is at least 30 years old. Likewise, in her education, she states her degree but does not give her graduation date since it would give away her age.

Tip
Dates in your Education section are optional. List them if they make you "look" the right age for the job you are going for. Delete them if they lead the reader to deduce that you are older or younger than you want to appear for the job.

The dates on Sally's resume are all honest, they just don't tell all. In the interview she will have the opportunity to sell herself with her enthusiasm, professional manner, and appropriate salary request—thereby fulfilling the employer's expectations of the ideal candidate.

How to Create an Older "Look" on Your Resume

Sam is a new grad who has worked in his dad's business all through high school and college. He's a remarkable achiever and is ready for more responsibility in the workforce than most his age. He applies for a position as a store manager, knowing that if he can just get his foot in the door he can convince the owner he can handle the job.

He decides that the employer is probably expecting to hire someone in his late 20s. So on his resume, Sam goes back in his work history eight years to when he started working for his dad in low-level positions and shows his progression over the following years. He states that he has a degree, but does not give the date since it might indicate that he is only 22.

Everything on Sam's resume honestly paints the picture of someone who has the experience and maturity of a 30-year-old without ever saying his age.

Commandments

Commandment V: Thou shalt not lie. You can be creative, but be honest. Of all the sections of your resume, your Work History is the most likely to be verified by a potential employer. Be sure your entries in this section coincide with the information your former employers will give.

Tip

Here's a quick and easy method for understanding how dates on your resume make an impression about your age. I call it my EPT formula (Experience Plus Twenty). Subtract the earliest date on your resume from today's date (using years only, no months). Add that number of years to 20 (as a ballpark figure for how old you might have been when your experience started) to get a total of "x." That means you are at least x years old.

For example, a resume written in 1996 with a work history that starts in 1980 tells the reader that the job applicant is at least 36 years old (16 years of experience + 20 = 36).

Disguising Employment Gaps

"What's wrong with a few gaps in my work history?" you might ask. "Isn't everyone entitled to a little time off?" Many responsible professionals have taken breaks in their careers to travel, take care of ill parents, recover from illnesses, or for other legitimate reasons.

But for some reason, employers don't like to see gaps in your work history. They would rather see the unemployed time explained, especially if the explanation is somehow connected to your job objective, or at least shows strength of character.

A void in your work history may cause the reader to think, "This person is hiding something," or "Here's someone who might have a problem" (such as substance abuse, incarceration, laziness, or instability). To gain the employer's trust, it's important to *justify your employment gaps*.

If you have a period of unemployment in your history, here are some ways of dealing with it:

➤ Use only years, not months, when referring to spans of time in your work history. This makes it quicker for the reader to grasp the length of time, and can eliminate the need to explain gaps that occurred within two calendar years.

Notice the gap in this presentation:

12/89–3/94	Manager	Friendly's Ice Cream Parlor, Trenton, NJ
2/87–1/88	Manager	Lyon's Restaurant, Milbrae, CA

Without the months, there is no apparent gap:

1989–1994	Manager	Friendly's Ice Cream Parlor, Trenton, NJ
1987–1988	Manager	Lyon's Restaurant, Milbrae, CA

➤ If your unemployment covers two calendar years or more, you need to explain the void. Consider all the things you were doing during that time (volunteer work, school activities, internships, schooling, travel, etc.) and present it in a way that's relevant to your job objective, if possible.

Someone looking for a medical sales position who took care of an ill parent for two years might say:

1984–1986   Home Care Provider for terminally ill relative

An applicant for a travel agent position could refer to a vacation:

1990–1991   Independent Travel: Europe, Asia, and South America

A mother wanting to reenter the job market as a teacher's aide might say:

1983–1989   Full-Time Parent and PTA Volunteer, St. John's Academy

➤ Even if your activities during your unemployment have no apparent relevancy to your job objective, you need to account for the gap. Just explain what you were doing in a way that is honest and feels comfortable to you. Don't refer to illness, unemployment (even if it is clearly due to a recession), or rehabilitation. These topics usually raise red flags, so avoid mentioning them at all cost. Think of something else you were doing during that time, even if it doesn't relate to your job objective, and refer to that activity instead of using a job title in your work history. Some suggested substitutes for a job title include:

Full-Time Parent	Professional Development
Home Management	Student
Family Management	Freelance whatever
Family Financial Management	Consultant
Independent Study	Contractual whatever
Personal Travel	Relocation from abroad
Adventure Travel	Volunteer
Travels to wherever	Civic Leader

Tip

If you include unpaid experience in your work history, be sure that you call this section either "Work History" or "History," not "Employment History," since "employment" implies that you were paid.

The following six resumes all have something in common: tricky work histories. If you're looking for a solution to a complicated history, one of these resumes may give you an idea for handling your situation.

Andrea R. Secore

41 Lucianna Drive • San Pedro, CA 95132 • **(408) 998-0253**

JOB OBJECTIVE

A position teaching preschool and elementary age children.

SUMMARY OF QUALIFICATIONS

- More than 20 years teaching preschool and elementary age children.
- Good communication skills with children and adults.
- Capable of leading projects. Supportive team worker.
- Experience working in low-economic and ethnic settings.

EXPERIENCE

WORK WITH CHILDREN

California State Preschool Program, a parent participation program:

- Taught children of low-income families from diverse cultural backgrounds.
- Incorporated parents into the program, being sensitive to the parents' needs for shared responsibility.
- Planned parent education programs and trained them in effective communications with children.
- Collaborated with fellow teacher to share ideas and solutions, as well as to train teacher aide in classroom management style and curriculum.

SCHOOL-COMMUNITY RELATIONS

San Pedro Elementary School

- Served on PTA board as president (2 years) and coordinator of parent services in the classroom (2 years).
- Taught Parent Educator Program (3 years). Co-planned curriculum, and facilitated classroom discussions on prevention of drug and alcohol abuse, and self-esteem.
- Volunteered extensively for classroom activities, field trips, etc., during my own children's school years.
- As member of School Site Council, planned use of state funds for school.
  - Identified the area of need; built a consensus of how to address it.
  - Applied for funding.

WORK HISTORY

Andrea was a mom reentering the workforce after many years of unemployment (her work in 1992 was done as a volunteer).

1992	**Childcare Teacher**	Westgate Baptist Church, Beaumont, TX
1976-92	**Full-time Parent**	San Pedro, CA and Nederland, TX
1969-76	**Classroom Teacher**	Texas State Preschool Program, Blair, TX
1967-69	**Classroom Kindergarten Teacher**	Chelsea Public Schools, Chelsea, MA

EDUCATION AND CREDENTIALS

B.S., Elementary Education, Lesley College, Cambridge, MA
California State Teaching Credential, K-9 and Early Childhood, lifetime
California Basic Educational Skills Test (CBEST), passed in 1990

Resume written in 1993.

Elizabeth A. Pameron

889 Oak Street • San Francisco, CA 94111 • (415) 889-3612

JOB OBJECTIVE
A position in the Creative Department

SUMMARY OF QUALIFICATIONS
- Experience working as part of professional creative teams in the areas of advertising, film production, and TV production.
- Skilled at promoting products and ideas through written and visual presentations.
- B.A. in Communications.

RELEVANT EXPERIENCE

1991-present **Independent Contractor in Creative Production**

"Zoli's Brain," a full-length feature film introduced to the Cannes Film Festival Committee.
- Provided support functions throughout most aspects of the creative process.
- Handled fundraising and onsite logistics.

"I Have a Dream," a Martin Luther King, Jr. 25th anniversary commemorative video shown on MTV.
- Performed creative and technical support for studio and location shoots.
- Worked with talent to facilitate ease of production.

"At Risk," a full-length independent feature film shot in Panavision.
- Assisted Art Director in set design and prop selection.

"Talk, Talk," a cable TV show produced by Studio 505 for Richmond Unified School District.
- Collaborated with director to create themes and studio ambiance.
- Functioned as camera operator, floor director, and editing assistant, as member of a small technical crew.

1991 **Production Intern**
PUBLICITY EXPRESS, Emeryville, CA
A direct advertising and PR agency that promotes entrepreneurial products.
- Assisted Creative Director in scripting commercial spots and handling client/public relations.
- Acted as liaison between Executive Producer and independent producers in coordinating props, talent, and locations for commercial shoots.
- Functioned as production, grip, and editing assistant.
- Frequently appeared as on-camera talent.

EDUCATION
B.A., Communications, St. Mary's College, Moraga, CA, 1990
Thesis: Children's Perspective of the Role of Mother in Advertising

Using a chronological format, Elizabeth presented her relevant freelance work as a valuable creative asset—which it was.

Resume written in 1993.

Rennie Murphy

456 Lyon Street • San Francisco, CA 94112 • (415) 242-5541

JOB OBJECTIVE: Assistant to the Art Director

SUMMARY OF QUALIFICATIONS

- Skilled at presenting technical and abstract concepts in a clear, concise, and detailed way.
- More than five years as a professional artist (photographer) who has coordinated sizable art projects.
- Strong background in layout and design.

PROFESSIONAL EXPERIENCE

1986-present **FREELANCE PHOTOGRAPHER**
Concurrent with: Medical Abstractor, 1991-present
Dr. Joseph Bernstein, San Francisco, CA

Notice the clever way Rennie showed that while she was doing office work, she was also working as a photographer, the truly relevant experience for her job objective.

- Created layout and design of over 80 four-color photographs of finished jewelry and precious metals. Photographed using 4x5 format and coordinated production of a 100-page annual catalog (for three years) at A.G. Findings & Manufacturing Co.
- Provided large format photography with challenging interior set ups that emphasized the qualities and specs of products. Photos used in brochure for Russell Range, a stove manufacturer.
- As photographer at Post Street Portraits, made portraits using 2-1/4 format, artificial light, and diverse studio backdrops.
- Photographed surgical procedures and did copy work of x-ray film for slide presentations to the American Medical Association.
- Other clients: The Miami Herald, Oracle, Allez (sportswear), Asanté Technologies, and Gray Line Tours.

1989-1991 **Faulkner Color Lab, San Francisco, CA**
TECHNICAL SALES REPRESENTATIVE, 1990-1991
CUSTOMER SERVICE REPRESENTATIVE, 1989-1990

- Initiated marketing ideas that targeted professional photographers and led to advertising programs currently in place.

1983-1985 **HMJ Corporation, Hollywood, FL**
MARKETING COORDINATOR

- Increased sales at least 15% by creating the company's first color brochure and implementing the first advertising campaign.
  - Selected products, oversaw photographer, wrote copy, and supervised production.
  - Coordinated national sales team of 15.

EDUCATION

Associate of Arts, Photography, 1987
Art Institute of Ft. Lauderdale, FL

Bachelor of Arts, International Relations, 1982
Florida International University, Miami, FL

Professional Development:
APA Seminars, 1991-present
San Francisco, CA

Corporate Art Consulting Class, 1995
Alumnae Resources, San Francisco, CA

— Portfolio available —

Resume written in 1995.

103

Ed Smith

8824 Fourth Street, Apt. 10 • San Francisco, CA 94117 • (415) 442-8854

Public Policy and Economic Analyst

- Communicate complex material in a clear and simplified manner.
- Analyze and develop options expediently.
- Understand the functionality of technical systems including telecommunications.
- Facilitate interdisciplinary team endeavors.

Experience

1991-present **Public Utilities Regulatory Analyst**
CALIFORNIA PUBLIC UTILITIES COMMISSION, San Francisco, CA

- Provide economic and technical expertise to commissioners and judges, and ensure compliance with the commission's decisions.
- One of four analysts currently developing policies and rules for local exchange competition in telecommunications.
- Developed options for restructuring the local switch transport market and analyzed their economic impacts.
- One of two analysts who calculated rates for Pacific Bell in Phase III of NRF, IRD.
- Lead technical analyst in the restructuring of the California gas industry through a capacity brokering program. Produced commission resolutions to implement the program for PG&E.

1990-1991 **Associate/Economic Consultant**
ICF RESOURCES, Fairfax, VA

- Served as economic consultant to corporations, utilities, and government agencies in the energy industry.
- Analyzed railroad behavior and investment patterns to develop an index of railrates for coal transportation.
- Provided analytical support in fuel procurement negotiations for several major utilities.

Concurrent with Education:

Fall '89 **Teaching Assistant, Mathematics**
UNIVERSITY OF CHICAGO, Chicago, IL

Fall '89 **Project Consultant**
ECONOMIC DEVELOPMENT COMMISSION OF CHICAGO, Chicago, IL

Summer '89 **Research Assistant**
ARGONNE NATIONAL LABORATORIES, Chicago, IL

Summer '87 **Student Intern**
STUDENT CONSERVATION ASSOCIATION, Lakeview, OR

By inserting the subheading "Concurrent with Education" in his work history, Ed explained why his earlier jobs were short-term.

Education

M.A., Public Policy, 1990
Research Project: The Effects of Deregulation Upon Airline Safety
The Graduate School of Public Policy Studies, University of Chicago, Chicago, IL

B.A., Economics, minor in Mathematics, 1988
The College of the University of Chicago, Chicago, IL

Resume written in 1995.

Joseph Williams
421 Jackson St.
San Francisco, CA 94121
(415) 532-9364

Foreign and National News Editor
with more than 20 years at prominent national publications

PROFESSIONAL ACHIEVEMENTS

1986-present SAN FRANCISCO CALL BULLETIN, San Francisco, CA
Foreign-National Editor

- Oversee national and international news coverage in the Sunday Call Bulletin (the 10th largest Sunday paper in the U.S.) and daily editions.
- Shaped news coverage for events such as:
    - The Balkans War
    - The Gulf War
    - Tiananmen Square
    - The decline of communism and disintegration of the Soviet Union
    - The Middle East peace process
    - The end of apartheid in South Africa
    - National elections
    - The Oklahoma City bombing
    - The Challenger disaster
- Established reputation for story selection and editing skills that produce an enterprising balance of news, features and graphic presentation.
- Manage reporters and a network of national and international stringers, developing stories and beat coverage.

1977-1986 SAN FRANCISCO CALL BULLETIN, San Francisco, CA
Assistant Features Editor

- Selected and edited features for Style section of daily and Sunday papers.
- Supervised layout and production.
- Broadened scope of coverage by developing a twice-weekly health page.

1975-1977 SAN FRANCISCO CALL BULLETIN, San Francisco, CA
Copy Editor, Night News Editor

Previous Experience
THE WASHINGTON STAR, Washington, D.C.
Staff Writer, 3 years

CONGRESSIONAL QUARTERLY, Washington, D.C.
Staff Writer, 4 years

Joseph introduced a subsection called "Previous Experience" so that he could use numbers of years for early jobs, instead of exact dates.

EDUCATION AND AWARDS

University of Michigan, B.A., Economics
Stanford University, Knight Journalism Fellowship
American Political Science Association, Reporting Award

Resume written in 1995.

Tracy L. Gent
1525 Yale Street, #1 • San Francisco, CA 94113 • (415) 250-4217

JOB OBJECTIVE: A position in fraud investigation

SUMMARY OF QUALIFICATIONS
- Top security clearance position in a U.S. Secret Service fraud investigation unit.
- Adept at uncovering fraudulent activity through item inspection and pattern identification.
- Skilled at working with credit bureaus, retailers, and consumers.

EDUCATION
B.S., Criminal Justice, emphasis: Private Investigation, 1991
    Northern Arizona University, Flagstaff, AZ
Diploma, Teller Training Institute, Concord, CA, 1986

EXPERIENCE

1993-present   U.S. SECRET SERVICE, San Francisco, CA
Counterfeit Squad Clerk
- Assist agents in investigation of cases by flagging suspicious patterns in counterfeiting.
- Examine bills to determine authenticity.
- Open new counterfeit cases using Master Crime Index and First Choice Database (national databases of criminal information).
- Prepare statistical reports for review by headquarters in Washington, D.C.
- Educate bank and retail personnel on how to identify and prevent fraud.
- Served as temporary replacement in the Financial Crimes Division.

1992-1993   BARCELON MANAGEMENT & ASSOCIATES, Orinda, CA
Administrative Assistant
- Provided administrative organization for this private firm contracted by HUD to manage low-income housing for the elderly and the handicapped.
- Interviewed residents for funding re-qualification, using a diplomatic approach to elicit financial information.

1990-1991   MC CAULOUS DEPARTMENT STORE, Lafayette, CA
Customer Service Representative, Credit Department
- Worked with TRW and CBI credit bureaus to clear customers' derogatory information.
- Investigated credit card problems: credit limits, lost and stolen cards, and collections.

1988-1990   **Full-time Student, Criminal Justice Program, Northern Arizona University**

Tracy inserted "Full-time Student" so she wouldn't have a gap in her work history.

1987-1988   WESTERN HYPERBARIC SERVICES, Richmond, CA
Research Assistant
- Maintained photographic and written medical records, used in insurance claims and litigation.

1986-1987   CREDIT BUREAU REPORTS, INC., San Ramon, CA
Credit Analyst
- Prepared credit reports for mortgage companies. Investigated reports using TRW and CBI. Persuaded credit, judgment, and collections contacts to remove derogatory data.

Resume written in 1994.

Getting More Mileage Out of Your Promotions

You can be especially proud of your work history if you've been promoted within a company. So go ahead, this is your chance to brag! Potential employers will be impressed by your promotions since they indicate *employment stability and high performance*. Here's how to show off your promotions in your Work History section.

Imagine that you have been promoted three times within a company called Harrison Productions. Notice what kind of impression you might make if you used this format:

1994–present	President	Harrison Productions, Springfield, IL
1993–1994	Vice President	Harrison Productions, Springfield, IL
1990–1993	Producer	Harrison Productions, Springfield, IL

At first glance, the employer is likely to think you are a job-hopper who had three jobs in four years. (Ouch!) Only upon closer examination might he or she understand that your three jobs were actually at the same company. But what if your reader doesn't take the time to figure that out? You will have made a negative impression when you had an excellent opportunity to make a positive one.

I suggest organizing the same information something like this:

1990–present   HARRISON PRODUCTIONS, Springfield, IL

                      President, 1994–present

                      Vice President, 1993–1994

                      Producer, 1990–1993

Notice how the second version makes it immediately clear that you were a loyal employee who had multiple promotions.

The good news is that this concept applies to both types of resume: chronological and functional, as demonstrated by the following three resumes.

FRANK MEYER
22 Hollister Place, San Francisco, CA 94102
(415) 446-9981

OBJECTIVE

Office Manager

SUMMARY OF QUALIFICATIONS

- 12 years office management experience in one of the nation's leading corporations.
- Consistent record of increasing productivity by maintaining effective interdepartmental relations and office systems.
- Excellent IBM and Macintosh skills.
- International background. Bilingual: German/English.

PROFESSIONAL EXPERIENCE

1982-present HEWLETT-PACKARD, INC., Palo Alto, CA

Administrative Secretary to Director, Corporate Communications, 1987-present
- Independently streamlined and managed this fast-paced department that generates and distributes annual, quarterly, and monthly publications with individual circulation of up to 120,000.
- Devised electronic network that facilitates immediate written communications with over 200 remote locations.
- Developed and managed budgets totaling $1 million. Prepared estimates and proposals for new publications.

Secretary to Vice President, Merchandising, Office Products, 1985-1987
- Set up and managed office procedures for the Merchandising Department, which produced a national wholesale office products catalog.
- Provided office support for 13 managers.

Secretary/Assistant to Manager, Office Services, 1983-1985
- Increased quality of office services for the 750-person headquarters building by improving customer service and inventory systems.

Assistant to Managing Director, California Training Academy, 1982
- Assisted the Director in setting up this training program for technical, media, and education professionals.

1976-1982 FOREIGN OFFICE, FEDERAL REPUBLIC OF GERMANY

Administrative Secretary to Consul General, San Francisco, CA
Secretary to Ambassador, Amman, Jordan
- Represented Federal Republic of Germany to foreign diplomats and maintained strict confidentiality as "right-hand" to the Consul General and the Ambassador.
- Served as translator to German officials during state visits.

EDUCATION

B.S. equivalent, University of Hamburg, Germany

Certificate, Graphic Design, University of California, Berkeley Extension

Certificates, Foreign Language Correspondent
    London Chamber of Commerce
    School of Foreign Languages, Hamburg, Germany

(cloud annotation:) Frank presented his multiple titles as subsets under Hewlett-Packard with achievement statements under each title. Nice graphics presentation!

(cloud annotation:) Resume written in 1994.

Elizabeth Henson

244 Bay Court • Sausalito, CA 94502 • Home: (415) 221-8432 • Work: (415) 443-7543

JOB OBJECTIVE: Collections Administrator

SUMMARY OF QUALIFICATIONS

- 10 years business experience including eight years in the financial services industry.
- Proficient at utilizing computer systems to produce analytical reports.
- Enhance operations through strong organizational and problem solving skills.

PROFESSIONAL EXPERIENCE

1991-pres. THE BANK OF CALIFORNIA, San Francisco, CA
Corporate Operations Manager
Banking Officer
Banking Assistant

> *Elizabeth listed her promotions at each bank in a concise list with overall achievements under them.*

- Retrieved data, analyzed information and spread financial reports for management, using mainframe and PC systems. LAN Administrator for two years.
- Bank certified to respond to credit inquiries using Robert Morris Associates criteria.
- Administered and monitored operational systems that satisfied auditors for four consecutive years.
- Reduced liability and standardized corporate banking operations by instituting risk management policies.
- Served as liaison to account officers, clients and bank departments, ensuring quality customer service through problem resolution.
- Supervised personnel; handled salary reviews, performance counseling and training.

1987-1990 GREAT WESTERN BANK, San Francisco, CA
Management Trainee
Administrative Assistant

- Compiled and calculated statistics for weekly and quarterly reports.
- Prepared human resources reports that included salary and turnover analyses.

1985-1986 UNIVERSITY OF SAN FRANCISCO, San Francisco, CA
Full-time MBA Student

1984-1985 ROUSE-TABOR CENTER, INC., Denver, CO
Assistant Marketing Manager

- Assisted in the development of annual calendar and budget for this large shopping center.
- Collaborated with merchants and management to produce joint promotions.

EDUCATION

MBA, Marketing, 1989
University of San Francisco, San Francisco, CA

BA, Administration and Legal Processes, 1984
Mills College, Oakland, CA

> *Resume written in 1995.*

Miles J. Rizkallah

2262 Banana Drive • Walnut Creek, CA 94124 • (510) 898-1174

Marketing Professional

Summary of Qualifications

- 13 years as a marketing professional for one the nation's leading corporations.
- Expertise in project management, marketing, and vendor relations.
- Computer proficient: Excel, PowerPoint, MS Word, Vizio, Lotus Notes, Microsoft Project.

Selected Accomplishments
at Chevron U.S.A. Products, Inc.

PROJECT MANAGEMENT
- Led a team of operations, advertising, and product development managers for the $200,000 launch of a new product.
- Coordinated analytical team efforts to standardize quality of service in 8500 retail sites.
- Increased sales and improved customer relations by developing Chevron International's first co-op advertising program.
- Organized sales retreats held in U.S. and overseas resorts for 50 agents from around world.
- Trained regional coordinators and outside consultants in new computer programs.

MARKETING
- Created "Who's Who," a 12-page, four-color brochure distributed world-wide that promoted Chevron as a valuable international player.
- Designed a $15,000 sales booth for international trade shows that displayed Chevron's cultural diversity.
- Produced "Technical Tables and Charts," a detailed, 50-page publication used by customers in the shipping industry. Updated content and image, dramatically increasing demand.

Work History

1981-present	**Chevron U.S.A. Products, Inc., San Francisco Bay Area**
	Business Analyst, 1995-present
	Marketing Specialist, 1991-1995
	Senior Marketing Assistant, 1989-1991
	Marketing Help Desk Representative, 1987-1988
	Collections Representative, 1986-1987
	Customer Representative, 1982-1986
	Administrative Assistant, 1981
1981-1982	**Saudi Research & Marketing, Inc., Houston, TX**
	Publication Subscription Manager

Here's how Miles demonstrated his many promotions at Chevron.

Education

B.A., Public Relations, minor: Business, San Jose State University, San Jose, CA, 1980

Resume written in 1995.

> **Tip**
>
> I always found the acronym "KISS" (Keep It Simple, Stupid) slightly offensive, but I have to admit, it's often true. This is one of those times: Use only years (not months) when referring to your work history, no matter what type of resume you use. Months complicate the presentation and make it harder (and therefore longer) for someone to figure out. Remember the eight-second scan? Providing just the years will help you pass the eight-second test.

Go For It

Good for you—you're armed with solutions to some tricky problems. Now you're ready to create the Work History section on your resume. Follow these instructions for the type of resume you are using.

Chronological Resume

➤ Determine how far back you want to go in your work history, based on the EPT formula you read about earlier in this chapter.

➤ List your job history as headings under "Professional History." Write the date (years only), job title, employer, and city (and the state, if necessary) of the jobs you have held until now.

➤ If the company you worked for is not known to your resume reader, you may need to give some explanation as to what industry it is in or what product it sells. If so, write a short overview statement immediately beside or under the company name. For example:

Smith & Associates, Phoenix, AZ
The nation's largest manufacturer of plastic containers

The following two resumes demonstrate the use of an overview statement to define the role of a company.

Leslie Lanier

32 Bryant Street • San Francisco, CA 94144 • (415) 883-9912

Positive, energetic **Creative Manager/Producer** of award-winning media for prominent national and local clients.

PROFESSIONAL EXPERIENCE

1991-pres.   **ACCOUNT MANAGER**
Zoe Street Pictures, Inc., San Francisco, CA
A poducer of creative corporate communications: multimedia, film, and video. Clients include:

Intel	Levi Strauss
Apple Computer	Clorox Company
Foote, Cone & Belding	Nestle Beverage Company
Ketchum Communications	California Lottery

- Increased billings 200% and established company as one of the premiere local producers of progressive media by introducing an innovative production approach that appealed to a wider client base.
  - Sought out innovative artists, writers, creative directors, graphic designers, computer animators, and musicians.
  - Customized creative teams for individual clients' project, image, and market.
  - Managed project from concept through post-production.
- Secured high volume of projects through the creative bidding process, making exciting and persuasive pitches.
- Increased production efficiency by managing multiple projects simultaneously including client relations, vendors, schedules, and deadlines.

1989-1991   **ACCOUNT MANAGER**
FM Productions, Brisbane, CA
A theatrical and stage design company started by Bill Graham. Budgets ranged from $20k to $1+M. Productions included:

Rolling Stones Steel Wheels Tour	San Francisco Black and White Ball
The Doors (movie set)	Corporate product launches

- Ensured smooth productions by supervising budgets, conceptual development, design, vendor coordination, and on-site event management of complicated projects.
- Maintained excellent client relations; strictly attended to details, deadlines, and budgets.

1988   **ASSISTANT TO DIRECTOR**
The Feud Company, New York, NY
A film company created to produce a movie based on *The Feud*, a Thomas Berger novel.

- As director's right hand, served as liaison to talent and department heads, and managed day-to-day details.
- Personally handled local bit and extra casting. Coordinated wardrobe, hairstyling, and makeup for extras.

1987   **ASSISTANT PRODUCTION MANAGER**
One Pass Film & Video, San Francisco, CA
Formerly the largest full-service film and video company in San Francisco.

- Scheduled and facilitated national commercial shoots. Booked freelance and in-house camera crews. Handled equipment and prop rentals.

EDUCATION

BA, Communication and Social Science, 1987
University of California at Berkeley, Berkeley, CA

> To define the organizations where she worked and to enhance her professional image, Leslie included an overview statement after each company name.

> Resume written in 1994.

112

Eldon Barrick

3320 14th Street • San Francisco, CA 94114 • (415) 229-3301

JOB OBJECTIVE: Accounting Manager

SUMMARY OF QUALIFICATIONS
- Seven years in finance management for organizations ranging from 30M-100M.
- Experienced supervisor with a management style that motivates staff productivity.
- Practical background in accounting.

PROFESSIONAL EXPERIENCE

1992-present **Accounting Manager and Human Resource Manager,** FWB, INC., San Francisco, CA
A hardware/software manufacturing concern that grew 38% each year during tenure.

Eldon's overview statements, near the beginning of each job entry, help the reader understand the significance of his achievements.

- Created accounting control systems from manual system, enabling existing staff to support growth at no increase in costs.
- Drafted and enforced accounting policies and procedures in compliance with GAAP that provided the basis for all departmental budgeting.
- Prepared and guided company through its first external audit, allowing FWB to address other forms of working capitalization.

1989-1991 **Accounting Manager,** CATHOLIC CHARITIES OF SAN FRANCISCO, San Francisco, CA
A non-profit corporation comprised of 36 agencies with an overall budget of 56M.

- Established separate accounting system to manage a 2M fund and oversaw its consolidation with agency financials.
- Streamlined AP/AR systems in compliance with federal and state fund restrictions.
- Helped division directors with budget drafts at RFP level.
- Ensured success of program funding by analyzing feasibility of program proposals.
- Identified agency's insurance needs and standardized coverage for all 11 divisions.
- Trained division and program directors to draft their own budgets and read financials, enabling them to control their programs.

1987-1989 **A/R and Credit Manager,** JASMINE TECHNOLOGIES, INC., San Francisco, CA
A hard drive manufacturer with 100M in annual sales.

- Cleaned up AR system and brought it within 90% of agreement, enabling company to borrow against that amount.
- Established credit and risk assessment policies.
- Assisted in accounting system conversion from manual to automated. Analyzed and balanced all accounts prior to conversion.

1982-1986 **Systems Analyst,** HELLER, EHRMAN, WHITE & MC AULIFFE, San Francisco, CA
The 65th largest law firm in the U. S. with multiple locations worldwide.

- Served as troubleshooter for accounting department's conversion to DEC/VAX 11/785.
- Provided system training and support to three departments.

1976-1982 **Manager,** DRUCQUER & SONS, LTD., Berkeley, CA
A retail store that expanded to two locations during tenure.

- Set up manual accounting system and established order policy.
- Supervised staff of eight and managed all aspects of the business.

EDUCATION
B.A., University of California at Berkeley, 1975
Dun & Bradstreet: Credit Risk Assessment, Credit Management, Finance Management

Resume written in 1994.

Functional Resume

➤ Figure out how far back you want to go in your work history, based on the EPT formula mentioned earlier.

➤ Fill in the Work History section by listing your work chronology, starting with your most recent position. Write the date (years only), job title, employer, and city (and the state, if necessary) of the jobs you have held until now.

The Least You Need to Know

➤ Use only years, not months, when presenting your work history.

➤ Avoid age discrimination by using the EPT formula.

➤ Disguise gaps in your work history by giving yourself a "job title" that sufficiently explains the unemployed span.

➤ Arrange your work history to show off your promotions within a company.

Chapter 8

Step Six—You've Got What It Takes

> **In This Chapter**
>
> ➤ Writing your resume is like writing your next job description
>
> ➤ Announce your skills by making them major headings in your functional resume
>
> ➤ Brainstorming for skill headings
>
> ➤ Prioritize your headings according to how you define your future

If you're writing a chronological resume, this section does not apply to you. That means you get a free ride to Chapter 9!

If you're writing a functional resume, however, you need to pay attention to this chapter. (If you're not sure which resume format you should use, go back to Chapter 3 for help in deciding.)

One of the key advantages to using a functional resume is that you get to define yourself by your skills, rather than according to your former job titles. That's why it's a good format for career changers. The way to put the spotlight on your skills instead of your work history in the functional resume is to create *skill headings*, which appear in the body of the resume. To see what I mean, take a look at the resume template on the following page that shows the skill headings highlighted.

The purpose of using the skill headings is to help the potential employer *quickly* identify you as someone with the abilities needed to do the job. (Don't forget you've got to make a good impression during the eight-second scan!) By keeping your skill headings brief and putting them in bold or large print, the reader will quickly define you by your skills, rather than by your previous job titles.

(Here's what I mean by "Skill Headings" on the functional resume.)

Name
Street • City, State Zip • phone

JOB OBJECTIVE
The job you want next

SUMMARY OF QUALIFICATIONS
- How much experience you have in the field of your objective, in a related field, or using the skills required for your new position.
- An overall career accomplishment that shows you'd be good at this job objective.
- What someone would say about you as a recommendation.

RELEVANT EXPERIENCE

MAJOR SKILL
- An accomplishment you are proud of that shows you're good at this skill.
- A problem you solved using this skill, and the results.
- A time when you used your skill to positively affected the organization, the bottom line, your boss, your clients.
- Awards, commendations, publications, etc. you achieved that relate to your job objective.

MAJOR SKILL
- A project you are proud of that supports your job objective.
- Another accomplishment that shows you're good at this line of work.
- Quantifiable results that point out your skill.

WORK HISTORY
19xx-present	Job Title	COMPANY NAME and city
19xx-xx	Job Title	COMPANY NAME and city
19xx-xx	Job Title	COMPANY NAME and city
19xx-xx	Job Title	COMPANY NAME and city

EDUCATION
Degree, Major (if relevant), 19xx (optional)
University, City, State

Commandments

Commandment I: Thou shalt not write about your past; thou shalt write about your future! Be sure to choose skill headings that are about your future job, not necessarily about your past employment. Many resume writers get confused about this point. Don't be one of them.

Help! Choosing Skill Headings

Imagine that you are an employer who is writing an ad for the job mentioned in your job objective statement. What skills would you list as requirements?

Let's say you're the manager of a retail store and you're looking for a Director of Customer Service. Your help wanted ad might read: "Applicant must be skilled in supervision and customer service." OK, now step back into the shoes of the job seeker. "Supervision" and "Customer Service" would be the two skill headings on your resume.

Commandments

Commandment II: Thou shalt not confess. In other words, you don't have to "tell all." Stick to what's relevant and marketable—a good guideline when it comes to choosing your skill headings. Highlight only the skills that support your job objective.

Let's role-play again: As a supervisor in a software development firm looking for a technical team leader, you might say: "Applicant must be proficient in computer programming and team leadership." Now, jumping back into the role of the job seeker, you understand that "Programming" and "Leadership" might be the two skill headings on your resume.

Tip

Make a list of all the things you'd love to have on your next job description, and another list of all the things you absolutely don't want in that description. Review both lists while creating your resume to make sure you market yourself *only* for your ideal job.

Take a look at the following six functional resumes for some examples. Notice how in each case, the skill headings define the job objective, not necessarily the job seeker's past work history.

117

JANE ROLLAND KING, M.P.A.

720 Ashland Ave., No. One • San Rafael, California 94122 • (415) 535-7923

OBJECTIVE

Community Coordinator

SUMMARY OF QUALIFICATIONS

- 10 years coordinating programs for nonprofits including 5 years organizing activities for substance abuse education and prevention programs.
- Success in working with high-risk populations of diverse backgrounds through individual and group engagement.
- Extensive office management, administrative, and supervisory experience.

EDUCATION

MPA (Master of Public Administration), Health Care Administration/Organization Change California State University, Hayward, 1994

Certificate in Therapeutic Recreation, California State University, Hayward, 1994

Supervision/Management Certificate, City College of San Francisco, 1984

B.A., San Francisco State University, 1977

RELEVANT ACCOMPLISHMENTS

PROGRAM COORDINATION

- Organized and scheduled over 360 programs a year for a prominent national nonprofit organization.
  - Supervised activities of 160 volunteers of all levels of experience. Recruited and trained 25 volunteers, being very selective so as to ensure safety and good public relations.
  - Personally facilitated groups ranging from 12-60, to educate participants about the healing value of nature.
- Led recreation outings that initiated and facilitated breakthroughs in behavioral change for substance abusers at Walden House.
- Co-led counseling sessions with women inmates of San Bruno County Jail regarding substance abuse, recovery, and health-related issues.

Jane's skill headings indicate that she has two major talents required for her job objective.

ADMINISTRATION

- Chaired monthly, quarterly, and annual strategic planning meetings for a well established nonprofit.
- Prepared 15 successful major grants for UCSF Medical Center programs.
- Performed multiple case management for two law firms, requiring strict attention to details, time lines, and accuracy.

COMMUNITY WORK HISTORY

1993-1994	Recreational Therapist	RCH, Inc. (formerly Recreation Center for the Handicapped), San Francisco, CA
1990-1992	Inner City Recreation Leader	Walden House, San Francisco, CA
1989-1992	Group Facilitator	San Bruno County Jail, San Bruno, CA
1981-1986	Program Director, Elected Leader	Sierra Club, San Francisco, CA

EMPLOYMENT HISTORY

1984-1993	Litigation/Legal Secretary	Rosenblum, Parish & Bacigalupi Severson & Werson, San Francisco, CA
1979-1984	Administrative Assistant	UCSF Medical Center, San Francisco, CA

PROFESSIONAL MEMBERSHIPS

American Society of Public Administration (ASPA)
American Therapeutic Recreation Association (ATRA)

Resume written in 1995.

Ann Harris
11 Los Alamos • Orinda, CA 94563
(510) 254-9931

Objective	Sales Representative in the interior environmental industry
Summary	• Experienced art consultant/sales representative to corporations and small businesses. • Hands on experience in redesign of residential and commercial properties. • Skilled at consultative sales based on product and industry knowledge.

Achievements

SALES

Because of Ann's skill headings ("Sales" and "Interior and Exterior Design"), the reader will see at a glance that Ann has the necessary skills for her job objective.

• As Sales Representative for the San Francisco Museum of Modern Art's Rental Gallery, managed approximately 100 accounts: large corporations, small offices, and residences.
- Increased revenue by persuading corporate decision makers to promote their company philosophy through public display of art.
- Assisted clients in choosing artwork that optimized budgets and created desired ambiance.
- Oversaw installations, artwork rotations, and contract renewals.
• As Membership Chair of the Art Guild, promoted the museum and increased the guild's membership 25% in one year through community presentations and direct mail campaigns.

INTERIOR AND EXTERIOR DESIGN

• Improved image and efficiency of Franklin and Pain by redesigning its eight-person office. Reallocated space, designed computer work stations, purchased furniture, and specified surface design.
• Consistently generated resale profits by redesigning and overseeing the remodeling of four residential properties. Projects involved:

Space planning	Landscape design
Lighting design	Structural renovations

Work History

1992-1994	**Franklin and Pain Financial Planning,** Concord, CA Project Manager
1984-1989	**San Francisco Museum of Modern Art,** San Francisco, CA Sales Representative/Art Consultant, Rental Gallery Membership Chairperson, Art Guild Board Docent Council Representative Art Department Assistant Chairperson Art Docent
1975-1992	**Independent Interior and Exterior Design/Remodeling** Project Manager

Resume written in 1994.

Education

B.A., San Francisco State University, San Francisco, CA
Graduate Studies, John F. Kennedy University, Orinda, CA

119

Amy K. Nederlof

1921 Pierce Street • San Francisco, CA 94114 • (415) 665-7956

JOB OBJECTIVE

Travel/Tour Guide with emphasis on outdoor adventure

SUMMARY OF QUALIFICATIONS

- Experienced at team-leading domestic and international group trips.
- Skilled at crisis management, safety compliance, and adherence to itineraries.
- Enjoy helping others explore their potential while having a great time.

RELEVANT EXPERIENCE

This resume defines Amy by her skill headings ("Customer Service" and "Adventure Travel"), not by her former job titles.

CUSTOMER SERVICE
- As counselor and instructor at camps while attending high school and university:
  - Taught and guided young adult campers from diverse backgrounds and with little to advanced levels of experience in:

backpacking	swimming	hydrosliding	canoeing
hiking	water skiing	kayaking	arts and crafts

  - Provided motivation, moral support, enthusiasm, and advice to ensure participants had a good time and met or exceeded their goals for personal growth.
- As an ESL teaching assistant at UC Santa Barbara, facilitated small groups of non-native English speakers, creating a non-intimidating atmosphere to encourage participation.
- Escorted about 40 campers by bus to and from the LA, Fresno, and San Francisco Airports for three summers.

ADVENTURE TRAVEL
- Assisted in an anthropological excavation of a Mayan site in a rain forest of Belize, which contributed to a reconstruction project for future tourism.
- Team-directed backpacking trips in Yosemite and Sierra National Forest.
- Planned itineraries and backpacked throughout Europe and Great Britain, being resourceful and composed in handling the unexpected.
- Served as a guide on a four-day canoe trip down the Colorado River for 15 novice canoeists.
- Team-led three, one-week trips throughout rural Mexico for 12 travelers by van. Encouraged cross-cultural relations while paying strict attention to safety and itinerary.

WORK HISTORY (Concurrent with Education)

Summers '90-'94	Gold Arrow Camp, Lakeshore, CA	Head Counselor, '94 Counselor/Instructor, '90-'93
Summer '89	Hume Lake Camps, Hume Lake, CA	Administrative Assistant
1990-94	YMCAs, So. CA	Counselor/Instructor

EDUCATION AND CERTIFICATIONS

B.A., Cultural Anthropology, University of California, Santa Barbara, 1994
    Undergraduate programs: Cité Universitaire, Paris, France
                            Anthropology Field Studies, Belize, Central America
                            Disneyland Public Relations Program, Anaheim, CA
EMT Certification (Emergency Medical Technician), 1994
First Aid and CPR Certification, 1994
Certified Life Guard, 1994

Resume written in 1994.

Keith Kliger

51 Patriots Street • San Francisco, California 94102 • (415) 533-2143

JOB OBJECTIVE

A position in technical writing

SUMMARY OF QUALIFICATIONS

- Eight years as a professional academic, business, and creative writer.
- Author of published articles and conference papers.
- Skilled at communicating technical information in a concise and clear manner.
- Taught English and writing at the university level.

RELEVANT EXPERIENCE

WRITING

"Writing" and "Research" (Keith's two skill headings) are two big clues that Keith has what it takes to be a technical writer.

- Authored analytical reports on MetLife's network development, used to design and implement organizational procedures.
- As writing instructor at Lehman College, taught creative and expository composition techniques to prepare students for academic research and the College Writing Exam.
- Edited business reports and correspondence for Virtual Laboratories, a computer graphics/3-D animation consulting company.
- Applied critical methodology in writing articles and papers on a wide range of creative and academic subjects, as a graduate student and teaching assistant.

RESEARCH

- Performed queries and analyses within multitask relational database programs to create technical reports for MetLife HealthCare.
- Conducted research and analysis at New York University on communication techniques for presenting complex concepts to diverse audiences.
- Guided individuals and groups in bibliographic research and fieldwork, as English Instructor at Lehman College and Teaching Assistant at New York University.

WORK HISTORY

1992-present	Research/Reporting Specialist	MetLife HealthCare, San Francisco, CA
1991	Business Writer	Virtual Laboratories, San Francisco, CA
1988-1990	Brokerage Clerk	Drexel Burnham Lambert, New York, NY
1987-1989	Adjunct Instructor, English Dept.	Lehman College, CUNY, Bronx, NY
1985-1988	Writer/Critic	High Performance magazine, New York, NY

EDUCATION AND PUBLICATION

M.A., Graduate School of Arts and Science, New York University, New York, NY
B.A., English Literature, Lehman College, City University of New York, Bronx, NY
cum laude and High Honors in English Department's Honors Program

Relevant Academic Experience:
Teaching Assistant, Graduate School of Arts and Science, New York University
Researcher/Co-Editor, Shubert Archive, New York, NY

Kliger, Keith, "The Wooster Group's The Road to Immortality," (a critical analysis of theatrical structure and technique), High Performance magazine, vol. #5, 1994

Resume written in 1994.

June C. Maynard
789 San Pablo Ave., #31
Brisbane, CA 94033
(415) 123-7531

OBJECTIVE

Executive management position with focus on organizational development and training

SUMMARY OF QUALIFICATIONS

- Over 15 years in management of human service organizations with consistent emphasis on team building and organizational development.
- Experienced at training assessment and facilitation.
- Skilled in staff development to meet individual and organizational goals.

PROFESSIONAL ACCOMPLISHMENTS

MANAGEMENT

The skill headings are like two ingredients in a recipe for "a management position in organizational development" (June's job objective).

- Improved cost effectiveness of Solano Napa Agency 30% by developing and redesigning programs based on client-centered decision making.
- Increased Independent Living's homeshare client participation more than 500% in three years though an intensive public information effort.
- Cleared a back log of 180 cases in six weeks using a team of existing staff at Mt. Zion.
- Elected by peers to represent Northern California at the Joint State and Area Agency Policy Development Committee.
- Team-drafted California Association of Area Agency Directors' position paper on community-based care.
- Led key aspects of the design and implementation of the Wisconsin Senior Statesmanship Program to educate consumers about the legislative process.

ORGANIZATIONAL DEVELOPMENT AND TRAINING

- Reconfigured the composition of staff to more accurately reflect the cultural and ethnic diversity of the Solano Napa Agency population.
- Used a collaborative approach to successfully build morale and team productivity during the downsizing of Solano Napa Agency.
- Co-founded the Wisconsin Adult Daycare Association to establish a support system for providers and standardize quality of services.
- Conducted national training conferences for Independent Living, attended by up to 200 social service providers per session.
- Designed and developed a long-term support model project for Agency on Aging that resulted in a cooperative effort between two competitive county departments.

WORK HISTORY

1990-1995	Executive Director	Solano Napa Agency on Aging, Vallejo, CA
1989-1990	Director of Aging	San Mateo County, Redwood City, CA
1985-1989	Assistant Program Coordinator	Mt. Zion Institute on Aging, San Francisco, CA
1982-1985	Homeshare Program Director	Independent Living, Inc., Madison, WI
1980-1982	Planner/Administrator	Agency on Aging, District I, Madison, WI
1976-1979	Ombudsman	Lt. Governor's Nursing Home Ombudsman, Madison, WI

EDUCATION

University of Wisconsin — Madison   M.S.S.W., 1975
B.A., Social Work, 1971

NTL Institute for Applied Behavioral Research, Alexandria, VA
Organizational Development and Training Program

Resume written in 1995.

Margaret R. Lindberg

7111 Fortunado Avenue • El Sobrante, CA 94560 • (510) 535-1265

JOB OBJECTIVE: An administrative support position

SUMMARY OF QUALIFICATIONS

- Experienced administrative professional with exceptional organizational skills.
- Ability to coordinate and supervise large administrative projects.
- Enjoy research and analysis of business and client patterns.
- Valuable client services representative.

PROFESSIONAL ACCOMPLISHMENTS

ADMINISTRATION

- Administered professional credentialing system, coordinated recruitment and orientation programs, and represented HEALS at business meetings.
- Trained and supervised clerical and temporary personnel, using a collaborative approach to achieve team success.
- Maintained over 3,000 client records utilized daily by doctors, technicians, and support staff at the Humane Society.
- Edited IPM's member-related documents and publications.

Margaret looks like a good candidate for an administrative support position with these three skill headings.

ANALYSIS

- Generated monthly analyses and reports on IPM's membership activity and HEALS' physician participation.
- Produced statistical documentation of client services at the Humane Society, used by management for annual review.

CLIENT SERVICES

- Resolved problems and formal complaints, and responded to inquiries from 27,000 HMO members, over 500 healthcare providers, and over 100 employer groups.
- As primary contact for clients and medical professionals at the Humane Society, addressed client needs, facilitated efficient service, and resolved problems.

WORK HISTORY

1990-1994   Administrative Support, Berkeley-East Bay Humane Society, Berkeley, CA
1988-1990   Logistical Support, Emily Damon Designs, El Cerrito, CA
1985-1988   Member Service Representative, IPM Health Plan, Vallejo, CA
1983-1985   Professional Relations Coordinator, HEALS Health Plan, Emeryville, CA

EDUCATION

BA, Sociology/Anthropology, Oberlin College, Oberlin, OH

Graduate coursework, California State University, Hayward
Organizational Management, Economics, Accounting

Resume written in 1994.

Skills List

Some functional resume writers get stumped trying to think of their skill headings. If you feel stuck, take a look at the following list of skills.

Notice that I've categorized this list according to four general occupational areas. Although you may want to focus on an area that's close to your job objective, I suggest you read through the entire list. Maybe a word in another category will inspire you to define your skill set in a way that is uniquely yours.

Business Management

Accounting	Management Consulting
Accounts Payable	Marketing
Accounts Receivable	Media Relations
Administration	Mediation
Advertising	Meeting Planning
Benefits	Negotiations
Budget Management	Office Management
Business Development	Operations
Client Relations	Order Fulfillment
Community Relations	Organizational Development
Conflict Resolution	Personnel
Consulting	Presentation Coaching
Copy Writing	Presentations
Corporate Giving	Product Development
Customer Service	Production
Executive Management	Project Management
Financial Management	Promotions
Human Resources	Public Relations
Insurance	Purchasing
International Relations	Quality Assurance
Inventory Control	Re-engineering
Inventory Management	Recruitment
Investor Relations	Retail Management
Leadership	Sales
Legal	Shipping

Speech Writing

Strategic Planning

Supervision

Training

Vendor Relations

Writing

Education

Administration

Admissions Evaluation

Classroom Management

Committee Leadership

Counseling

Curriculum Development

Interdisciplinary Teamwork

Parent Relations

Program Development

Research

Teaching

Tutoring

Engineering and Technical

Analysis

Computer

Conversions

Customer Support

Data Collection

Database Management

Design

Development

Documentation

Engineering

MIS

Planning

Presentations

Programming

Research

Survey Coordination

System Design

System Evaluation

Systems Analysis

Team Leadership

Team Work

Technical Support

Technical Writing

Nonprofit Management

Advocacy

Board Relations

Calendar Management

Community Outreach

Consensus Building

Counseling

Development

Event Planning

Financial Management

Fundraising

Grant Proposal Writing

Leadership

Major Donor Giving

Media Relations

Needs Assessment

Program Coordination

Program Development

Project Coordination

Public Relations

Public Speaking

Recruiting

Service Delivery

Solicitations

Staff Management

Volunteer Recruitment

Volunteer Management

Writing

The Least You Need to Know

➤ Your skill headings become subheadings under your Relevant Experience section.

➤ Choose skill headings that define your job objective, not your job history.

➤ Make your skill headings easy to read by keeping them short and by setting them off with bold or slightly larger type.

➤ Prioritize your skill headings so your strongest one comes first.

Step Seven— Be a Winner!

Most resumes are so dry you need to drink a couple of glasses of water just to get through them. That's because they focus on boring job duties. Although the reader wants to know what you've done, he or she is even more concerned with whether you achieved the desired results on the job.

Commandments

Commandment III: Thou shalt not write job descriptions; thou shalt write about achievements. Talk about your experience in terms of achievements instead of monotonous job descriptions. Achievements will impress the reader, make your resume far more interesting to read, and stimulate productive conversation during the interview.

In this chapter, you determine what your relevant achievements are and learn how to put them on your resume, so you can get the most out of every word.

Dynamite Achievement Statements

Nab the employer's interest right away with an achievement-oriented resume. By writing about your experience in terms of achievements, not job descriptions, you'll convey three things:

Tip
Achievement statements on your resume can trigger some good conversation about your strengths during the interview.

➤ You have the experience and skills to do the job.

➤ You're good at this work and at using these skills.

➤ You like your work. (You must! There's pride in your statements.)

The achievement statements that I'm talking about in this chapter are in the center part of your resume, as shown in the following two resume templates—chronological and functional formats respectively.

(Here's where the achievement statements go on your chronological resume.)

Name
Street • City, State Zip • phone

JOB OBJECTIVE
The job you want next

SUMMARY OF QUALIFICATIONS
- How much experience you have in the field of your objective, in a related field, or using the skills required for your new position.
- An overall career accomplishment that shows you'd be good at this job objective.
- What someone would say about you as a recommendation.

PROFESSIONAL EXPERIENCE
19xx-pres. **Company Name**, City, State
JOB TITLE
A brief description of the organization
- An accomplishment you are proud of that shows you're good at this profession.
- A problem you solved and the results.
- A time when you positively affected the organization, the bottom line, your boss, your co-workers, your clients.
- Awards, commendations, publications, etc. you achieved that relate to your job objective.

19xx-xx **Company Name**, City, State
JOB TITLE
A brief description of the organization
- A project you are proud of that supports your job objective.
- Another accomplishment that shows you're good at this line of work.
- Quantifiable results that point out your skill.

EDUCATION
Degree, Major (if relevant), 19xx (optional)
University, City, State

(Here's where the achievement statements go on your functional resume.)

Name
Street • City, State Zip • phone

JOB OBJECTIVE
The job you want next

SUMMARY OF QUALIFICATIONS
- How much experience you have in the field of your objective, in a related field, or using the skills required for your new position.
- An overall career accomplishment that shows you'd be good at this job objective.
- What someone would say about you as a recommendation.

RELEVANT EXPERIENCE
MAJOR SKILL
- An accomplishment you are proud of that shows you're good at this skill.
- A problem you solved using this skill, and the results.
- A time when you used your skill to positively affected the organization, the bottom line, your boss, your clients.
- Awards, commendations, publications, etc. you achieved that relate to your job objective.

MAJOR SKILL
- A project you are proud of that supports your job objective.
- Another accomplishment that shows you're good at this line of work.
- Quantifiable results that point out your skill.

WORK HISTORY
19xx-present	Job Title	COMPANY NAME and city
19xx-xx	Job Title	COMPANY NAME and city
19xx-xx	Job Title	COMPANY NAME and city
19xx-xx	Job Title	COMPANY NAME and city

EDUCATION
Degree, Major (if relevant), 19xx (optional)
University, City, State

Brainstorming for Stellar Achievements

Here are some questions to help you think of relevant achievements for your resume:

➤ What work-related projects are you proud of that relate to your job objective?

Example: Increased productivity 20 percent as lead engineer on Hewlett-Packard's HMS technical team.

➤ What are some quantifiable results that point out your ability?

Example: Drove profits from $20 million to $34 million by directing a national celebrity marketing campaign.

➤ When have you demonstrated PAR (Problem, Action, Result)? What was the problem, what was your action to remedy it, and what was the result?

Example: Reduced theft 47 percent by instituting "Shoppers' Spy," a tight yet discreet security program.

➤ When did you positively affect the organization, the bottom line, your boss, your co-workers, or your clients?

Example: Enhanced staff morale through a six-month incentive program that also instigated a major increase in sales.

➤ What awards, commendations, publications, etc. have you achieved that relate to your job objective?

Example: Awarded "Top Salesperson" three consecutive years.

➤ How is success measured in your field? How do you measure up?

Example: Selected by the NIH to represent the United States at the International AIDS Conference in Brazil.

> **Tip**
>
> Name dropping is the name of the game. Look for opportunities to enhance your image by slipping in names of impressive people, companies, or organizations.

➤ Are you good at using the skills required for this job? When have you demonstrated that to be true?

Example: Used advanced CAD tools to create a totally new look in video game modeling.

➤ What activities, paid and unpaid, have you done that used skills you'll be using at your new job?

Example: Offered academic counseling to 40 students at "Make It Happen," a volunteer program at Sanford High School.

➤ When did someone "sit up and take notice" of how skilled you are?

Example: Commended for achieving 97 percent of production goal in an industry where 85 percent is considered high.

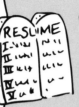

Commandments

Commandment IV: Thou shalt not write about stuff you don't want to do again. When you create your achievement sentences, be careful not to emphasize any aspect of the experience that you don't enjoy doing. Only stress the parts of the achievement that you would like to repeat.

Who's Your Audience?

Your resume is about your future, not your past. Based on this principle, keep in mind while you write your resume that your audience is the hiring manager for the position mentioned in your job objective statement. In order to sell yourself to this potential employer, talk about yourself in ways that are meaningful to him or her. In some cases, you may need to:

➤ Translate terminology to downplay differences between your past experience and your job objective

➤ Select only aspects of your achievements that paint a picture of you at your next job

➤ Prioritize your points so that your most relevant achievements are emphasized

Now let's take a closer look at these three methods of presenting achievements.

Downplay Differences

Use more generic terminology to downplay the differences and emphasize the similarities between your previous position and your job objective. Take a look at the following examples.

Elizabeth was a nurse who was applying for a customer service position at a department store. She used generic terms when referring to her hospital work so the reader would see that her customer service skills were just what he needed in his department store.

Instead of:

Explained medical procedures and equipment to Hamilton Medical Center patients and their families to enable them to make wise decisions regarding surgery, care, and discharge.

132

Elizabeth wrote:

Educated clients about new products and procedures at the medical center, and assisted them in making personal decisions based on financial, lifestyle, and timeline concerns.

When Charles exited the military and wanted a job in corporate public relations, he phrased his statements using civilian terminology to de-emphasize his career transition.

Instead of:

Managed public relations for the U.S. Navy's "Fleet Week," a $1.5 million celebration that drew 50,000 civilians.

Charles wrote:

Managed public relations for a $1.5 million celebration sponsored by the Bay Area's largest employer and attended by some 50,000 people.

Keep it Relevant

Your achievements are made up of several aspects, some of which have nothing to do with what you will offer your next employer. Use your resume to draw parallels (not point out disparities) between your past and future so that the employer will see you as someone who is qualified for the job. Make an impression that you're a good fit by presenting only those aspects of your achievements that relate to your job objective. Here are some examples.

Henry was an excellent event planner who wanted to use his organizational skills in a new field: graphic layout for a daily newspaper. He knew he could not assume the reader would conclude, "Since this job seeker can plan events, he can lay out newspaper copy." So Henry took extra care to draw the parallels between the two occupations.

Instead of:

Produced social and business events for up to 2,000 people, managing budgets, catering, entertainment, and logistics.

Henry wrote:

Maintained a perfect record of on-time delivery of at least 20 projects a month, involving tight time, budget, and space constraints.

Commandments

Commandment I: Thou shalt not write about your past; thou shalt write about your future! Select from your past only those parts of an achievement that paint a picture of you at your next job.

As a horticulturist, Patty realized that the part of her job she liked the most was answering clients' questions. When she wrote her resume for a job as a travel agent, she emphasized her customer service skills and downplayed her scientific expertise.

Instead of:

Provided scientific information on thousands of plant species, as the lead horticulturist of the country's most prestigious botanical garden.

Patty wrote:

Assisted customers in selecting from more than 2,000 options by patiently answering questions and educating them about costs and benefits.

First Things First

Prioritize your statements, so the one most relevant to your new job is first.

For example, as a former office manager, 75 percent of Andrea's time was spent processing administrative paperwork, and less than 25 percent was spent on training and supervision. She wanted to get a job as a corporate trainer. So she prioritized her achievement statements to stress the training experience, even though it was not her primary responsibility.

Instead of:

➤ Supervised administration of firm's largest litigation department with more than 300 cases per week.

➤ Led office to achieve "#1 Team" award by motivating staff to take a customer service approach to all internal and external interactions.

➤ Trained 13 employees on new automated accounting system, providing classroom sessions, individual coaching, and written instructions.

Andrea reordered her statements to read:

➤ Trained 13 employees on new automated accounting system, providing classroom sessions, individual coaching, and written instructions.

Commandments
Commandment V: Thou shalt not lie. You can be creative, but be honest.

➤ Led office to achieve "#1 Team" award by motivating staff to take a customer service approach to all internal and external interactions.

➤ Supervised administration of firm's largest litigation department with more than 300 cases per week.

Lights, Camera...Action Verbs!

You may have lights and cameras, but it's not a movie until there's action. Likewise, your resume needs dynamic language to make it sing. To deliver the most punch in your achievement statements, *use an action verb at or near the beginning of each line.* Action verbs make your resume more powerful by describing how you accomplished your goals.

> **Tip**
>
> Avoid using the term "responsible for." This phrase doesn't clearly describe your level of involvement. Did you think of an idea that others carried out, or did you work overtime to implement every detail of a project? Be sure to give yourself full credit by using action verbs to indicate exactly what your role was.

The following list of verbs is categorized under two headings: "Management" and "Communication." Which verbs most powerfully describe your achievements?

Management	augmented	conceptualized
accelerated	authorized	conducted
accomplished	bid	consolidated
achieved	boosted	consummated
activated	budgeted	contracted
added	built	controlled
administered	capitalized on	converted
advanced	carried out	coordinated
allocated	caused	corrected
analyzed	centralized	cultivated
anticipated	certified	cut
appointed	chaired	decided
appropriated	championed	defined
approved	collaborated	delegated
arranged	completed	delivered
assigned	conceived	designated
attained	concentrated	determined

developed	guided	motivated
devised	handled	multiplied
directed	headed	netted
dominated	heightened	obtained
doubled	hired	opened
downsized	implemented	orchestrated
drove	improved	organized
earned	incorporated	oversaw
empowered	increased	performed
endorsed	induced	piloted
engineered	initiated	pioneered
enhanced	installed	planned
enlarged	instituted	positioned
enlisted	integrated	precipitated
established	intensified	presided
evaluated	introduced	prioritized
exceeded	invested	processed
executed	launched	produced
expanded	led	promoted
expedited	lowered	proposed
facilitated	magnified	purchased
financed	maintained	ran
focused	managed	ranked
forced	marketed	rated
forged	maximized	re-engineered
fostered	merged	reached
founded	met	realized
fulfilled	minimized	recommended
gained	mobilized	recruited
generated	modernized	reduced
governed	modified	regulated
grew	monitored	rejuvenated

remedied

renewed

represented

resolved

restored

restructured

revamped

reviewed

revitalized

revived

revolutionized

scheduled

secured

served as

set

shepherded

sold

solved

started

steered

stimulated

streamlined

strengthened

structured

succeeded

supervised

synchronized

systematized

targeted

trained

tripled

triumphed

turned around

underwrote

unified

united

upgraded

upheld

verified

won

Communication

addressed

adjudicated

advertised

advised

advocated

annotated

announced

answered

appeased

arbitrated

argued

articulated

asserted

assuaged

assured

authored

bargained

briefed

campaigned

canvassed

clarified

coached

coined

collaborated

communicated

compelled

compiled

composed

compromised

conversed

converted

convinced

corresponded

couched

counseled

created

defined

delivered

demonstrated

demystified

depicted

described

detailed

developed

dictated

discussed

drafted

edited

educated

elucidated

encouraged

explained

expounded

expressed

facilitated

formulated	pressured
guaranteed	proclaimed
guided	promoted
illustrated	prompted
impressed	proofread
influenced	proposed
informed	publicized
inspired	reassured
instigated	recommended
instructed	reconciled
interpreted	remarked
intervened	represented
interviewed	settled
intonated	(disputes)
lectured	specified
litigated	spelled out
lobbied	spoke
mediated	stated
moderated	stimulated
motivated	stipulated
negotiated	stressed
ordered	swayed
outlined	taught
penned	trained
persuaded	translated
phrased	urged
pitched	verbalized
preached	voiced
prepared	won over
presented	wrote

How'd the Other Guys Say It?

A quick look at what others have written might give you the jump start you need for writing about your own achievements. The following achievement statements were taken from several different resumes:

➤ Restructured entire Service Department, resulting in more efficient outreach programs.

➤ Initiated procedures to increase employee productivity while reducing stress levels.

➤ Successfully explained and demonstrated technical products in lay terminology to prospective buyers.

➤ Negotiated the sale of $100,000 worth of unprofitable inventory.

➤ Created sales and marketing programs that increased shopping center profits by 33 percent.

➤ Won more than 80 percent of cases, delivering persuasive arguments as legal representative for corporate clients in administrative law hearings.

➤ Increased MediSave's stock value five-fold in nine months by repositioning the product and company.

➤ Convinced more than 400 commuters to carpool, reducing the number of vehicles on the road by 225 per year.

➤ Managed a national and international sales force of 32 manufacturers' representative companies for Teekel Press, a publisher of photographic greeting cards.

Tip

Ever wonder why newspapers use one-inch columns instead of printing across the full width of the page? Because it's quicker to read short lines than long ones. That's a tip you can use in formatting your resume. Keep your line lengths short—about five inches if possible.

➤ Exceeded delivery performance by 10 percent, taking it from 85 percent to a record 95 percent in an industry where the norm is 75 percent.

➤ Managed the sales and full P&L for 20 stores in Northern California region.

➤ Handled daily news coverage of the San Francisco 49ers and Oakland A's, involving extensive travel.

➤ Authored two published pieces on international touring, which demystified the hardships and emphasized the rewards of independent travel.

➤ Reconciled differences among personnel, creating a more cohesive team spirit.

Go For It

Now that you've composed your achievement statements, it's time to put them into your resume format. Follow these directions for the type of resume you are creating.

Writing Achievement Statements for a Chronological Resume

If you're writing a chronological resume, your achievement statements should appear under the company name where you performed the achievement. For help, see the resume template that appears earlier in this chapter, and the following six chronological resumes from real job seekers.

> **Tip**
>
> After you've listed your achievement statements, prioritize them within each section so that the most relevant and most impressive one appears first.

DEBBIE WINTERS
SENIOR PRODUCTION MANAGER

2824 Wilsohn Avenue
Apple Creek, CA 88376
(501) 112-6532

SUMMARY OF QUALIFICATIONS

- 13 years experience in print production management for Fortune 500 companies.
- Excellent project manager. Skilled at resolving "unsolvable" problems and keeping projects moving forward.
- Successful at project P&L responsibility.
- Quick study who enjoys new challenges.

PROFESSIONAL EXPERIENCE

1987-present SOUTHERN MARKETING GROUP, San Francisco, CA
A West Coast based marketing and sales promotion agency providing in-store promotion, direct mail, and event marketing expertise.

Business Manager, Creative Services Group/Director of Production Services, 1992-present
Creative Services Manager, 1990-1992
Production Manager, 1987-1990

- Managed highly visible national promotions (creative development through print production and delivery) with budgets up to $3M. Fortune 500 clients included:

Compaq Computer	Levi Strauss
California Milk Board	VISA
Baskin Robbins	Nestles

> *Dynamic action verbs make Debbie's achievements even more impressive.*

- Consistently secured lowest prices by seeking out most efficient technology, maintaining strong business relations with vendors, and negotiating aggressive contracts.
- Collaborated with account and creative staff and clients at initial phases of projects to ensure cost appropriate products and timely deliveries.
- Generated added value by locating rare services, technologies, materials, and talents.
- Cut ordering errors and production/administration time by initiating new bidding, budgeting, and vendor communications systems. Worked with MIS group on development and set up.
- Generated $100K additional annual profit by introducing and overseeing the development of an in-house Macintosh based design and pre-press department.

1985-1986 JAMES DESIGN, San Francisco, CA
A design studio used by large advertising agencies for special assignments.

Production Manager/Art Director

- Managed collateral printing and direct mail for large clients such as:

Pacific Northwest Bell	Paramount Pictures
Washington State Apples	Easton Sporting Goods
Del Monte Food Services	Ready-Care

- Hired and coordinated teams of photographers, illustrators, writers, and models, frequently resolving personality, time, and cost differences.
- Protected Shubin against liability by working with legal staff regarding contract negotiations.

— Continued —

1983-1985   TYPE GRAPHIC DESIGN STUDIOS, San Simeon, CA
A design studio with in-house presses owned by Blake Printery, the largest printer in the central coast of California.
Graphic Designer
- Gained hands-on printing and pre-press experience as primary graphic designer of catalogs, newsletters, and wine labels.

1982-1983   KRSN-TV, San Simeon, CA
The #1 TV station on the central coast of California.
Production Manager/Graphic Designer
- Created all on-air graphics and operated controls to integrate graphics into live news broadcasts.
- Produced print collateral and direct mail for sales staff.

1978-1982   CAL POLY EXTENDED EDUCATION OFFICE, San Simeon, CA
Graphic Specialist
- Designed 60-page course catalog distributed quarterly to approximately 50,000 residents.
- Increased enrollment in non-credit courses 600% and credit courses 58% by improving catalog distribution without increasing costs.

EDUCATION

B.A. Graphic Design and Reproduction, 1981
     California Polytechnic State University, San Luis Obispo

M.A., History, 1978
     University California at Santa Barbara

B.A., History, 1976
     California Polytechnic State University, San Luis Obispo

Resume written in 1995.

Debra Willis

314 Forest Avenue • San Jose, CA 95138 • Work: 408-661-2246 • Home: 408-831-0094

JOB OBJECTIVE

Manager, Client Education and Training

SUMMARY OF QUALIFICATIONS

- Nine years as a marketing professional with recent experience as manager of successful client education and training programs.
- Creator of seminars that result in lead generation and improved client relations.
- Recognized as a supervisor who builds interdepartmental team rapport.

PROFESSIONAL EXPERIENCE

1993-pres. **Paris & Daily, Inc.,** San Jose, CA
MANAGER, CLIENT EDUCATION AND TRAINING, 1994-pres.
SEMINAR AND TRADE SHOW MANAGER, 1993-1994

- Manage the customer product training program that educates an average of 350 clients per month throughout California.

Look at all those quantified results! Debra's achievements shine in the dark!

- As supervisor of 4 full-time trainers, 10 contract field trainers, a training supervisor, and a seminar coordinator, gained a reputation as a creative leader who initiates interdepartmental cooperation.
- Collaborated with technical staff to develop "Introduction to CD-ROM," a 1-hour seminar that increased sales 33% in the first 2 months. This seminar became the primary sales tool and was presented 388 times in 1994.
- Contribute to product development by communicating customer feedback and suggestions for product enhancements through trainer-engineer meetings.
- Manage 35 trade shows per year, including booth and promotions development. Established an attendee database that enabled efficient follow-up on leads.
- As member of executive marketing team, participate in strategic and budget planning.
- Currently developing a VAR program that will involve over 100 vendors.

1989-1992 **Ardenwood & Associates,** San Jose, CA
CLIENT RELATIONS ADMINISTRATOR

- Created and managed the firm's first marketing efforts, which improved client relations through corporate communications, seminars, special events, and partner retreats.
- Increased efficiency and quality of new business proposals by establishing a 1-stop resource center for marketing collateral.
- Managed vendor relations and served as spokesperson to community organizations.

1986-1989 **RBH Allround,** San Jose, CA
DIRECTOR OF MARKETING

- Achieved sales goals by developing and executing marketing plans: national trade shows, promotions, corporate communications, special events, and community relations.

1984-1986 **San Jose Chamber of Commerce,** San Jose, CA
ASSISTANT MANAGER, SMALL BUSINESS DEPARTMENT

- Developed and produced 24 small business education programs throughout the year.
- Organized fundraising events and started the Woman Entrepreneur of the Year Program.

EDUCATION AND AFFILIATION

B.A., Sociology/Psychology, University of San Francisco
Continuing Education: Marketing, Management, and Communications
Member, Leadership San Francisco

Resume written in 1995.

Sally S. White

2197 Union St. • San Francisco, CA 94109 • (415) 721-9327

Special Gifts Development Officer

SUMMARY OF QUALIFICATIONS

- Over six years as Major Gifts Development Officer for a metropolitan United Way which raised over $50M annually.
- 20 years experience in nonprofit management.
- Ability to maximize productivity through volunteer training, motivation, and recognition.

PROFESSIONAL ACCOMPLISHMENTS

1995-pres. **International Diplomacy Council (IDC)**, San Francisco, CA
DIRECTOR OF VOLUNTEERS

- Increased special event fundraising 14.5% by managing IDC's first annual silent auction.
- Recruit, train, and manage 40+ regular volunteers who perform over 50% of the organization's program development, marketing, public relations, and event planning.

1988-1994 **United Way of Southeastern PA**, Philadelphia, PA
CAMPAIGN DIRECTOR, SPECIAL GIFTS

When the employer read Sally's resume, I'll bet he thought, "I'd like Sally to achieve these kinds of results for me!"

- Led the Philadelphia Alexis de Tocqueville (ADT) Campaign ($10K+ annual individual donors), which ranked #1 in the country for five consecutive years.
  - Raised $5M per year.
  - Obtained $1M challenge match for new ADT givers.
  - Program won United Way of America's most prestigious fundraising award, the Fleur de Lis, for four years running.
- Established leadership giving program for donors with salaries of $50K or more
  - Leadership givers now donate 13% of overall United Way campaign.
  - Program won the United Way of America Award in the Special Markets Category.
- Increased major giving 10%, individual giving 6% despite overall 4% campaign decrease.
- Generated $1M per year by rejuvenating the planned giving program to focus on a campaign approach to endowment building.
  - Created Bequest Society and Honor Roll to recognize donors of $25K+.
- Served as consultant on major giving to United Ways throughout U.S. and Canada.
  - Delivered seminar for 18 major giving staff for United Way of Tri-State, New York.
  - Led conference session on major donors for United Way of Canada's annual meeting.
  - Served as resource specialist for two-day major gift development seminar for United Way of Toronto volunteers and staff.

1986-1988 **International Visitors Center**, Philadelphia, PA
DEPUTY DIRECTOR

- During the Bicentennial of the U.S. Constitution, developed and managed The Pew Charitable Trust funded program to educate 3,000 professionals from 100 countries about nation-building.
- Prepared corporate executives and government officials to participate in special forums with international visitors.
- Trained volunteers to promote program's mission via individual and group presentations.

— Continued —

Sally S. White
Page 2

1984-1986 **University of Pennsylvania,** Philadelphia, PA
ADVISOR, OFFICE OF INTERNATIONAL PROGRAMS

- Co-created three new international student programs. Conducted needs assessment and data analysis; developed program plan.
- Designed internships for undergraduate and graduate students.

1975-1984 **University of Iowa,** Iowa City, IA
DIRECTOR OF PROGRAMS

- As Executive Director of Women's Institute for Community Leadership, taught policy making skills to women who later became influential community leaders.
- Chaired university task force that set up international alumni organizations worldwide.
- Served as on-site consultant to Iowa Alumni Associations in Asia.
- Founded the Council of International Visitors of Iowa City, still considered the primary international programming agency in the area.
- Organized memorial scholarship and obtained endowment funds.

1972-1975 **Congressman Edward Mezvinsky,** First District, IA
CONSTITUENT RELATIONS OFFICER, Iowa City Office

EDUCATION

M.S.W., Social Policy Program and Planning, University of Iowa, Iowa City, IA
B.A., Political Science, Chatham College, Pittsburgh, PA

United Way of America course:	Mega-Gifts	
University of Pennsylvania:	Major Giving	Individual Giving
	Planned Giving	Prospect Research

PROFESSIONAL AFFILIATIONS

Member, NSFRE: Committees: Franklin Forum, Annual Awards, Friends Project
Former Member, National Committee on Planned Giving
Former Vice Chair, Delaware Valley Planned Giving Council

COMMUNITY INVOLVEMENT

Member, Board of Directors/Chair, Development Committee, Hydrocephalus Association
Fundraiser, Chatham College Alumnae Association
Member, Russian Hill Neighbors

Resume written in 1995.

Jon Carter

4672 Union Street • San Francisco, CA 93211 • (415) 664-8854

Sales Professional

Business Development
Marketing
Sales Management
Product Development

PROFESSIONAL ACCOMPLISHMENTS

1991-pres. **Telegraph Hill Club**, San Francisco, CA
MEMBERSHIP REPRESENTATIVE

- Produced 70% of sales for this high-end athletic club with 1,500 members.
- Achieved a 30% close rate on 50-70 cold calls per day.
- Ranked #1 sales rep among the nine clubs of the parent company, Western Athletic Clubs, which generates over $30M annually.
- Stabilized revenue by initiating a corporate membership program that now realizes 30% of club's income.
- Increased market share and reduced attrition by expanding product line.
- Received the "Service Star Award" for outstanding customer service, presented to only 14 of the 4,000 employees company wide.

Numbers, dollar signs, percentages…Wow! Jon knows how to get results!

1988-1990 **McGraw-Hill College Textbook Division**, San Francisco, CA
SALES REPRESENTATIVE

- Attained "#1 Sales Rep" in Northern California for exceeding sales goals 20%.
- Managed a client base of colleges and universities representing approximately $1M in textbook sales per year.
- First rep in the country to achieve major sale of first edition physics book by an unknown author.
- Developed profitable publishing contract between Stanford University professor and McGraw-Hill.

1986-1988 **Georgia Pacific**, Denver, CO
SALES REPRESENTATIVE

- Averaged $20K per day in inside and outside sales for this construction materials distributor.
- As product manager, increased revenue by revamping the roofing sales program.

EDUCATION

B.A., Economics, University of Colorado at Boulder, 1985
Member, Chi Psi Fraternity
Graduate, Dale Carnegie Sales Course

Resume written in 1995.

Mary Henderson

339 Terrace Place • San Francisco, CA 99712 • (415) 773-9886

PROFILE

- 12 years as a professional in the lending industry.
- Excellent record of approving and selling loans profitably.
- Adept at every aspect of the loan process from origination through reconveyance.

PROFESSIONAL EXPERIENCE

1981-1993 GEORGE FRIEND MORTGAGE COMPANY, San Francisco, CA
A small lending firm making quality loans that consistently realized profits throughout my tenure.

Vice President, 1986-1993
Loan Officer, 1981-1986

- Produced more than 50% of the company's business by establishing a network among local real estate brokers and generating referrals.
- Developed and maintained more than 60 private loan portfolios with total values in excess of $18 million.
- Achieved profitable revenue growth annually.
- Handled all phases of the loan evaluation from application through approval, including on site appraisal.
- Managed escrow process including the preparation of loan documents.
- Serviced all loans generated, utilizing trust fund and loan servicing software.
- Coordinated the transition of office operations to a computerized system.

Each one of Mary's successes from top to bottom is impressive!

1980-1981 CALIFORNIA TITLE COMPANY, Redwood City, CA
Bookkeeper

- Handled accounting for escrows and prepared operational financial statements.

LICENSURE

Licensed Real Estate Broker

Resume written in 1993.

Frank Helman
3392 Fairmount Dr.
Cape Elizabeth, CA 97882
(329) 662-9571

OBJECTIVE

Executive Management Consultant

SUMMARY OF QUALIFICATIONS

- Expertise in transition management due to mergers, downsizing, expansion, and change in ownership.
- Confident approach to identifying problems, designing solutions, and building consensus.
- Adaptive to various personalities and management styles.

PROFESSIONAL ACCOMPLISHMENTS

1979-1993   **Executive management positions** in a successful frozen food commodity company that transitioned through four ownerships/organizational configurations in 14 years.

Penn-Fresh Grown, Inc.	Vice President Marketing & General Manager, 1991-1993
	Director of Sales, 1989-1991
Original Veg. Products	General Manager, 1986-1989
Express Fresh-Grown, Inc.	Vice President of Sales and Administration, 1982-1986
Fresh Grown, Inc.	Executive Vice President, 1979-1982

- Drove the company from $7 million to $18 million in revenues in two years as Vice President of Sales and Administration.
- Recommended plan of action that turned around Production Department and retained $8 million in revenue.
- Maintained continuity of $5 million in annual sales and reduced administrative overhead by creating consulting position for veteran sales executive.
- Built a cohesive team spirit throughout the company by designing a program that recognized competing management objectives, created common goals, and provided measurement incentives.
- Strengthened morale and reduced recruiting costs by promoting cross-training and internal promotions.
- Through proactive employee relations, maintained a 100% retention rate despite changes in ownership and organizational size/structure.

(Note bubble: Love these action verbs and quantifiable results! Each accomplishment is credible and enticing.)

1978-1979   University of California, Berkeley, CA
Project Director (contractual), Health Data and Management for HEW Region X

1975-1977   Health Wise Association, Portland, OR
HMO Management Consultant

1974-1975   United Health Cooperative, Portland, OR
Assistant to CEO

1972-1974   American Health Planners, Bakersfield, CA
Planning Administrator

EDUCATION

Masters of Health Administration, University of California, Berkeley, CA
Bachelor of Arts, Liberal Arts, Occidental College, Pasadena, CA

(Note bubble: Resume written in 1994.)

Writing Achievements for a Functional Resume

If you're a functional resume writer, your achievement statements should appear under the appropriate skill heading. See the resume template that appears earlier in this chapter, and the following six functional resumes.

> **Tip**
>
> Many times functional resume writers make the mistake of writing accomplishment statements without indicating where the achievements took place. This makes the reader uneasy since he or she has no way of referencing the experience. The solution? *Give each accomplishment credibility by saying where it happened.*

Here are three ways to indicate where your success took place:

➤ Incorporate the name of the organization or your position into the sentence:

Managed Harrington Department Store's $1.5 million budget.

Collaborated with executives to create a new marketing strategy, as member of the St. Francis Board of Directors.

➤ Reference the organization or your position at the end of the statement:

Managed budget of $1.5 million. (Harrington Department Store)

Collaborated with executives to create a new marketing strategy. —Member, St. Francis Board of Directors

➤ Group achievements together according to where they happened, still keeping them within skill categories. This, in effect, becomes a hybrid resume based on a functional format (this is discussed in detail in Chapter 14):

Harrington Department Store

Managed the store's $1.5 million budget.

St. Francis

Collaborated with executives to create new marketing strategy.

Wendi Packerson

490 Twonscend Street
San Francisco, CA 94909
(415) 826-8921

OBJECTIVE

A position as Editorial Assistant for the Clairmont Times

HIGHLIGHTS

- Five years in a business environment, coordinating writing projects from research to publication.
- Skilled at using a keen sense of investigation along with a friendly personality to uncover sought-after information.
- Ability to "read between the lines"; a well-tuned "B.S. indicator."

RELEVANT SKILLS & EXPERIENCE

WRITING

- Instigated change of a 10-year policy by writing a provocative eight-page memorandum proposing the restructuring of accounting procedures. (Sunset Oil)
- Authored script for 25-minute documentary on the Himalayas, sold to Smith College. (independent project)
- Wrote copy, designed layout, and oversaw production for nationwide ad campaign. Company mentioned in *Time* magazine as a result of the ad. (Paris Anton Enterprises)

RESEARCH

- Interviewed principals to gather details and substantiate a position on financial dealings. (Anderson Company)
- Researched feasibility of projects to weed out unworkable plans; presented recommendations to General Manager. (Paris Anton Enterprises)
- Uncovered financial discrepancies which led to the exposure of a long-standing problem in the Accounting Department. (Sunset Oil)

The name within the parentheses at the end of each achievement statement tells the reader where Wendi performed her achievement.

PROJECT COORDINATION

- Oversaw the start-up and operation of a mail order project involving advertising, data entry, shipping, and accounting. (Paris Anton Enterprises)
- Built coalition of investors to resolve payment of company's debt. (Anderson Company)
- Collaborated with 33 climbers and 200 porters to organize logistics of a dangerous six-week expedition in the Himalayas. (independent project)

WORK HISTORY

1988-present	*Financial Researcher*	Anderson Company Inc., San Francisco office
1985-1987	*Start-up Consultant*	Home Office, San Francisco
1984-1985	*Project Manager*	Paris Anton Enterprises, Saco, TX
1981-1983	*Revenue Accountant*	Sunset Oil Company, Houston, TX

EDUCATION

Bachelor of Arts, Journalism, New York University, Albany, NY

Resume written in 1993.

Doris Ferguson

4525 Springer Avenue • Oakland, CA 94504 • (510) 526-7341

JOB OBJECTIVE

A position in Human Resources with emphasis on Training and Recruiting

HIGHLIGHTS OF QUALIFICATIONS

- 14 years as an administrative professional within prominent corporations, who has contributed to the success of programs through training and recruiting.
- Knack for putting people at ease, enabling them to learn easily and quickly.
- Very strong background in computer operations: mainframe and PCs (IBM and Macintosh).

EDUCATION

B.A., Human Services, concentration: Human Resources/Communications, March 1995
Holy Names College, Oakland, CA
Relevant classes: Labor Law   Psychology and Personality
                    Organizational Behavior   Group Processes and Communication
                    Human Services   Essentials of Effective Speech

Certificate, Computer Operations/Word Processing, 1989
Lawton Business School, Oakland, CA

RELEVANT EXPERIENCE

TRAINING / PRESENTATIONS

- Trained personnel in DOS/MVSE hardware and software operations at Computer Science Corporation, a service bureau for small businesses statewide.
- Wrote and updated "easy-to-follow" technical manuals used by all computer operations personnel at Computer Science Corporation.
- Due to advanced computer skills, informally trained co-workers during Clorox Marketing Department's computer conversion.
- Supervised paid and volunteer staff who handled logistics for health care education sessions for Kaiser Hospital patients.
- Taught summer class in English Arts to prepare students for entry into new grade levels at public school. Developed lesson plans and teaching materials that addressed needs of a multicultural classroom.
- Won two Toastmaster awards for delivering prepared and spontaneous speeches.

Each of Doris's achievement statements includes the name of the organization where it took place. This lends credibility to the claim.

RECRUITING

- Interviewed and hired candidates for Kaiser's special employment program, using a personable style that put applicants at ease and revealed their true skills and personality.
- Recruited reliable and competent volunteer staff, using a careful selection process to ensure quality of Kaiser's Health Education Program.

WORK HISTORY

1992-1994	The Clorox Company, Oakland, CA	Secretary
1990-1992	Bank of America, Oakland, CA	Senior Secretary
1989-1990	Kaiser Hospital, Oakland, CA	Administrative Secretary
1987-1988	AT&T, Pleasanton, CA	Engineering Clerk
1981-1986	Computer Science Corporation, Oakland/L.A.	Senior Computer Operator

Resume written in 1995.

SHARI TAYLOR
3513 Langstrom Street • San Francisco, CA 94115
(415) 518-4498

OBJECTIVE

An administrative support position in an arts/design organization

SUMMARY OF QUALIFICATIONS

- 10 years' experience in administrative support, working in arts oriented and international environments.
- Proven ability to coordinate events from in-house meetings to art festivals.
- Enjoy organizing projects efficiently to get the job done.
- Experienced with WordPerfect 5.1 and Unisys systems.

RELEVANT EXPERIENCE

Events Coordination

Notice how Shari tells the reader where each achievement took place by weaving the name of the organization into the sentence.

- Co-directed Cine de las Americas, the first North and South American animation festival which led to coalitions between U.S. and international filmmakers.
- Coordinated two annual trade seminars and six sales trips to Pacific Rim countries for Pacific International Commerce and Planning Corporation.
- Provided reception and hospitality for Pacific International's foreign clients.
- Arranged travel and accommodations for training staff at the Equal Opportunity Office (EEO) at the National Park Service, Western Region.

Project Organization

- Administered the Minority Business Export Program for Pacific International.
  - Coordinated management and technical consulting services for clients.
  - Established a resource library, used to assist new businesses interested in exporting products.
- Streamlined the Dental Research Foundation accounting system at University of the Pacific (UOP), greatly improving accuracy and efficiency.
- Managed the administration of educational programs presented by EEO.
- Oversaw daily EEO office operations.

Basic Bookkeeping

- Performed bank reconciliations, tracked expenditures, and produced monthly financial reports for 30 accounts, (representing revolving assets of $156,000 for dental research at UOP).
- Managed tracking of all purchase orders, annual operating program funds, A/P, and A/R at Western Region Office of National Park Service.
- Assisted the Bookkeeper at Pacific International.

WORK HISTORY

1989-present	**Secretary**	University of the Pacific (UOP), San Francisco
1987-89	**Equal Opportunity Assist.**	National Park Service, San Francisco
1983-86	**Program Administrator**	Pacific International Commerce & Planning Corp., S. F.
1981-83	**Volunteer Coordinator**	Mexican Museum, San Francisco
1981-86	**Freelance Filmmaker**	San Francisco Area

EDUCATION

B.A., Fine Arts, San Francisco Art Institute, 1980
Business Administration coursework,
San Francisco Renaissance Center for Education & Technical Training, 1991

Resume written in 1995.

Dorothea Conger

3290 Paramount Street • Oakland, CA 94603 • (510) 576-8697

JOB OBJECTIVE: Hospice Program Manager

SUMMARY OF QUALIFICATIONS

- As current Acting Hospice Program Manager, prepared to take a proactive approach to healthcare reform.
- 11 years as a practicing nurse with a wide range of clinical specialties.
- 2 years as an accomplished Hospice Case Manager.
- Demonstrated strengths in planning, organizing, problem solving, and communication.

RELEVANT ACCOMPLISHMENTS

LEADERSHIP AND MANAGEMENT

Each of Dorothea's accomplishments are believable because she says where they happened.

- As Acting Hospice Program Manager, developed a plan to restructure Hospice to improve quality of service and accommodate a growing census without increasing costs.
- Fulfilled a two-year commitment to restructure the leadership and organization of the Evangelical Free Church of Oakland. Attendance increased 300%.
- Made presentations on behalf of Hospice at the Family Conference, CPMC volunteer training, and a Contra Costa County high school.
- Led a team of 31 Team Missions International teenagers to India for six weeks to build an orphanage and visit nationals in hospitals and villages.

AIDS AND HOSPICE CARE

- Managed a caseload of 15 clients. Received exemplary evaluations; maintained timely completion of records; and received numerous commendations from families.
- Frequently handled complicated cases. For example: Educated and led a team that provided counseling and care to a 12 year-old AIDS patient and her family.
- Utilized a diverse clinical background to manage a wide range of cases and offer advice to colleagues.

WORK HISTORY

1992-present	Visiting Nurses and Hospice of San Francisco, CA
	Acting Hospice Program Manager
	Case Manager
1990-1992	Highland General Hospital, Oakland, CA
	ER Charge Nurse
1990-1992	Agostini and Associates (registry), Orinda, CA
	ICU, ER, PICU Nurse
1985-1990	St. Francis Medical Center, Peoria, IL
	Neuro ICU and ER Charge Nurse, Life Flight Nurse

EDUCATION AND CERTIFICATIONS

ADN (1985) and Certificate of Practical Nursing (1983), Carl Sandburg College, Galesburg, IL
Accepted into BSN External Degree Program, Graceland College, Lamoni, IA

Advanced Cardiac Life Support Provider and Instructor	Trauma Nurse Specialist
Certified Emergency Nurse (C.E.N.)	Life Flight Specialist
Mobile Intensive Care Nurse (M.I.C.N.)	Poison Nurse Specialist

Resume written in 1994.

153

Samantha C. Edgar

153 Grand Avenue • Kensington, CA 94708 • (510) 332-9453

Objective	Psychosocial Rehabilitation Case Manager
Summary	• Experience as a case manager in a vocational/academic skills development program for adults with psychological disabilities.
	• Work effectively with consumers, individually and in groups.
	• Competent at case record keeping and administration of programs.

Experience

PSYCHOSOCIAL REHABILITATION

Transitions to College Program, College of San Mateo
• Manage caseload of 35 students with severe psychological disabilities who are transitioning from residential treatment to academic/vocational education.
• Maximize students' strengths by coaching them individually, assessing their needs, and customizing curriculum.
• Teach "Skills Development for Career Growth," a class designed for adolescents and adults with psychological disabilities.

PROGRAM DEVELOPMENT

Transitions to College Program, College of San Mateo
• As member of interdisciplinary committee, continually develop and evaluate the program which has grown from 20 to 108 students in two years.
• Serve as liaison among the community, mental health agencies, and the college to coordinate rehabilitation efforts for program participants.

COUNSELING

Psychological Services, College of San Mateo
• Counsel 10 students a week regarding career, social, academic, and family issues. Students come from a wide range of ethnic and economic backgrounds.
• Provide crisis intervention.

Samantha categorized her achievements according to where they happened, making this a hybrid resume based on the functional format.

Work History

1993-present	Counselor, Psychological Services COLLEGE OF SAN MATEO, San Mateo, CA
1992-present	Psychological Disabilities Counselor Transitions to College Program COLLEGE OF SAN MATEO, San Mateo, CA
1992	Survey Conductor, Stanford Alcohol Study STANFORD SCHOOL OF MEDICINE, Palo Alto, CA
1991-1992	Volunteer Food Server, Dining Room for Homeless ST. ANTHONY'S FOUNDATION, San Francisco, CA
1980-1990	Manager, MIRACLE MUSHROOM, San Francisco, CA
1978-1980	Administrative Assistant MORGANELLI HUMAN ARCHITECTS, San Francisco, CA
1973-1978	Waitress, SIR FRANCIS DRAKE HOTEL, San Francisco, CA

Education

MA, Counseling Psychology, College of Notre Dame, Belmont, CA, May 1994
Thesis: Teachers' Perceptions Regarding Students with Psychological Disabilities
National Scholastic Honor Society, Delta Epsilon Sigma

B.F.A., New School of Social Research, New York, NY, 1973

Resume written in 1994.

Maria A. Sanchez

44 Clairmont Street, #6 • San Francisco, CA 94123 • (415) 449-1184

JOB OBJECTIVE

Event Coordinator with emphasis on trade show production

SUMMARY OF QUALIFICATIONS

- Experienced at managing details and completing projects on time.
- Dedicated team player who has a positive approach to problem solving.
- Commitment to customer service.

RELEVANT ACCOMPLISHMENTS

PROJECT MANAGEMENT

As Corporate Meeting Planner Assistant
- Assisted in the production of seminars for up to 300 people.
  - Compiled a master list of RSVPs and participated in on-site registration.
  - Circulated among participants throughout event to answer questions and ensure smooth flow of logistics.
- Gathered information on California recreation/entertainment corporations that offer company discounts.

As Broker Service Representative
- Collaborated with account executives to review top accounts and define sales strategies.

As Lead Underwriting Assistant
- Supervised four assistants who handled a large volume of administrative and client relations work each day.
- Trained new assistants in northern and southern California.

As C-Span Promotion Intern
- Provided research and technical assistance for the production of 30-second promotional videos aired nationally.

It's easy to see where Maria's achievements took place because she grouped them according to job title (a hybrid resume based on the functional format).

CUSTOMER SERVICE

As Broker Service Representative
- Handled about 60 phone calls a day regarding rates, programs, and problems.
- Expedited special client requests by re-prioritizing and guiding projects through the system.

As Lead Underwriting Assistant
- Served as liaison among underwriters, clients, and staff. Prepared letters of approval, denial, and suspension.

WORK HISTORY

1991-present	Headlands Mortgage Company, Larkspur, CA
	Broker Service Representative, 1992-present
	Lead Underwriting Assistant, 1991-1992
1990	Benham Capital Management Group, Mountain View, CA
	Corporate Meeting Planner Assistant

EDUCATION

1989	BA, Communications, University of California, Santa Barbara, CA
	Promotional Video Intern, C-Span, Washington, D.C.

Resume written in 1994.

The Least You Need to Know

➤ Don't write boring job descriptions—write powerful achievement statements.

➤ Use terminology that has meaning to the potential employer.

➤ Start lines with action verbs.

➤ Prioritize bulleted points within each section so the statement with the most impact comes first.

➤ Functional resumes should include where an achievement took place.

Chapter 10

Step Eight— Where'd You Learn That?

In This Chapter

➤ How to create a proper Education section

➤ How to list college degrees

➤ What if you have college experience but no degree?

➤ Listing a new high school diploma

➤ What about the not-so-new high school graduate?

Your resume is looking pretty good, isn't it? You've resolved your work history problems, written dynamite achievement statements, made claims that blow your competition out of the water...you're on a roll! Only a few more things to consider for your resume and you'll be ready to drop it in the mail.

In this chapter, I share some helpful hints on how to make the most of your academic, professional, and vocational training.

The ABCs of Your Education

Your education is almost always a point of interest to a prospective employer. The Education section is usually positioned at or near the end of the resume, as noted on the following template.

(Here's where the Education section usually appears.)

Name
Street • City, State Zip • phone

JOB OBJECTIVE
> The job you want next

SUMMARY OF QUALIFICATIONS
> - How much experience you have in the field of your objective, in a related field, or using the skills required for your new position.
> - An overall career accomplishment that shows you'd be good at this job objective.
> - What someone would say about you as a recommendation.

PROFESSIONAL EXPERIENCE

19xx-pres. **Company Name**, City, State
JOB TITLE
A brief description of the organization
- An accomplishment you are proud of that shows you're good at this profession.
- A problem you solved and the results.
- A time when you positively affected the organization, the bottom line, your boss, your co-workers, your clients.
- Awards, commendations, publications, etc. you achieved that relate to your job objective.

19xx-xx **Company Name**, City, State
JOB TITLE
A brief description of the organization
- A project you are proud of that supports your job objective.
- Another accomplishment that shows you're good at this line of work.
- Quantifiable results that point out your skill.

EDUCATION
> Degree, Major (if relevant), 19xx (optional)
> University, City, State

Exceptions to the Rule

Commandments

Commandment V: Thou shalt not lie. You can be creative, but be honest. If you're tempted to lie about a degree or certification, resist! Getting caught with your hand in the cookie jar could put your job on the line.

In some cases, however, it's better to place the Education section under the Summary of Qualifications section near the beginning of the resume. You might want to place it here if:

➤ Your education is highly relevant to your new position.

➤ You're a new graduate and you want to show off your degree.

➤ You have no employment experience in the field you are going into, but have a degree or training in that field.

Commandments

Commandment I: Thou shalt not write about your past; thou shalt write about your future! Instead of listing all the classes and workshops you attended, list only the ones that support your job objective.

College Degrees

Perhaps the most common listing for the Education section on a resume is a college degree. Let's begin by talking about degrees and related information.

Commandments

Commandment II: Thou shalt not confess. In other words, you don't have to "tell all." Stick to what's relevant and marketable. It's OK to delete information (such as degrees) that makes you look overqualified.

If you have one or more college degrees:

➤ State where each degree was received. You don't have to put down all the different schools you attended leading up to achieving your degree.

➤ Dates are optional. They sometimes indicate how old you are and how current your knowledge is, so be conscious of that when you decide whether or not to include dates.

➤ Majors, minors, theses, dissertations, internships, projects, papers, and coursework should be listed only if they are relevant to your job objective.

➤ You can spell out a degree (Bachelor of Arts) or use the representative letters (BA or B.A.).

Take a look at Fredona's resume on the following page to see how she showed off her college degrees.

Warning

Don't look overqualified for the job. For some positions your college degree might scare the pants off an employer. When in doubt, leave the degree off.

Degree Pending

If you are currently in a relevant educational or training program but have not yet finished, list the program and name of the institution you are attending, followed by the date you intend to finish, or a phrase such as "currently enrolled," "anticipated completion: Spring '97," "in progress," or "six months completed."

See Annie's resume later in this chapter for a demonstration of this point.

Degree Equivalent

If you achieved a degree equivalency through a less traditional or non-American system, state your experience in terms of its equivalency; for example, "B.A. equivalent, St. Paul University, Paris, France."

Take a look at Guy's resume later in this chapter. He has both a degree equivalent and additional training.

Fredona Riekels
RN, MS, CNA

1362 Palmer Avenue • Muskegon, California 00327 • Tel: (331) 556-9932 • Fax: (331) 556-2479

Health Care Administrator

with 20 years combined experienced:

        Project Management
        Standards Development/Quality Assessment and Improvement
        Staff Training and Development
        Client Services

EDUCATION

MS, Nursing Major with dual focus: Administration and Education, 1985
Thesis: Identification of Family Problems During the Treatment Stage of Cancer
University of Oklahoma, Oklahoma City, Oklahoma

BS, Nursing, 1973
University of Arizona, Tucson, Arizona

BA, History of Art, 1967
University of Michigan, Ann Arbor, Michigan

Continuing Education
Numerous courses to maintain **Certified Nurse Administrator** status, 1989-present

Western Network for Nurse Executives Program, 1988
University of California at Berkeley

> Fredona placed her Education section near the top of her resume because her degrees are highly relevant to her profession.

PROFESSIONAL EXPERIENCE

1986-1994   **St. Agnes Medical Center,** Fresno, California
                DIRECTOR PATIENT CARE SERVICES, 1991-1994
                DIRECTOR MEDICAL/SURGICAL, 1986-1991

Managed operating budgets up to $14M, 382 FTEs, and 272 patient beds for this 326-bed accredited, not-for-profit, regional, acute care facility with extensive managed care and outpatient services.

- Revitalized Quality Assurance Program by developing high standards, promoting extreme nursing staff involvement, establishing interdepartmental problem solving, and transitioning to Quality Assessment and Improvement.

- Played primary role in achieving JCAHO accreditation and placement within top 10% of facilities nationwide.

- Improved staff productivity, patient satisfaction, and quality of care.

  - Empowered staff by decentralizing management and decision making within patient care services. Reorganized, trained, and supported staff to ensure success of structural transition.

  - Restructured systems for delivery of care including staff roles and interdepartmental reporting.

  - Introduced new communication and computer technology involving 20 hospital departments.

  - Aligned FTEs with volume and cost variations by introducing staffing by Hours Per Patient Day (HPPD) to replace staffing ratios and static patterns.

  - Improved communication and conflict resolution by providing 20-hour training program, Increasing Personal Effectiveness, for over 500 personnel.

  - Developed cooperative rapport with Finance, Human Resources, Information Systems, Pharmacy, and Laboratory Departments.

(Continued)

St. Agnes Medical Center (Continued)

- Recruited 13 British nurses (five of whom have stayed for more than five years) as a result of three trips to London. Worked with advertising agency, State Board of Nursing, and immigration attorney.
- Represented the hospital through newspaper and TV interviews about innovative solutions to health care problems.
- Oversaw remodeling of three major units. Merged intensive and cardiac care into one critical care unit.
- As Acting Critical Care Manager for nine months, turned around critical care management through team building, empowerment, and responsibility clarification.

1983-1986   **HCA Northwest Hospital,** Tucson, Arizona
MANAGER SURGICAL/ORTHOPEDICS

Played major role in the start-up of this new 150-bed, for profit, acute care community hospital.

- Developed and managed a 28-bed surgical unit.
- Managed a 24-bed ortho/neuro unit and hospital-wide messenger service.
- Started the nursing Quality Assurance Program and chaired its committee.
- Implemented the HCA Patient Classification System.
- Established HPPD staffing guidelines for all nursing units.
- Successfully prepared Med/Surg units for initial JCAHO accreditation.

1982-1983   **University of Oklahoma, College of Nursing,** Tulsa, Oklahoma
TEACHING ASSISTANT

1981-1982   **CSI Productions,** Tulsa, Oklahoma
RESEARCHER AND WRITER
Wrote narratives for this producer of health care training materials on Cardiac Monitoring, Medicating the Patient, and Antiembolism Stockings.

1978-1981   **Gila Pueblo College,** Globe, Arizona
NURSING INSTRUCTOR
- Saved the nursing program by achieving 100% graduate passing rate on State Board Exams, a drastic improvement from previous years' unacceptably low rates.
- Redeveloped entire content of first year associate degree nursing program to update information and improve presentation.
- Obtained three full nursing scholarships from local civic groups.

1974-1978   **Hospitals in Arizona and Oklahoma**
CLINICAL PATIENT CARE positions: Charge Nurse, IV Therapist, Staff Nurse

AFFILIATIONS

World Affairs Council

Nursing Administrators Council (NAC) of Central San Joaquin Valley
- As President, established NAC as a voice of influence on nursing and health care in the valley.

Organization of Nurse Executives, California (ONE-C)

Sigma Theta Tau, National Nursing Honorary Society

Resume written in 1994.

ANNIE JONES
11 Teralinda Ct., Danville, CA 94765, (510) 978-4623

JOB OBJECTIVE

A position in organizational systems management

PROFILE

- Expertise in developing and managing organizational systems that:

Facilitate efficiency	Encourage creativity
Promote responsible behavior	Respond to change
Optimize the group's diversity	Build team spirit

- Committed to improving the environment through research and education.
- Particular skill in empowering others to acknowledge and articulate their value and role in an organization/society.

EXPERIENCE

1993-present **Facilitator, Navy Program for Personal Responsibility**
The Prevent Office, University of Arizona, NAS Alameda, CA

- Facilitate weekly classes for 20 Navy personnel from diverse cultural backgrounds, promoting personal responsibility through communication and appropriate lifestyle behaviors. Topics include:

Decision Making and Problem Solving Strategies	Interpersonal Skills
Personal and Organizational Values and Conflicts	Resistance to Addictions

1989-1993 **Manager, Project Management and Contracts**
Accounting Manager
Barakat & Chamberlin, Inc., Oakland, CA

An international consulting firm specializing in projects that address energy efficiency.

- Facilitated forums for organizational dialogue, encouraging excellent communication among all levels of personnel (president through support staff).
- Improved client relations by establishing procedures and training staff how to develop strong consultant-client rapport.
- Worked with consulting staff to provide tools and resources needed to effectively manage their projects.

1984-1989 **Independent Bookkeeping Contractor**

1978-1984 **Full-time Parent**

1975-1978 **Paralegal**
Pillsbury, Madison & Sutro, San Francisco, CA
Wolf, Block, Schorr and Solis-Cohen, San Francisco, CA

EDUCATION

Candidate, Master's Program, Social and Cultural Anthropology
California Institute of Integral Studies, San Francisco, CA

B.A., Anthropology and Social Studies
Macalester College, St. Paul, MN

When Annie wrote her resume, she had not yet completed her master's degree, so she put "Candidate." Good call!

COMMUNITY SERVICE

Moraga Junior Women's Club:	Chair, Soviet/US Visitors Program
	Co-Chair, Art Auction and Fundraiser
Donald Rheem Elementary School:	Volunteer Teacher, Parent-Educator Program
	Treasurer, Parents Club
	Co-Chair, Animal Days Program

Resume written in 1996.

Guy Deminier

1924 California Street, San Francisco, CA 94117   (415) 427-9421

JOB OBJECTIVE: Director of Customer Service

SUMMARY OF QUALIFICATIONS

- 20 years as department manager with experience in internal and external customer service.
- Excellent supervisory skills which enhance employee skills to produce quality work.
- Computer literate: DOS, Windows, and Macintosh.

PROFESSIONAL ACCOMPLISHMENTS

MANAGEMENT

Resolution Credit Services, Corp.

- Monitored $500,000 per month in expenses and compiled data for upper management.
- Decreased expenditures 35% by standardizing purchasing procedures.
- Created and directed all administrative procedures for this 58-person financial firm affiliated with Xerox Corporation.
- Wrote six manuals (70-100 pages each) to clarify responsibilities of accounts payable, telecommunications, records, check processing, and administrative support.

Fireman's Fund

- As manager of 28 employees, increased productivity, morale, and individual and team initiative by fostering employee career development within the company.
- Improved staff performance evaluations by upgrading job descriptions.
- Created and administered a $850,000 annual budget.
- Established workflow priorities and monitored activities of four supervisors and their staff.

CUSTOMER SERVICE

Fireman's Fund

- Created system for identifying and notifying past-due accounts, recovering $236,000 of uncollected premiums from previous years.
- Used a diplomatic yet firm approach to resolve accounting disputes with customers, agents, and sales staff.
- Encouraged interdepartmental cooperation by providing excellent internal customer service to four departments.

Resolution Credit Services, Corp.

- Resolved client issues promptly as liaison to branch offices and attorneys.
- Anticipated and handled hardware, software, and other equipment problems, achieving minimum of downtime for six departments that work with offices in other U.S. time zones.

WORK HISTORY

1995	Administrative Assistant	Medical Review Group, San Francisco
1986-1994	Supervisor, Administration	Resolution Credit Services, Corp., San Francisco
1984-1986	Family Management	Les Sables d'Olonne, France
1973-1984	Manager, Policy Administration	Fireman's Fund Insurance, San Francisco

EDUCATION

B.A. equivalent, French, Sorbonne, Paris, France
Teacher's Training Course, International Language Center, London, England

Since the name of Guy's diploma is in French, its significance might not be understood, so he called it "B.A. equivalent."

Resume written in 1995.

College Experience But No Degree

If you went to college but do not intend to get your degree in the immediate future:

➤ Write your area of study and the name of the college. For instance: Liberal Arts, Antioch College, Yellow Springs, OH.

➤ If you attended several schools without completing your degree requirements, list only one or two schools. Listing more than that might make the reader think you tend to move around a lot without finishing things.

Angelique's resume on the following page employs this concept.

New High School Diploma

If you are a new high school graduate:

➤ Write the name of your high school and year of graduation.

➤ If you have enrolled in a college, say so; for example, "Enrolled in St. Mary's College, Moraga, CA."

Frank's resume later in this chapter presents his high school diploma.

Not-So-New High School Diploma

If you received your high school diploma more than two years ago and have no additional schooling, you do not need to have an Education section on your resume unless the job you are applying for specifically asks for a high school diploma. If it does:

➤ Put "Graduate" or "Diploma," followed by the name of your high school.

➤ Stating your graduation date is optional.

Examine C'Ann's Education section on her resume later in this chapter to see how she handled her "no degree" situation.

Angelique Braun

495 Sea Cliff Drive • San Francisco, CA 94121 • (415) 555-2177

JOB OBJECTIVE

Bookkeeper/Accountant

HIGHLIGHTS OF QUALIFICATIONS

- Experienced Bookkeeper/Accountant for small and medium-sized businesses.
- Ability to work independently.
- Strong list of references.

PROFESSIONAL EXPERIENCE

1977-present BOOKKEEPER/ACCOUNTANT

Selected Clients/Projects

Michael Smith, CPA, San Francisco, CA
Blue Nile Cafe, San Francisco, CA
Star Mountain Texaco, San Francisco, CA
The Walters Marketing Group, San Francisco, CA
Paintings '80, San Francisco, CA
Fleur D'Alsasce Restaurant, San Francisco, CA
Mark-Thomas Corporation, San Francisco, CA
Cleaveland Consulting Group, Redwood City, CA

Michael Smith, CPA

- Prepared federal and state tax returns for corporations, partnerships, individuals, and estates.
- Maintained general ledgers and prepared financial statements for assigned clients.
- Prepared payrolls, quarterly federal and state payroll tax returns, and state sales tax returns.

Blue Nile Cafe and Star Mountain Texaco

- Set up company books, maintained general ledgers, and prepared Schedule C and partnership returns.

The Walters Marketing Group

- Maintained general ledger, accounts receivable, and accounts payable. Prepared financial statements.
- Prepared payroll, federal and state payroll tax returns, and sales tax returns.
- Assisted in the conversion to computer generated accounting.

EDUCATION

Accounting
University of California Berkeley Extension, San Francisco, CA
Healds Business College, San Francisco, CA
San Francisco State University Extension, San Francisco, CA

Computer
Computer Options, San Francisco, CA

Angelique highlighted her relevant college coursework even though she did not obtain a degree.

Resume written in 1995.

Frank Jordan
P.O. Box 51
Bayview Meadow, ME 03907
(207) 444-3321

OBJECTIVE: Bus Driver

SUMMARY OF QUALIFICATIONS

- Dependable, hard worker who can be counted on to "get the job done."

- Excellent driving record; always give first priority to safety.

- Friendly and well liked; good at customer relations.

- Available to relocate.

EXPERIENCE

1994-96   **Driver/Tour Guide**   Trolley Tours, Bay Meadows, ME
- Drove small tour bus through scenic parts of this resort, pointing out sites, providing friendly service, and assisting senior citizens.
- Did light repair work as needed.
- Recognized as #1 employee within this company of 15.

Summer '93   **Sales Representative**   Recycled Tractor Parts, Townsend, ME
- Sold used tractor and equipment parts by phone and over the counter.
- Handled inventory, shipping, and nationwide teletype service.

Summer '92   **Driver**   Paris Oil Recycling, Paris, ME
- Picked up and delivered waste oil (until business was sold).

EDUCATION
Diploma, Wells High School, Wells, ME, 1994

Since Frank is a new high school graduate, he mentioned his diploma under Education.

Resume written in 1996.

C'ANN P. PARKER
1212 Fourteenth St., #642
Oakland, CA 94607
(510) 428-9632

OBJECTIVE: To retain insurance company relations, as new owner of Middlebrook Insurance Agency

★ Reliable reputation among Bay Area attorneys.

★ Proven ability to work profitably with home office.

★ Currently developing underwriting practice at Middlebrook Insurance Agency.

PROFESSIONAL ACCOMPLISHMENTS

CLIENT RELATIONS

As Branch Manager, Bonding Service, National Insurance:

• Developed and serviced a loyal client base, almost doubling branch premium dollars from $190,000 to $365,000 per year.
- Gained a reputation among attorneys for providing timely service/markets.
- Recaptured accounts lost during departure of previous branch manager.
- Offered additional services to gain accounts.
- Generated new business through regular court appearances.

As Vice President, Middlebrook Insurance Agency:

• Secured clientele, based upon my established reputation among local attorneys.

UNDERWRITING

As Branch Manager, Bonding Service, National Insurance:

• Authorized to execute under power of attorney in all counties in California, with underwriting authority up to $50,000. Branch bond amounts ranged from $6,000 to $3,000,000.
• Simplified application form to more effectively gathered underwriting data.
• Established and implemented more efficient procedures for home office approval, reducing turnaround time from three days to eight hours.
• Dealt directly with surety home office in Plainfield, IL.
• Gained extensive knowledge of litigation process as it relates to judicial bonds.
• Negotiated with brokerage firms to perfect surety positions.

MANAGEMENT

As Branch Manager, Bonding Service, National Insurance:

• Developed a user-friendly billing system that increased efficiency and promptness of premium collections.
• Managed office relocation, keeping down-time to a minimum.
• Maintained regular communications with home office, reporting monthly totals and branch activities.

WORK HISTORY

1995-pres.	**Vice President**	Middlebrook Insurance Agency, Oakland, CA
1989-94	**Branch Manager**	Bonding Service, National Insurance, Oakland, CA
1981-89	**Operations Manager**	Window Covers, Inc., Palm Springs, CA

C'Ann chose not to include an Education section on her resume since she did not attend college. This approach is perfectly acceptable.

Resume written in 1995.

The Least You Need to Know

➤ List only degrees, courses, training sessions, and workshops that are relevant to your job objective.

➤ If you have a degree or credential that makes you look overqualified for the job, don't put it on your resume.

➤ Dates are optional in the Education section. If they tell the reader more than you want, leave them out.

Chapter 11

Step Nine— Extra Goodies

In This Chapter

➤ Where to put professional affiliations, community service, and other information on your resume

➤ How to deal with an employer's request for your salary history

➤ Putting personal data on a resume

➤ What about names and addresses of references?

Your destination is within sight—you don't even need binoculars to see the resume-shore anymore! There are a few more sections that might appear on your resume; things like professional affiliations, community service, computer skills, and personal interests.

In this chapter, you learn where to list all of your remaining relevant information. And you'll find out why some information—such as references, salary history, and personal data—may not belong on your resume at all.

Other Sections on Your Resume

At this point, you may be left with only laundry lists of technical, personal, and professional details that don't fit in the primary sections of your resume. Even if you feel like just throwing them in a pile at the bottom of the page, don't! Instead, create one or more logical sections that will spark the employer's interest.

Community Service

What you do in your unpaid time may say more about what kind of person you are than what you do for employment. If you feel that your volunteerism makes a statement about your dedication, character, or social awareness, or in any way enhances your qualifications for your next job, a section called "Community Service" is the place to list it.

Dates are optional; if you list them, you should present your volunteer work in reverse chronology (your most recent work first). If you don't use dates, list your community service according to impact (the most relevant first).

Professional Affiliations

Professional associations to which you currently belong or have once belonged can be listed either alphabetically or in order of relevance to your profession under a section called "Professional Affiliations." If you currently hold or have held an office, that should also be noted here.

Publications and Awards

Articles, books, chapters in books, and research papers that you have authored or co-authored belong in a section called "Publications and Awards." Usually, dates accompany this information, necessitating that they be presented in reverse chronology (the most current date first). List any honors, awards, and grants you have received that support your job objective. You can arrange this list according to date received (if you give the date), or by relevance to your next job (if you don't provide the date).

Computer Skills

If you have computer skills that are important to your next job, you can highlight them under a special section called "Computer Skills." Your list might include hardware, software, languages, systems, and networks with which you have experience.

Personal Interests

Some job seekers like to have a section called "Personal Interests" in which they can list travel, sports, religious, political, and other personal activities. The Personal Interests section is optional and should be included only if you feel your personal activities:

➤ Add to your qualifications as a candidate for your job objective.

➤ Say something about your character which might be valued on the job.

There's controversy among professional resume writers as to whether personal interests are appropriate on a resume. Employers have favorably reacted to them about half the time—some find them irrelevant, others find them interesting and valuable. Although many have said they wouldn't hold it against a job seeker for including that sort of information, consider whether stating your personal activities might create undesired conflict with your reader's views and preferences. A potential conflict of interest could arise over issues such as race, religion, unions, and other controversial topics.

Here are some assumptions an employer might make from the following listings on resumes:

➤ An applicant who lists "Board of Trustees, St. Anne's Episcopal Church" is indicating that she is actively involved in her church. While some employers may welcome this involvement, others may feel uncomfortable with it.

➤ An applicant who writes "Member, Gay and Lesbian Couples United" on his resume tells the reader that he is probably homosexual. Such a disclosure may or may not create a favorable impression with a hiring manager.

➤ The owner of a non-union company might feel threatened by an applicant who lists "Organizer, Teamsters, Local Chapter 47092," since he may be worried the applicant will want to unionize his company.

Is Anything Missing?

Other headings that might appear on your resume include: "Exhibitions," "Research," "Lectures," "Licenses," and "Certifications." Or you may choose to combine two related headings (such as "Education and Certifications").

On the next few pages, you'll find five resumes that have extra sections. Notice how these sections support the job seekers' job objectives.

Commandments

Commandment I: Thou shalt not write about your past; thou shalt write about your future! Every word on your resume should paint the picture of you on your next job—even ones listed in your extra sections.

Bonnie Sykes

993 Hamilton Place • Los Angeles, CA 94332 • (805) 113-5432

Logistics Executive

with expertise in:

Customer Relations	Distribution Systems
Strategic Planning	Operations Analysis
Retail Services	Team Leadership

SELECTED PROFESSIONAL ACHIEVEMENTS

1976-present GOTCHA SPORTSWEAR, Los Angeles, CA

Director, Retail Services, 1992-present
Manager, Customer Service, 1990-1992
Manager, Distribution Systems and Services, 1986-1990
Manager, Distribution Administration, 1984-1986
Senior Distribution Analyst, 1981-1983
Distribution Analyst, 1979-1981
Financial Analyst, 1977-1979
Manager, Training and Accuracy Control, 1976-1977

- Played executive role in the $10M, four-year re-engineering initiative for Gotcha's U.S. $200M business.

- Managed closure of two distribution centers totaling 750K sq. ft. and started up two new distribution centers totaling 1.5M sq. ft. Planning and execution:

Inventory ($50M) and systems migration	Order processing and fulfillment
Physical product movement	Sales coordination
Staff development	

- Saved over $2M in logistics related customer claims and increased retail product sell-through by introducing a new customer service concept that built liaisons between company logistics personnel and retail counterparts.

- Supervised direct staff of 10 and indirect reports of 40 who planned and managed the company's 1984 Olympics Host Program for over 500 retail executives and sweepstakes winners.

- Earned one team and two individual Gotcha Awards, the company's highest distinction for superlative professional achievement.

EDUCATION

M.S.W., California State University, San Francisco
B.A., California State University, Sacramento

PROFESSIONAL AFFILIATIONS

Featured speaker and member:	Council of Logistics Management
	National Retail Federation
	American Apparel Manufacturers Association
	International Customer Service Association
Featured speaker:	Strategic Research Institute
Member:	VICS (Voluntarily Inter-industry Communications Standards) Committees

> Bonnie's professional affiliations were relevant to her job objective, so she listed them under a heading called just that.

> Resume written in 1994.

Ryan Christoff

1420 Lombard Street • San Francisco, CA 94108 • (415) 932-1596

JOB OBJECTIVE

A position in Marketing / Sales with REI sporting goods

QUALIFICATIONS

- Three years as member of a sales team with a substantial retail client base.
- Natural ability to promote products and build rapport through listening and communication skills.

MARKETING / SALES ACCOMPLISHMENTS

- Achieved highest bonus level for exceptional performance on sales team with a targeted client base of retail and institutional accounts.
- Promoted within this team headed by three financial consultants who worked for two major investment firms and went on to form their own company under the Smith Barney umbrella.
- Generated sales through weekly phone calls to account base of 150 clients.
- Commended for building strong rapport with clients by understanding their needs and clearly explaining products.
- Created "syndicate calendars," marketing pieces used by the sales, trading, and research departments.
- Served as liaison between parties to coordinate schedules, payments, and allocations.

WORK HISTORY

1992-present   Member of Sales Team that worked for:
Smith Barney, San Francisco, 1995-present
PaineWebber, San Francisco, 1993-1995
Alex Brown, San Francisco, 1992-1993

1989-1991   Waitperson   Bart and Yeti's Restaurant, Vail, CO

EDUCATION

B.A., Psychology, Fort Lewis College, Durango, CO, 1988

ADVENTURE / SPORTS

- Completed a two-month solo trip throughout Central and Eastern Europe.
- Actively participate in sports:

Triathlons	Hiking
Downhill skiing	Cycling
Back country skiing	Swimming
Running	Camping

Since Ryan's personal travel and sports are key qualifiers for the job he's going for, he created a section in his resume called "Adventure/Sports." Very fitting!

Resume written in 1995.

Nanci M. Mish

267 Frontier Avenue, #2 • Sunnyvale, California 94316-6342 • (408) 553-8564

ADMINISTRATIVE PROFESSIONAL
with strengths in:
Project Management
Office Management
Executive Support
Team Building

PROFESSIONAL EXPERIENCE

1985-present **XEROX CORPORATION - PALO ALTO RESEARCH CENTER**
Executive Secretary/Member Support Staff, Palo Alto, CA, 1989-present
Office Manager/Member Support Staff, Portland, OR, 1985-1988

- One of first five members of research team that consults with corporate and institutional clients regarding their document creation and publishing problems.

- Logistics manager of research team awarded for successful completion of educational project for Harvard Business School.
  - Honorary MBA from Harvard Business School.
  - Excellence in Science and Technology Award plus $1,000, Xerox's second highest employee award.

- Co-planned "Vision & Values" and "Milestones & Goals" statements for the team.

- One of five originators of "Office of the Future," a successful pilot project involving two sites connected by audio/visual communications through a gateway (phone lines).

- Supervised construction/remodeling and furnishing of offices in Portland and Palo Alto. Set up administrative operations for both 10-person sites.

- Managed the physical facilities including compliance with corporate requirements.

- Office manager for 10 research and marketing professionals. This included customer contact, consultant contracts, accounting, budgets, purchasing, travel, and conferences. Commended for best record keeping in the corporation.

1981-1985 **R. HOE & CO.,** Portland, OR
Executive Secretary

- Provided office management and administrative assistance to President and Vice President of this lumber equipment manufacturer.

EDUCATION

Honorary MBA, Harvard Business School, Cambridge, MA
Business and Business Law, Portland State College, Portland, OR
Xerox Training: Leadership Through Quality

COMPUTER SKILLS

Sun Sparc Station	MS Word
Macintosh	FrameMaker
IBM	MacDraw

By having a special section for computer skills, Nanci sends a clear signal that she wants to use these talents on her next job.

Resume written in 1994.

Lauri Kaufman

221 41st Avenue, Denver, CO 88421   (415) 338-5521

JOB OBJECTIVE: Executive Director of Performing Arts for Children

SUMMARY OF QUALIFICATIONS

- Four years experience in a nonprofit art organization. Positions included: Board Member, Fundraiser, Event Planner, and Newsletter Editor.
- Committed to motivating children through art, education, and recreation.
- Published writer and skilled presenter.

RELEVANT ACCOMPLISHMENTS

FUNDRAISING AND PUBLIC RELATIONS

Denver Museum of Modern Art

- Directed fundraising committees that produced events including lectures, balls, parties, receptions, and home, gallery, and corporate tours.
- Served on Modern Art Council, the primary fundraising arm of the museum.
- As a founding member of the Young Donors Committee, recruited new members and solicited higher level of financial commitment from existing members.
- Promoted educational and fundraising events by producing a bi-monthly newsletter with circulation of 250.

Finley Galleries

- Wrote press releases and designed invitations that generated full-house attendances at exhibitions.
- Interviewed and quoted in national magazines.
- Wrote and co-designed exhibition catalogs.

ADMINISTRATION

Finley Galleries

- Managed day-to-day operations for the largest art gallery in San Francisco.
- Conducted monthly fiscal analysis, set goals, and led management-level meetings to plan revenue generating strategies.
- Hired, trained, and supervised staff.

PROGRAM PLANNING AND SUPPORT

Denver Museum of Modern Art

- Co-Chaired "Art Sandwich-In," an ongoing lecture series that drew full capacity. Continually evaluated effectiveness of themes, promotions, and services.

Finley Galleries

- Developed and managed twice-yearly openings to promote local artists.
- Wrote three articles published in *Art of California* and *Fine Art and Antiques International* magazines.

— Continued —

177

Lauri Kaufman
Page 2

WORK HISTORY

1993-present	Independent Art Consultant	Denver, CO
1987-1993	Director/Curator	Finley Galleries, Denver, CO
1985-1987	Full-time Student	University of Colorado, Boulder, CO
1983-1984	Athletic Coach	Winter Park Ski Team, Winter Park, CO
		Boulder High School, Boulder, CO

EDUCATION

B.A., University of Colorado, Boulder, CO, 1979-1982, 1985-1987

> Lauri's extra sections tell a lot about her personality: well traveled, art enthusiast, and socially concerned citizen. All are supporting qualities for her job objective.

TRAVEL AND STUDY ABROAD

Europe, Africa, Latin America, and Southeast Asia

COMMUNITY SERVICE

Denver Museum of Modern Art, 1990-present

Contemporary Extension:	Executive Board Member, Newsletter Editor and Publisher, Events Chair
Young Donors Committee:	Executive Board Member
Modern Art Council:	Co-Chair of "Art Sandwiched-In," Auction Committee Member, Fundraiser

World Affairs Council, Member, 1991-present

Denver Art Academy, Judge, M.F.A. Exhibitions, 1992, 1993

Resume written in 1995.

Dianne Henderson

478 Hearst Street • Berkeley, CA 94704 • Office: (510) 221-7754 • Home: (510) 237-9543

JOB OBJECTIVE

Reengineering Consultant

HIGHLIGHTS OF QUALIFICATIONS

- Accomplished Reengineering Manager with proven ability to design and implement processes for organizational improvement.
- Eight years as an effective manager within the nonprofit and for-profit sectors.
- Recognized throughout career for initiating productive change.

PROFESSIONAL ACCOMPLISHMENTS

1992-present   University of California, Berkeley
REENGINEERING PROJECT MANAGER, Office of Residential Programs, 1993-present

- Manager of the reengineering process for a student services unit with 396 employees.
- Facilitated a reengineering training retreat for 21 managers.
- Collaborated with 10 managers to establish the unit's first vision and mission statements.
- Wrote project management guidelines and determined appropriate software to manage the implementation of the reengineering process.
- Gathered reengineering recommendations from internal and external customers by conducting focus groups and Internet forums.
- Presented three reorganization proposals based on research and analysis of existing services and needed improvements.
- Currently creating a multi-media presentation to market the benefits of the reengineering project to executive managers and employees.

RESIDENTIAL LIFE COORDINATOR, 1992-1995

- Developed a two-year restructuring proposal to save $200,000 and improve customer service. Proposal resulted in my promotion to Reengineering Project Manager.
- Redesigned and streamlined a recruitment and selection process for 150 staff members.
- Analyzed services and reorganized a program serving 1100 students from 20 countries.
- Managed the overall operations of a complex that housed 1000 students.
- Supervised and evaluated 80 staff members via eight coordinators.

1991-1992   University of Houston, TX
COORDINATOR, Housing and Dining Services Department

- Managed the overall operation of a residential facility for 1300 students.
- Created and instructed a 16-week training seminar for 100 employees.
- Chaired a committee that implemented a selection process for 65 new staff members.
- Produced a summer conference for 400 students from China and Spain.
- Supervised 84 staff members via four assistant coordinators.

1985-1991   Southern Illinois University, Carbondale, IL
PROGRAM TRAINING COORDINATOR, State of Illinois Special Project, 1991

- Designed the first "train the trainer" course to teach 25 educators to train 700 employees.

FULL-TIME STUDENT, 1985-1991

— Continued —

Dianne Henderson, Page Two

1985-1987   **Shoney's South Corporation, Carbondale, IL**
RESTAURANT MANAGER

- Managed a full-service restaurant and catering service that seated 300.
- Trained and supervised 32 employees and managed their payroll and benefits.
- Administered complex allocations of $600K in annual revenue.
- Evaluated costs, inventory, and service contracts.
- Oversaw preventive maintenance for the facility and equipment.

EDUCATION

Master of Arts, Education (Specialization: Higher Education), 1991
Summa Cum Laude
Southern Illinois University, Carbondale, IL
Coursework included: Recruitment and Evaluation   Research and Evaluation
                       Training Theories and Application   Tests and Measurements

Bachelor of Arts, Psychology (Specialization: Industrial and Organizational), 1989
Cum Laude
Southern Illinois University, Carbondale, IL
Coursework included: Management   Industrial Psychology
                       Business Communications   Personnel Psychology
                       Organizational Behavior   Psychology of Leadership

Professional Training, 1992-1995
IMPAQ   Taking Advantage of Change
Pappas Consulting Group Inc.   Reengineering in Higher Education
Price Waterhouse   Reengineering Human Resources
Fred Pryor Seminars   Project Management
                                   How to Manage Multiple Priorities
                                   Self Directed Work Teams
                                   How to Develop & Administer a Budget
                                   Business Writing For Results
Empower Perspectives   Conflict In Organizations
University of California, Berkeley Diversity Facilitator Training
                                   Customer Survey Methods
                                   Developing Budget Initiatives

Readings:
Reengineering the Corporation by James Champy and Michael Hammer
Reengineering Management by James Champy
Business Reengineering: The Survival Guide by Andrews & Stalick

RECOGNITIONS

National Association of Female Executives
          Honorary Membership 1995
University of California, Berkeley
          Chancellor's Recognition for Diversity Education 1992, 1993, 1994, 1995
          Chancellor's Outstanding Staff Award nominee 1994
American College Personnel Association
          Multicultural Program Award nominee 1994
Western Association of College Housing Officers
          New Professional Award 1994

The Recognitions section on Dianne's resume is a nice finishing touch to a marketing piece that already shines with accomplishments.

Resume written in 1995.

What Not to Put on Your Resume

Knowing what to leave off your resume can be just as important as knowing what to include. The following sections show you some items that are best left off your resume.

Salary History

Although some job advertisements ask for a resume and salary history, the two do not go together. *Discussion about salary belongs in the interview,* not on the resume. It is to your advantage not to make a monetary request before an interview. Indicating salary requirements before the interview may increase your chances of being screened out and decrease your bargaining power during salary negotiations.

If you feel obligated to address salary in order to fulfill the employer's initial application requirements, do so in your cover letter, not on your resume. Speak in generalities, such as: "My salary in previous positions ranged from $X to more than $Y, accompanied by benefits." Or simply indicate that you would prefer to discuss salary during the interview.

Talking directly about salary expectations in a letter is tricky. I suggest that you first find out what the position typically pays (you can do this by asking a job counselor or employment agency, or by reading ads for similar jobs in the newspaper). Then mention your salary expectations in your cover letter, using language that gives you room for negotiations, such as: "I am looking for a position in the $X to $Y salary range."

References

Addresses and phone numbers of references should not be a part of your resume. They belong on a separate sheet of paper that you bring to the job interview.

Also, a big thumbs down to including "References available upon request" at the bottom of your resume. It's unnecessary, since the reader will assume that you have references and he or she knows to ask for them when the time comes.

Personal Data

Including information about your age, sex, marital status, and health is not appropriate for resumes being used in the United States. If you are applying abroad (in Europe or the United Kingdom) however, it might be expected.

The Least You Need to Know

➤ Take inventory of the relevant information that you still want to include and list that data in appropriate sections at the end of your resume.

➤ Sections that you may want on your resume include "Community Service," "Professional Affiliations," "Awards," and "Computer Skills."

➤ Items that should not appear on your resume include salary history, references, and personal data.

Great Expectations

See, it didn't take you 34 days to reach your goal the way it did Columbus. I knew you could do it. But before you start stuffing envelopes and announcing your career move to the world, take one more minute to review the Top Ten Checklist in this chapter as well as the tips on printing and circulating your resume. Then you'll be armed with a winning strategy for getting your resume out on the job market.

The Top Ten Checklist

Take your pencil in hand (or get out a box of gold stars) and give yourself credit for each one of the items on this list that you've completed. No need to get nervous—it's not a test. It's just a way to assure you that you've done the best job possible with your resume:

1. Your name appears in the top center or on the upper right-hand side (not in the upper left-hand corner) of the page.

2. Your resume starts with a brief and clear job objective statement or a strong indication of what position you are seeking.

3. Everything on your resume supports your job objective.

4. Achievements, rather than job descriptions, are stressed.

5. Achievement statements start with action verbs and do not contain vague terms such as "responsible for."

6. There are no paragraphs anywhere on the resume. Bulleted statements make achievements quick and easy to read.

7. Statements and sections are prioritized so that the most impressive information comes first.

8. Your resume fits on no more than two pages. The exception to this two-page limit applies to resumes (also called curriculum vitas) for the academic and scientific communities.

9. If you have a two-page resume, "Continued" appears on the bottom of page one, and your name and "Page Two" is placed at the top of the second page.

10. There are no misspellings, grammatical errors, or other mistakes.

Tip

Show your resume to friends and people you respect, then evaluate their feedback and make adjustments appropriately. The ultimate test for whether you have a good resume, however, is to send it to employers. If it gets you job interviews, you have a great resume!

Warning

Typos on a resume are deadly! Make sure yours is typo-free by using your spell checker (if you're working on a computer), proofreading thoroughly, and asking someone else to check it once more.

The Big Production

You're getting close to the finish line...you're ahead of your competition...and it looks like you're going to be a winner. Just a few more steps and you'll be there.

Now you need to get your resume printed and reproduced. If possible, get your master resume produced on a computer, and print it out on a letter-quality printer (laser, ink jet, or the like). Avoid using a dot-matrix printer—you'd be better off using an electric typewriter. Your master printouts should be on white paper of any weight.

Once you have your master printed, it's off to a copy center, unless you have access to a high quality copier. Don't order a whole slew of copies—start with the number you think you'll need for two weeks of your job search. By copying in short runs, you'll be a lot more inclined to adjust your marketing approach as you pursue your ideal job. That's really important—you need to be prepared to change your job objective and tweak your resume, if necessary, as you get feedback from employers along the way.

Tip

When mailing your resume, use a large 9 × 12-inch envelope instead of the standard 4 × 9-inch business envelope. This allows it to arrive without creases that crack the print (which happens no matter how you reproduce your document).

Choosing Paper

Your next step is to select paper that's appropriate for the type of work you're going after. It makes sense that someone going for a CEO position is going to have higher-end paper than someone seeking a clerical position. I personally don't like fancy textured or "parchment" sheets—they look pretentious. I like good old plain white that has just a little more weight than the standard 20-lb. paper used for copying. That extra weight sends a subconscious message of quality to the reader without screaming out, "This is expensive paper!" One administrative assistant pointed out to me, "When the paper is too thick, it jams up the copier. That makes me mad and I'm apt to throw the resume away." Oops! Better not get on the wrong side of an administrative assistant who, at that moment, wields the fate of your career. Solution: Choose something a little heavier than 20-lb. but not as thick as card stock.

Ah, I can just see it now—your chin lifted high and chest puffed out as you walk out of the copy center with your stack of fresh resumes. You're ready to conquer the world!

Good Circulation

Congratulations! You've finished writing and copying your resume. It looks and sounds great. Now what? You need to get your marketing sheet into the hands of potential employers. A good job search strategy uses more than one means of resume distribution to ensure success. Read on for some ways you can get your resume into circulation.

Personal Contacts

Networking among friends, family, business associates, and people with influence in your field is the most valuable means of getting an interview. Be sure to contact everyone you know who might be helpful in this regard and supply them with your resume and networking cards (now you get to use the networking cards you're going to create in Chapter 16) so they can pass the news of your job search on to hiring managers.

Companies You'd Love to Work For

You may have a company in mind that you would love to work for. Even without knowing if there are any job openings, you can submit your resume to human resources or the manager of the department in which you're interested, using a job objective and resume construction that clearly indicates your relevant skills.

Job Postings and Job Hotlines

Many career centers, state agencies, and nonprofit organizations have on-site job listings and telephone job hotlines. Some organizations charge a fee for using them. Others may ask you to do volunteer work to "pay" for the services they provide. To find such organizations, look in the yellow pages under employment-related headings such as "Career Centers," where you should find private, nonprofit, and state-run agencies.

On-Line Resume Databases

On the Internet and other on-line services, you can post your resume in databases for thousands of employers to see. Once you've placed your resume on-line, pretend that you're an employer and download it, if possible, to be sure it looks the way you want it to look when the real employer receives it off his or her on-line service. (More on this type of resume distribution in Chapter 18.)

Recruiters

Collaborating with a recruiter is a free and usually painless way to submit your resume to employers. Recruiters usually specialize according to industry (for example, computer or pharmaceuticals) or profession (for example, sales or executive management). When showing your resume to a recruiter, be open to his or her suggestions for adapting it to a particular field or company. You can find a recruiter by looking in the yellow pages under job-related headings such as "Employment Agencies," or ask a career counselor who works in your field.

Job Fairs

Attending a job fair can be an efficient way to talk to representatives from several companies in one day. Be sure to bring many resumes, comfortable shoes, and lots of stamina since you're likely to find yourself in large crowds and long lines. Job fairs are usually advertised in the newspaper, or on the radio or television.

Newspaper Ads

Although "help wanted" ads are considered by many to be the least effective place to land a job, don't exclude them from your strategy. Many prominent companies use the classified ads as a successful recruiting method. A well-written resume accompanied by a cover letter can grab the reader's eye and secure an interview, despite the overwhelming amount of competition that newspaper ads generate.

Mass Mailings

To conduct a mass mailing, you need a qualified, up-to-date mailing list of potential employers. There are several books available that catalog employers by industry and location. You can also hire an information researcher to create a mailing list to your specifications. Locating an information researcher isn't easy. I suggest asking at a career center or looking on-line under career-related subjects to see if one is listed.

Tip
Don't staple your resume if it's more than one page long. Paper-clip it to your cover letter instead.

When evaluating the results of your mailing, keep in mind that a response of 3 to 4 percent for a commercial direct mailing is considered successful. You can use a similar measuring stick for the effectiveness of your resume mass mailing.

The Least You Need to Know

➤ Go over the Top Ten Checklist to double-check that you did everything you were supposed to do on your resume.

➤ Produce your resume on a letter-quality printer or electric typewriter.

➤ Reproduce your resume on a high quality copier, using appropriate paper.

➤ Devise a strategy for distributing your resume, using several approaches to ensure your success.

➤ Get yourself poised to listen to feedback; and be ready to use that feedback to hone this marvelous marketing piece—your resume.

Part 3
So, You Need a Special Resume

When I go to the grocery store, I like lots of variety, especially when it comes to the cookie aisle. I like to choose from as many different kinds of chocolate chip cookies as possible, just to be sure I'm getting the best. And once I get my package home, I examine each cookie and pick the one that has the most chocolate chips. And you thought you were picky! Yep, I've been persnickety since I was a kid, and probably always will be.

That's the kind of discriminating attitude I expect you to have when it comes to deciding which resume format to use. Now that you know all about chronological and functional resumes from Parts 1 and 2, I'm going to tell you about some spin-offs on these two formats. At the end of this part, you can pick the format that's right for you.

Chapter 13

Achievement Resumes

In This Chapter

➤ Why employers like this powerful approach

➤ How your achievement resume will make you look like a winner

---

Of all the resume formats, the achievement resume is the one I find most powerful. It doesn't fit all job seekers' situations, but when it does, it has tremendous impact. The achievement resume is frequently the most effective way to stop a potential employer in his or her tracks and get the salary dollars rolling in an upward direction. Bet you'd like that to happen to you!

This chapter explains what an achievement resume is and helps you decide whether it's the right format for you.

Why Employers Like This Powerful Approach

Here it comes again: the old "less is more" slogan.

Saying less is more effective than saying a lot, and that's what the achievement resume is all about: brevity and punch! With a few strong accomplishments, an achievement resume can generate more questions and interest than pages of details.

Take it from a pro, this type of resume works well for sales professionals, top-level executives, and those who want to keep the spotlight on just a few successes from their whole career.

Imagine how short and powerful a former U.S. president's resume could be. Take Jimmy Carter. Although he could fill pages and pages with achievements, he doesn't need multiple-pages to make his point. At most, two lines will get him in the door for any interview he's after:

➤ 39th President of the United States.

➤ Negotiator of 1979 Camp David accords between Egypt and Israel.

Tip
A confident resume (and a good achievement resume definitely overflows with confidence) places you in an excellent position to negotiate your salary.

Likewise, Ronald Reagan's resume might read:

➤ 40th President of the United States.

➤ Known as the "Great Communicator" who drastically improved U.S. relations with the Soviet Union.

The achievement resume is also a marvelous way to throw attention onto your strengths while de-emphasizing a weak or complicated employment history. Using this format, I've created dynamite resumes for many a client whose career history was a mess.

You're Going to Look and Sound Impressive!

An achievement resume looks like a functional resume except that it does not have skill headings in the body of the resume. Instead it just lists five or six strong, relevant achievements under a main heading such as "Professional Accomplishments" or "Selected Achievements."

The following template represents an achievement resume. You'll also find six achievement resumes by real job seekers. An easy scan of these resumes will tell you that the job seeker in each case is a winner in his or her field. That's the beauty of this format!

Warning

Remember, the following template is not a boilerplate (a form in which you simply answer the questions, and you're finished). The bulleted statements in the template are ideas that I might suggest if I were sitting next to you as you create your resume. Since not all of them will apply to your situation, answer only the ones that give you the opportunity to support your job objective. If these brain-ticklers aren't enough, check out the brainstorming exercises in Chapters 6 and 9.

(Achievement Template)
Name
Street • City, State Zip • phone

JOB OBJECTIVE
The job you want next

SUMMARY OF QUALIFICATIONS
- How much experience you have in the field of your objective, in a related field, or using the skills required for your new position.

- An overall career accomplishment that shows you'd be good at this job objective.

- What someone would say about you as a recommendation.

SELECTED ACHIEVEMENTS
- An accomplishment you are proud of that shows you'd be valuable to your next employer.

- Another achievement that demonstrates you have the skills to produce results.

- A project you are proud of that supports your job objective.

- A problem you solved using the skills required for your job objective.

- A time when you used your skill to positively affect the organization, the bottom line, your boss, your clients.

- Awards, commendations, publications, etc. you achieved that relate to your job objective.

WORK HISTORY
19xx-present	Job Title	COMPANY NAME and city
19xx-xx	Job Title	COMPANY NAME and city
19xx-xx	Job Title	COMPANY NAME and city
19xx-xx	Job Title	COMPANY NAME and city

EDUCATION
Degree, Major (if relevant), 19xx (optional)
University, City, State

193

Craig Jevan

4133 Prairie Street, #2 • Berkeley, CA 94707 • (510) 622-4198

JOB OBJECTIVE

Member of Creative Team with emphasis on Graphic Design

SUMMARY OF QUALIFICATIONS

- Skilled fine artist with experience in applied graphics.
- Competent in:
  - Quark Express
  - PageMaker
  - Adobe Illustrator
  - Design Studio
  - Freehand
- Designed promotional pieces for clients including:
  - Starbucks Coffee Company
  - University of Oregon
  - Alexander Valley Vineyards
  - U.S. Navy

Here's a great technique for making special talents pop out—put them in columns.

GRAPHICS PROJECTS

With five achievement statements, Craig sends the message that he's completed some notable graphics projects.

- Designed several Starbucks' promotional T-shirts worn by all Portland store employees.
- Team-developed scratcher card game to boost morale of U.S. Naval personnel in Long Beach. Co-designed game card that reached total production of 900,000.
- Combined computer and applied graphics in designing the cover for *The Hearst Corporation Plans Book* for the University of Oregon.
- Designed POP standup card for Alexander Valley Vineyards, displayed in San Francisco Bay Area stores.
- Created numerous promotional pieces for university and community events.

WORK HISTORY

1987-pres.	Freelance Graphic Designer	Eugene, OR and Oakland, CA
1992-pres.	Lead Clerk	Starbucks Coffee Company, Portland, OR/Oakland, CA
1991-1992	Desk Top Publisher	Kinkos Copies, Eugene, OR

EDUCATION

B.A., Graphic Design/Fine Arts, University of Oregon, Eugene, OR, 1991
Internship: Project Coordinator, MWR Marketing, Long Beach, CA

— Portfolio available —

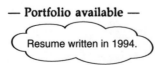
Resume written in 1994.

Cathleen Forest

441 Sunset Drive • Lahaina, Maui, HI 94901 • (808) 528-7721

JOB OBJECTIVE: Inside Sales Manager

SUMMARY OF QUALIFICATIONS

More than 10 years as a Sales Manager who consistently takes salesforces to the top.

Risk smart sales professional who knows how to improve and promote product lines.

Highly motivated self-starter and problem solver.

Increased sales up to 300% through excellent customer relations.

Featured in *Boston Magazine* and a national sales magazine for an exceptional sales program.

SALES ACCOMPLISHMENTS

Consistently ranked top sales person within first month of employment at every company and went on to train sales forces in winning techniques.

Broke records in initial, referral, and repeat sales through unique quality customer service.

Drove local and regional sales groups to the top of division by improving sales dollars per purchase, sales per hour, items per purchase, and referrals.

Trained and supervised an average of 12 employees a year over a 10-year period in sales and customer service. Resolved employee-management conflicts to keep focus on sales.

Designed and implemented a door-to-door sales program that increased sales, productivity, and profit while reducing turnover of personnel.

Reduced delinquent accounts by 40% and collected $250K in less than three months by redesigning collection policy.

Planned and directed marketing strategies including advertising, promotions, and tradeshows.

Improved inventory standards resulting in reduced shortages.

> Strong verbs help the reader understand the impact of Cathleen's accomplishments.

WORK HISTORY

Sales Consultant	Maui businesses, 1993-present
Telemarketing and Inside Sales Manager	Infotech Automation, Pasadena, CA, 1992
Manager	Leather Etc., Hermosa Beach, CA, 1991
Sales/Business Manager	Frank Burstein, D.D.S., Pasadena, CA, 1988-1990
Sales Trainer	LNS Portrait Studio, Manchester, NH, 1986-1987
Sales Manager	Newton Greenhouse, Newton, MA, 1985-1986
Manager	Merry Maids, Arlington, MA, 1983-1985
Sales Manager	Star TV, Needham, MA, 1982

EDUCATION

B.A., Sociology, minor in Psychology, Harvard University, Cambridge, MA

Resume written in 1995.

Tonia Ann Ford

1069 Granville Circle • San Bruno, CA 94054 • (415) 243-8566

ADMINISTRATIVE MANAGER

- 20 years experience directing and implementing complex organizational and technological changes.

- Recognized leadership skills and a natural talent for relating to people of various ethnic, socioeconomic, and educational backgrounds.

- Customer-focused management style.

- Ability to find innovative solutions to resource constraints.

QUALITY MANAGEMENT ACCOMPLISHMENTS

- Implemented two major organizational changes in the U.S. Naval Facilities resource and information management administration. Commended for relocating and retraining personnel while maintaining quality customer service.

- Directed the conversion from hierarchical to relational information systems at the U.S. Naval Facilities. Recognized by technical team for using effective training and internal marketing to achieve management and staff "buy-in" of this major change.

- Developed a self-directed team to conduct process analysis in preparation for decentralization of 50 IRS controller operations. Trained staff in the practical and theoretical aspects of process improvement.

- Reduced U.S. Naval Shipyard's unreconciled material costs $1M by reorganizing administrative procedures, introducing a new information system, and directing the first complete physical inventory certified by the GAO.

- Improved goal tracking at U.S. Naval Facilities by analyzing the workload evaluation process, assessing its validity, and convincing headquarters to revise the methodology.

Tonia's five achievements make it clear she can handle the job as administrative manager.

WORK HISTORY

1991-present	Internal Revenue Service, San Francisco	Program Manager, 1992-present Senior Budget Analyst, 1991-1992
1974-1991	U.S. Naval Facilities, San Bruno	Director Workload Analysis, 1980-1991 Program Analyst, 1977-1980 Accounting Manager, 1974-1977

EDUCATION

B.S., Organizational Behavior, University of San Francisco, 1989

Resume written in 1994.

Susan Bonetti

332 Pacific Street • San Francisco, CA 94122 • (415) 992-7613

JOB OBJECTIVE

Manufacturer's Sales Representative in the fashion industry

HIGHLIGHTS

- 10 years as a sales professional with management experience in the fashion industry.

- Proven ability to develop exclusive client bases in high-end markets.

- Combine a passion for fashion and travel with an accomplished sales savvy.

SALES ACCOMPLISHMENTS

- Managed sales and procurement of fashion accessories for Tina Z, an upscale boutique featuring French and Italian sportswear. Achieved growing profitability throughout tenure.

These great sales achievement statements say where they took place.

- Consistently met personal sales goals at Lexus of Stevens Creek, using a consultative approach to sell high-end luxury automobiles to a wide range of personalities.

- Ranked "Top Salesperson in Northern California" at Raytheon Data Systems. Sold largest single order in San Francisco office.

- Rated #1 salesperson for selling highest dollar volume among 35 sales agents at Pacific Union Brokerage.

- As Account Executive for Racal-Milgo, traveled throughout eight western states selling data communications equipment to military installations.

WORK HISTORY

1993-present	Sales and Leasing Consultant	LEXUS OF STEVENS CREEK, San Jose, CA
1990-1993	Real Estate Agent	PACIFIC UNION, San Francisco, CA
1988-1989	Extensive travel in Europe and Asia	
1986-1988	Partner/Accessories Buyer	TINA Z BOUTIQUE, St. Helena, CA
1984-1985	Account Executive	RACAL-MILGO, Oakland, CA
1981-1984	Account Manager	RAYTHEON DATA SYSTEMS, San Francisco, CA

EDUCATION

Liberal Arts, West Valley College, Saratoga, CA

Numerous sales courses including Mike Ferry Sales Training

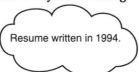

Resume written in 1994.

Linda A. Bastein

3452 Franklin Road • Lafayette, CA 94549 • (510) 332-1145

JOB OBJECTIVE

Sales Consultant/Representative

SUMMARY OF QUALIFICATIONS

- Nine years as a business development manager, using a collaborative approach to build an international clientele.

- Intuitive interpersonal skills. Ability to think on my feet and use humor to mix easily with people.

- Comfortable working with cross-cultural and multi-functional teams.

RELEVANT ACHIEVEMENTS

- Generated international business by developing X.NET promotional material that was included in Microsoft's developers' package.

- Managed X.NET's broker relations, which generated accounts with Fortune 500 clients including:

Bank of America	Cincom
Hewlett Packard	First Interstate Bank
Wells Fargo Bank	

- Solicited donations within an affluent community for organizations including American Cancer Society, American Association of University Women, and Lafayette Arts and Science Foundation.

- Served as active member of fundraising team, which doubled contributions for Saklan Valley School through donor solicitations and event planning.

- Made persuasive presentations before multi-city councils in San Francisco Bay Area, which influenced tax funding of public school bussing.

These achievement statements use the column technique to draw attention to noted clients.

WORK HISTORY

1985-present	Business Development Manager, X.NET, Inc., Lafayette, CA
1992-1993	Business Manager, Reliez Valley School Bus, Lafayette, CA
1974-1976	Sales Representative, Portal Travel Agency, San Francisco, CA
1972-1985	Full-time parent/fundraising volunteer

EDUCATION

Resume written in 1994.

B.A., Psychology, University of California at Berkeley, 1970
M.A. Program, Counseling Psychology, San Francisco State University, 1970-1973

Katherine E. Barnes

44 Oakdale Avenue • Napa, CA 92774 • (707) 992-1184

JOB OBJECTIVE

Private Investigator

SUMMARY OF QUALIFICATIONS

- Fine-tuned research, interviewing, and fact finding skills.
- Ability to establish rapport with a wide range of people.
- Integrate intuition, common sense, and logic to draw conclusions. On many occasions, demonstrated the ability to "read" people accurately.
- Background in accounting and auditing.

RELEVANT EXPERIENCE

- As a young teenager, verified a family "skeleton" rumor by researching county and financial records, school yearbooks, and questioning people. Found answers and remained quiet for years.
- Worked in a probation office during high school and college summers, accompanying state police on cases including domestic violence, child neglect, family disputes, and traffic violations.
- As a young adult, was approached for recruitment twice by federal officials.
- Based on my detailed description, line-up identification, and court testimony, a criminal who had attacked me and five other women (none of whom would testify) was caught and convicted.
- Without the help of the police, recovered personal stolen property by questioning witnesses and tracing leads into a dangerous part of a foreign city.
- Investigated a case involving a dishonest South African diamond dealer and recovered payment for my mother-in-law's $20,000 diamond.
- Following my common sense and without adequate proof, I confronted an employee concerning missing funds. She subsequently resigned and problems were resolved.
- Instinctively knew a business partner was not paying federal and state payroll taxes. Over objections of other owners, investigated the partner and proved her guilt. Negotiated a settlement with the IRS and EDD.
- Based on intuition, warned my ex-husband about two of his clients. They are now in prison for white collar crime.

(Cloud note at left: Most of these accomplishments came from unpaid experience.)

WORK HISTORY

1993-1994	Survey Interviewer, Study on Aging, The Buck Center, Novato, CA
1987-1992	Partner and General Manager, Stonehouse Farms (equestrian training facility and land investment company), Lakeview Terrace, CA
1986	Accounting Consultant, Pasadena Senior Center, Pasadena, CA
1983-1985	Accountant, Robert D. Gourley and Associates (CPA firm), Arcadia, CA
1982	Travel around the world
1980-1982	Full-time Student
1977-1979	Real Estate Agent, Villa Properties, Pasadena, CA

EDUCATION

Manhattanville College, Purchase, NY
   B.A., Political Science
California State University at Los Angeles, Los Angeles, CA
   Accounting
   Psychology
CPA examination, passed

(Cloud note: Resume written in 1994.)

Go For It

It's time to sit down at your computer or get out your pencil and paper, and use the resume template shown earlier in this chapter as a guide to create your own achievement resume. All the principles in Part 2 apply here (using action verbs, writing punchy summary statements, and so on). The only difference is the midsection where you're going to write just a few smashing accomplishments that shoot you light-years ahead of your competition. That's right—no boring job descriptions, no skill headings, just the cream from the top of your career. Like I said, you're going to look great!

The Least You Need to Know

➤ A resume that exudes confidence is hard for an employer to resist.

➤ Emphasize only selected achievements that say you're the best person for the job.

➤ De-emphasize a tricky employment history by placing it concisely at the bottom of the page.

➤ Start salary negotiations at a higher level because your resume presents you as one of the best in your field.

Chapter 14

The Best of Both Worlds: Hybrid Resumes

In This Chapter

➤ Getting creative with standard resume formats

➤ When to use a hybrid based on the chronological resume

➤ The advantages of using a hybrid based on the functional resume

So, you like both the chronological and functional resume formats, but neither one is quite right for your situation. You can combine the benefits of both formats by creating a *hybrid*. Creating a hybrid resume is kind of like borrowing from two recipes to come up with that wonderful entree!

Let's say you have the perfect situation for writing a chronological resume (based on what you learned in Chapter 3), but you want to highlight your transferable skills as well. You could start with the chronological structure and then add skill headings under "Professional Experience."

On the other hand, you might be the ideal candidate for using the functional resume (based on what you learned in Chapter 3), but you may be worried that the functional resume won't be well received by a conservative employer. In that case, you could start with the basic functional layout, then add subheadings comprised of the name of the company where your achievements took place, and...voila! You have a functional resume that looks somewhat like the traditional chronological resume.

Let's take a look at these two types of resume hybrids and how they might be advantageous to you.

Hybrid Based on the Chronological Resume

At first glance, the hybrid based on a chronological resume looks like a chronological format because the job seeker's achievements are presented as part of the work history in the body of the resume. The difference is that the achievement statements under each job heading are listed under skill subheadings. The following table shows you an example of what I mean; skill subheadings have been inserted into the Professional Experience section of a chronological resume.

1989–1994   Marketing Director, Fairfield General Company, Franklin, MA

Management

➤ Started the company's marketing department, which now creates promotional strategies for all 46 national branches.

➤ Directly supervised 16 managers who oversaw the work of 14 graphic designers, 10 copywriters, and 12 vendors.

Marketing

➤ Increased sales by 40 percent by launching three new products in the first year.

➤ Achieved significant return on advertising by creating a campaign that made "Fairfield" a household name.

When should you consider using a hybrid based on the chronological format instead of the regular chronological resume? If you fit into one of the following circumstances, think about designing a hybrid:

➤ *You're looking for a promotion.* If you want to use your resume to get a position that's a rung higher on your career ladder, the skill subheadings will help the employer see right away that you've already used the skills required for the next position without having to read the small print.

➤ *You're switching industries.* If you want to continue doing the same kind of work you've been doing but you want to change industries, the hybrid based on the chronological format can be a great promotional tool for you. This format will encourage the employer to identify you by your job titles and skills, even though your work history is from a different industry.

➤ *Your job titles are nondescript.* If your job titles don't express the level of responsibility you actually held, having skill subheadings in your Professional Experience section will help. This is frequently the case for government and university employees, where titles such as "Assistant, Level III" tell the reader almost nothing about the job.

To see this hybrid theory in action, take a look at the following template that represents a hybrid based on the chronological resume. It's followed by six sample resumes used by real job seekers.

(Hybrid Template based on Chronological Format)

Name
Street • City, State Zip • phone

JOB OBJECTIVE
The job you want next

SUMMARY OF QUALIFICATIONS
- How much experience you have in the field of your objective, in a related field, or using the skills required for your new position.
- An overall career accomplishment that shows you'd be good at this job objective.
- What someone would say about you as a recommendation.

PROFESSIONAL EXPERIENCE

19xx-pres. **Company Name,** City, State
JOB TITLE

MAJOR SKILL
- An accomplishment you are proud of that shows you're good at this profession.
- A problem you solved using this skill, and the results.

MAJOR SKILL
- A time when you positively affected the organization, the bottom line, your boss, your co-workers, your clients.
- Awards, commendations, publications, etc. you achieved that relate to your job objective.

19xx-xx **Company Name,** City, State
JOB TITLE

MAJOR SKILL
- A project you are proud of that supports your job objective.
- Another accomplishment that shows you're good at this line of work.

MAJOR SKILL
- Quantifiable results that point out your skill.

EDUCATION
Degree, Major (if relevant), 19xx (optional)
University, City, State

Rita Matajak

1410B Brookwood Street • Berkeley, CA 94301-5342 • (510) 553-8634

JOB OBJECTIVE

Environmental Health & Safety Coordinator

SUMMARY OF QUALIFICATIONS

- 10 years as an Environmental Compliance Professional with recent experience in Environmental Protection and OSHA compliance.

- Demonstrated ability to build rapport and resolve complex issues among multiple entities with conflicting interests.

- Working knowledge of industrial and research settings.

PROFESSIONAL EXPERIENCE

1991-present **Environmental Compliance Specialist**
LAWRENCE BERKELEY LABORATORY (LBL), Berkeley, CA

Leadership
- As Facility Coordinator for a building on UC Berkeley Campus, closed out 80% of 1800 deficiencies, turned around maintenance and custodial standards, implemented a recycling program, and improved security.

- As Chairperson of the Life Sciences Division Safety Committee, revitalized the group, improved productivity, increased recognition within LBL, and facilitated a self-assessment inspection program.

- Served as liaison between Principle Investigators and Environmental Health and Safety (EH&S) Division. Developed strategies for EH&S compliance including OSHA and waste management.

- As Manager of the Medical and Biohazardous Waste Program, developed a comprehensive compliance document including a generator's guide and training plan. Program was fully implemented in only six months.

Compliance Enforcement
- Conducted advice visits to hazardous and mixed waste generators to review procedures, labeling practices, and adherence to accumulation time limits.

- Updated and managed the Underground Storage Tank (UST) Program, which included the creation of four-page Monitoring Plans that were used as models by the Department of Energy (DOE).

- Coordinated certification of tanks and secondary containment for five Permit-by-Rule (PBR) Hazardous Waste Treatment Units. Ensured upgrades were in compliance and directed the permit writing effort.

- Set up a Waste Minimization and Pollution Prevention Program, which included a two-year implementation schedule and met California SB-14 Hazardous Waste Source Reduction, EPA, and DOE requirements.

> Rita's resume uses the chronological format as a foundation and adds skill headings within that structure.

— Continued —

Rita Matajak
Page 2

1990-1991   **Environmental Compliance Consultant**
SAIC (Science Applications International Corp.), Pleasanton, CA
An environmental consulting firm providing support to DOE facilities.

- Developed and wrote the first-ever Quality Control Inspection Plan/Procedure to monitor quality assurance of Lawrence Livermore National Laboratories' Hazardous Waste Management storage and treatment facilities. Plan was incorporated into their Part B Permit.

- Audited hazardous waste management facilities and Waste Accumulation Areas (WAAs) for compliance with EPA and Cal-EPA regulations, and DOE policies. Waste included: Hazardous
Radioactive, high and low level
Mixed

1986-1990   **Environmental Program Manager**, 1989-1990
Environmental Compliance Specialist, 1989
Chemist, Materials Engineering, 1986-1989
U.S. NAVY, NADEP, Alameda, CA
An aircraft re-work facility comprised of 150 manufacturing shops and a materials engineering laboratory.

- Ensured EH&S compliance in 100 WAAs by performing frequent surveillance and enhancing the training program.

- Co-developed directives for issues including waste minimization, solvent substitution, recycling, chemical storage, fire safety, and OSHA standards.

- Directed preparation of individual shop contingency plans for the site Hazardous Material Management Plan.

1983-1985   **Physical and Inorganic Chemistry Advanced High School Teacher**
U.S. PEACE CORPS, Kenya, East Africa

1980-1983   **Chemist**, 1983
Lab Technician, 1980-1982
IT CORPORATION, Martinez, CA
A hazardous waste disposal company.

EDUCATION

B.S., Biochemistry, San Francisco State University, San Francisco, 1978-1981

Seminars:	OSHA/RCRA	Hazardous Materials
	Hazardous Waste	Medical Waste
	Emergency Preparedness	Radioactive and Mixed Waste
	Fire Safety	Underground Storage Tanks

Resume written in 1996.

Paul Feldman
Executive Management Professional
951 Lucite St. • Berkeley, CA 94707 • (510) 525-8523

QUALIFICATIONS
- 11 years progressive leadership experience for a San Francisco company recognized as the best in its field.
- Success in managing 65% of organization's total revenue and expenditure, affected by multiple markets and fluctuating economy.
- Excellent supervisor who motivates staff by instilling confidence and dedication.

PROFESSIONAL EXPERIENCE
1985-present **The Recorder**, San Francisco, CA
Associate Publisher, 1993-present
General Manager, 1989-1993
Director of Legal Information Services, 1987-1989
Calendar Manager, 1985-1987

By adding skill headings to this chronological format, we can easily see Paul's areas of responsibility.

BUSINESS
- Manage a $3M annual print budget, requiring creative negotiations with vendors to maintain quality, despite 40% rise in paper costs.
- As director of the $600K legal advertising budget, achieve consistent sales in a declining market.
- Approve all capital acquisitions (approximately $100K per year) for the entire company.

PROJECT INITIATION
- Cut costs 40% by creating a 45-user, in-house editorial and production system.
- Doubled subscriptions by establishing a daily stand-alone supplement that provides crucial legal information to over 80,000 industry professionals.
- Increased sales market 30% through expansion of courtroom coverage from one to six counties.

SUPERVISION
- Hired, trained, and supervise 15 art, production, MIS, advertising, and clerical personnel, using a management style of staff empowerment and delegation.
- Motivate an interdepartmental team of 45 to consistently meet two publication deadlines per day (500 per year).
- Maintained excellent retention rate, experiencing turnover only due to employee advancement or education.

1981-1983 **Peace Corps**, Sierra Leone, West Africa
Volunteer, Agriculture Extension Officer

EDUCATION
B.A., Political Science, Wabash College, Crawfordsville, IN, 1981
Internship, U.S. Representative Tom Kindness, Washington, D.C., 1979

Resume written in 1996.

Larry Anderson

47 Serramonte Ave. • San Antonio, TX 94965 • (448) 281-8502

SUMMARY OF QUALIFICATIONS

- Accomplished Assistant Vice President in The Easter Seal Foundation.
- Doubled donations during the '91 Campaign, achieving stretch goal of $1 million.
- Allocated $1.6 million to community service agencies.
- Enjoy motivating and establishing rapport with volunteers, donors, and co-workers.

PROFESSIONAL EXPERIENCE

1990-present THE EASTER SEAL FOUNDATION, San Antonio/Andrews County, TX
ASSISTANT VICE PRESIDENT
Manage a wide range of activities within the organization, including:

Fundraising • Manage four fundraisers with a $1.2 million goal - 22% over last year. • Manage 125 existing corporate accounts; develop new accounts with high potential for giving. • Develop leadership giving. • Speak before community and corporate groups to solicit funds.

Allocations and Agency Relations • Allocated $1.6 million after reviewing fiscal stability, board governance, and program services of 54 Andrews County Easter Seal agencies. • Serve as liaison to coordinate activities.

Staffing Committees • Staff the Marketing, Agency Relations, Special Events Committees, creating effective teams of volunteers.

Volunteer Management • Recruit, develop, and manage high-level volunteers.

Special Events • Conceive and produce special events through out the year, including public relations events and prestigious fundraising galas.

Skill headings as subsets under the place of employment define Larry as someone who qualifies for his job objective.

LOANED EXECUTIVE
- Sponsored by Shell Oil to fundraise for the '91 Easter Seal Andrews County Campaign.
- Personally doubled annual donations, raising more than $330,000 from local businesses, schools, and city officials. • Contributed 1/3 of overall stretch goal of $1 million.

1988-89 GENERAL FOODS CORP, Houston, TX
PUBLIC RELATIONS ASSISTANT
- Assisted in corporate and product public relations during leveraged buy-out.
- Collaborated on PR strategies. • Co-managed sensitive internal issues such as layoffs and restructuring due to buy-out.

1984-90 LKA Business Services, Houston, TX
CONTRACTOR
- Provided sales and administrative assistance to nonprofit and for-profit organizations in the Houston area.

EDUCATION

B.S., Psychology, Kent State University, Kent, OH

Resume written in 1995.

Terri Ann Whitaker
505 Acadia Drive • Petaluma, CA 94954 • (707) 765-6237

JOB OBJECTIVE
Legal Secretary

SUMMARY OF QUALIFICATIONS
- 13 years as a legal secretary for two prominent law firms.
- Specialization in litigation support.
- Experienced at integrating interpersonal and professional skills to facilitate the objectives of a legal team.

PROFESSIONAL EXPERIENCE

1982-1994　**Legal Secretary**
PILLSBURY MADISON & SUTRO, San Francisco, CA

Litigation, 1989-1994
- Provided legal and administrative support for one partner and two associates who specialized in underwriters' insurance and international securities litigation.
- Managed voluminous amounts of paperwork, gaining a reputation for providing information accurately and promptly.
- Frequently asked by co-workers to clarify litigation procedures.

Notice how Terri's skill headings emphasize the areas of legal work she'd like to pursue.

Estate Planning/Administration, 1982-1989
- Played a supportive role on a legal team comprised of an attorney, a paralegal, and myself.
- Commended for accuracy in preparing and assembling legal documents and correspondence for large complicated estates.

1981-1982　**Legal Secretary**
EMARD & PERROCHET (formerly ACRET & PERROCHET), San Francisco, CA

Maritime Law
- Handled correspondence and prepared legal documents for two partners involved in personal injury cases aboard cruise ships.
- Gained basic knowledge of legal procedure including litigation.

EDUCATION
Degree: Legal Secretary
Heald Business College, San Francisco, CA
Legal Secretary Procedures
University of California, Berkeley Extension, San Francisco, CA
English
California State University, San Francisco, CA

Resume written in 1994.

Sharon L. Mitchell

442 Carol Lane • Lafayette, California 99442 • (510) 994-2271

JOB OBJECTIVE

Administrative Assistant

SUMMARY OF QUALIFICATIONS

- Nine years as an administrative support professional in a corporation that provides confidential case work.
- Skilled researcher, writer, editor and proofreader.
- Easily master meaning and spelling of industry terminology.
- Proficient in WordPerfect; 70+ WPM.

PROFESSIONAL EXPERIENCE

1985-1994   **Medical Records Department Staff Member**
Elizabeth Heights Medical Center, San Francisco, CA

Writing and Editing
- Authored article on professional transcription and dictation practices, published in the *Journal of the American Medical Record Association*.
- Wrote article about how to produce an organization's periodical, published in the *Minnesota Journal of Education*.
- Drafted and edited procedural manuals and job descriptions for the records department.

Organizational
- Researched all dictation and word processing systems available, evaluated each according to criteria and made recommendation to department director.
- Coordinated installation of word processing network and digital dictation system. Worked effectively with four departments to meet deadlines.
- Organized all aspects of a transcription symposium for 100 people.

Clerical
- Transcribed detailed medical reports. Edited sentence structure to clarify meaning and protect the organization from litigation.
- Increased word processing productivity by creating macros and using customized abbreviation software.

This hybrid allows Sharon to capitalize on her accomplishments for just one employer.

EDUCATION

B.S., English, Mankato State University, Mankato, MN
Journalism, Marquette University, Milwaukee, WI

Resume written in 1994.

Linda Ng

662 Knight Lane • San Rafael, California 99217 • Telephone/Fax **(415) 993-2845**

OBJECTIVE

Position in Faculty of Law, University of Hong Kong,
teaching California Real Estate Transactional and Land Use Law

SUMMARY OF QUALIFICATIONS

- Practical experience in California Real Estate Transactional and Land Use Law.
- Skilled at teaching law, both in classroom and individual settings.
- Conversational in Cantonese.

PROFESSIONAL EXPERIENCE

1989-1992   **TRANSACTIONAL ASSOCIATE**

FORSYTH, BRINKS, LOWMAN & FORESTER, San Francisco, California, 1990-1992

Real Estate Transactions

- Structured acquisition and disposition of four properties (totalling $2 million) within required time to obtain tax deferral.
- Negotiated with U.S. Fish and Wildlife Service and the Nature Conservancy (a nonprofit environmental organization) to sell two parcels and to grant two easements, involving complex California title insurance issues.
- Minimized tax liability and potential environmental liability of foreign buyers by creating California corporations, which acquired the property.
- Drafted joint venture agreements between developer and city school district for construction of two schools.
- Formed and maintained corporations, and created general and limited partnerships, for acquisition of property.
- Prepared numerous purchase and sales agreements, commercial leases, and other real estate contracts.

Land Use

- Critiqued federal, state, and city mandated environmental documents (Environmental Impact Statements, Environmental Impact Reports, and General Plans) for development of real estate.
- Co-wrote land use regulations section of a Specific Plan for the joint development of eight parcels.

BRANDEISE, LEWTON, FRIEND & POWELL, San Rafael, California, 1989
Specialized in commercial lease agreements negotiated by this real estate law firm.

- Compared terms of letter of intent with initial draft of commercial lease.
- Reviewed leases and recommended revisions to protect the client's interest and obtain leasehold benefits.

Since Linda has so many achievements from her most recent place of employment, the skill headings break them up, making them easier to read.

(Continued)

TEACHING EXPERIENCE

UNIVERSITY OF THE NEVADA, LAWRENCE SCHOOL OF LAW, Reno, Nevada

1988-1989   **ASSISTANT EDITOR,** *LAWARENCE LAW JOURNAL*

- Supervised 30 student writers, teaching them specific techniques to analyze changes in state legislation.

1987-1988   **MENTOR,** MOOT COURT COMPETITION

- Taught students to write concise briefs and to make persuasive oral arguments.
- Lectured on:
  Structuring briefs and citation formats
  Effective presentation styles
  Court etiquette
- Tutored one student who qualified for the competition as the Best Moot Court Advocate.

1985-1989   **TUTOR**

- Informally tutored students in difficult subjects.
- Developed concise course outlines and used them as tutoring aids.

EDUCATION

UNIVERSITY OF THE NEVADA, LAWRENCE SCHOOL OF LAW, Reno

J.D., 1989
Class Rank: Top 25%
Dean's Honor List: 2 years
Traynor Honor Society
Outstanding Graduating Senior Award
President, Asian American Law Students Association

UNIVERSITY OF WASHINGTON, Seattle

B.S., Economics, 1984
Legal Intern, Student Legal Clinic

PROFESSIONAL AFFILIATIONS

State Bar of California, Real Property Section
Asian American Bar Association, Co-chair of Education Committee
Bar Association of San Francisco

Resume written in 1994.

Hybrid Based on the Functional Resume

The hybrid based on the functional resume looks almost like a functional format. Its work history is concise and placed at the bottom of the page, and achievement statements are categorized according to skill headings in the body of the resume. What makes it a hybrid is that under the skill headings there are subheadings that indicate where the achievements took place.

As I mentioned in Chapter 3, one of the biggest objections to the functional format is that most resume writers fail to say where each achievement took place. The hybrid based on the functional resume not only identifies where each achievement happened, it announces it loud and clear through subheadings in the body of the resume, similar to the subheadings in the chronological format. That's the advantage—the hybrid looks similar to the chronological resume (and therefore familiar to the employer), yet it has the structural advantage of the functional resume.

To understand this better, look at the way the achievement statements are categorized in the following table.

MANAGEMENT

Fairfield General Company

➤ Started the company's marketing department, which now creates promotional strategies for all 46 national branches.

➤ Directly supervised 16 managers who oversaw the work of 14 graphic designers, 10 copywriters, and 12 vendors.

Indigo International Inc.

➤ Introduced an automated resume scanning system that eliminated 50 work hours per week.

➤ Improved team spirit by including department representatives in corporate decision making.

MARKETING

Fairfield General Company

➤ Increased sales by 40 percent by launching three new products in the first year.

➤ Achieved significant return on advertising by creating a campaign that made "Fairfield" a household name.

Indigo International Inc.

➤ Wrote a 25-page proposal that outlined strategies for reaching long-and short-term goals.

I recommend the hybrid based on the functional resume for job seekers who have chosen the functional format and who have several achievements from one place of employment.

The following template shows a hybrid based on the functional resume. The template is followed by six sample resumes for real job seekers.

Tip

Your juiciest information should appear near the top of your resume. Prioritize your achievements so that the most impressive ones appear at the top of each section.

(Hybrid Template based on Functional Format)

Name
Street • City, State Zip • phone

JOB OBJECTIVE
The job you want next

SUMMARY OF QUALIFICATIONS
- How much experience you have in the field of your objective, in a related field, or using the skills required for your new position.
- An overall career accomplishment that shows you'd be good at this job objective.
- What someone would say about you as a recommendation.

RELEVANT EXPERIENCE

MAJOR SKILL

Company where the following achievements took place
- An accomplishment you are proud of that shows you're good at this skill.
- A problem you solved using this skill, and the results.

Company where the following achievements took place
- A time when you used your skill to positively affected the organization, the bottom line, your boss, your clients.
- Awards, commendations, publications, etc. you achieved that relate to your job objective.

MAJOR SKILL

Company where the following achievements took place
- A project you are proud of that supports your job objective.
- Another accomplishment that shows you're good at this work.

Company where the following achievements took place
- Quantifiable results that point out your skill.
- A time when someone took notice of your skill.

WORK HISTORY
19xx-present	Job Title	COMPANY NAME and city
19xx-xx	Job Title	COMPANY NAME and city
19xx-xx	Job Title	COMPANY NAME and city
19xx-xx	Job Title	COMPANY NAME and city

EDUCATION
Degree, Major (if relevant), 19xx (optional), University, City, State

Arlene A. Borrows

4792 Pramount Street • San Francisco, CA 94661 • (779) 374-9115

JOB OBJECTIVE

A sales position

SUMMARY OF QUALIFICATIONS

- Enthusiastic and motivated; sincerely enjoy developing and maintaining excellent customer relations.
- Outstanding ability to understand others' needs and offer solutions.
- Resourceful and innovative; proven talent to adapt quickly to challenges.
- Commended for top-notch organizational skills.

RELEVANT ACCOMPLISHMENTS

SALES/INTERPERSONAL RELATIONS

Word Processing Contractor:

- Consistently developed new business, despite slow economy, through prospecting, persuasive presentations and persistent follow-up.
- Easily developed rapport with clients, quickly assessing needs and responding effectively to pressure and deadlines.

Assistant to Executive VP of Production, Orion Pictures:

- Handled phones for this successful VP working with celebrities and politicians. Used diplomacy to accommodate demanding schedules and powerful personalities.
- Negotiated terms with vendors for special events.

Inside Sales Representative, New Zealand Milk Products:

- Resolved customer service problems, i.e., deliveries, quality control.

The subheadings under Arlene's skill headings make it easy for us to see where each accomplishment took place.

PROJECT MANAGEMENT

Assistant to Executive VP of Production, Orion Pictures:

- Planned private screenings for 50-100 VIPs. Evaluated needs for the event, personally invited guests and handled on-site logistics.
- Maintained an extremely high-profile appointment schedule with prominent directors, producers and actors. Managed correspondence, film proposals and expenses.
- Supervised immediate support staff.

WORK HISTORY

1989-present	Word Processing Contractor	San Francisco
1987-1988	Assistant to Executive VP of Production	Orion Pictures Corporation, Los Angeles
1985-1986	Booking Assistant	Creative Artists Agency, Los Angeles
1983-1985	Inside Sales Representative	New Zealand Milk Products, San Francisco

EDUCATION

B.A., Political Economics, University of California, Berkeley

Interior Design Program, Canada College, Redwood City

Resume written in 1995.

Kristan M. Bunnin

334 Fillmore Street, #209 • San Francisco, CA 94123 • (415) 442-8864

JOB OBJECTIVE

A position in Fundraising

SUMMARY OF QUALIFICATIONS

- Experienced at fundraising and public relations work for nonprofit organizations and political leaders.
- Talent for generating support for causes that increase awareness and community involvement.
- Skilled at fostering relationships with people from diverse cultural and economic backgrounds.

EXPERIENCE

FUNDRAISING / PUBLIC RELATIONS

Fundraiser for College Kids, a nonprofit organization dedicated to getting and keeping at-risk youth on the college track.

Kristan used a clever technique of categorizing her accomplishments by "employer" and putting them under the appropriate skill heading.

- Played key role in focusing the fundraising committee. Clarified goals, set priorities, and created action plans.
- Organized a pubic relations/fundraising event to attract 500 supporters who see the need to "make a difference" through education.

Public Relations for Political Figures

- Represented Speaker O'Neill to the public, explaining his platform, answering questions, and responding to complaints by phone and through correspondence.
- Prepared packets for public appearances, debates, and press conferences for Governor Dukakis during his presidential campaign, frequently responding to public controversies.
- Served as front-end person to Senator Alan Cranston, handling hundreds of phone calls per day from a diverse constituency of 30 million.

ADMINISTRATION

- Created and maintained donor database for College Kids that has recently experienced a dramatic expansion.
- As assistant to political figures, managed extremely busy calendars that juggled numerous meetings, press conferences, and media events.
- Wrote commemorative announcements and letters on behalf of Senator Alan Cranston.

RELEVANT WORK HISTORY

| 1993-present | Fundraiser | College Kids, San Francisco/Los Angeles, CA |
| 1991-1993 | Financial Aid Advisor | National University, Los Angeles, CA |

(Mostly concurrent with education)

1985-1989	Assistant to political figures:	Congressional Office of Thomas P. O'Neill, Jr.
		Dukakis/Bentsen Campaign
		Office of Senator Alan Cranston
		Congressional Office of Ike Skelton

EDUCATION

B.A., National University, Los Angeles, CA, anticipated 1995
Grant Proposal Writing , Alumnae Resources, San Francisco, 1995

Resume written in 1995.

216

Dianne M. Sterling
883 Fulbright Street • Fremont, CA 97112 • (510) 229-9623

MANAGEMENT CONSULTANT
with emphasis on:
Seminars and Training • Organizational Development • Financial Management

SUMMARY OF QUALIFICATIONS

- 20 years of broad based management experience with a realistic understanding of what it takes to achieve business growth and success. Owner of a successful small business.
- Excellent background for teaching organizational and individual effectiveness:
    BA, Business Management
    MA, Psychology
    Ongoing training toward Ph.D., Organizational Development
- Talent for seeing the "big picture," pinpointing organizational objectives, and setting goals and priorities to achieve them.
- Articulate and persuasive in written and verbal presentations.

PROFESSIONAL ACCOMPLISHMENTS

BUSINESS MANAGEMENT

As a Business Owner / Manager:
- Created and managed a successful small consulting firm for individuals and organizations regarding:

Management success	Conflict resolution
Troubleshooting	Board meeting facilitation
Organizational development	Financial management / accounting
Productivity	Personnel administration

Dianne's hybrid based on a functional resume is appreciated by employers because it looks like a chronological resume.

- Wrote vision statement and business plan based on pragmatic and philosophical objectives.
- Built a strong client base primarily from referrals.

As a Financial Manager and Sales Manager:
- Conducted management troubleshooting and designed simplified and comprehensive systems to resolve issues.
- Built consensus throughout the organization by writing clear policy and procedure manuals.
- Reduced DSO of receivables from 120 days to less than 30 days by installing programs that maintained efficiency.
- Increased cash flow by maintaining an accurate cash position, records, controls, and transfers.

SEMINARS , TRAINING , AND COACHING
- Consulted to Board members, executives, and management to provide clear leadership toward company mission.
- Motivated personnel at all levels of the organization to achieve excellence. Offered

Seminars	Coaching
Training sessions	Personal example

- As a coach and therapist, worked with individuals and groups on:

Self-motivation	Effective communications
Stress reduction	Anger management
Presentation skills	Balancing work and personal life

— Continued —

Dianne M. Sterling
Page 2

WORK HISTORY

1987-present   Dianne M. Sterling Consultancy, Corte Madera, CA
           Consultant, Seminar Leader, Coach, and Psychotherapist

1987-present   Import International, Mill Valley, CA
           Business Consultant, 1993-present
           Controller, 1989-1993
           Accounting Manager, 1987-1989

1980-1987   Fennegan Corporation (subsidiary of Motorola, Inc.), Daly City, CA
           Corporate Credit Manager

1977-1980   Holiday Clubs International (subsidiary of Holiday Inns), Sausalito, CA
           Accounting Manager

1974-1976   Fraser's (subsidiary of Harrod's of London), Glasgow, Scotland
           Sales Manager

EDUCATION

MA   Psychology, 1988
           John F. Kennedy University, Orinda, CA

BA   Business Management, 1986
           Sonoma State University, Rohnert Park, CA

Resume written in 1994.

Darleen Collier

831 Walnut Grove Way • Marin City, CA 94219 • (415) 832-0931

JOB OBJECTIVE

A training position with a focus on team building

HIGHLIGHTS OF QUALIFICATIONS

- 16 years in leadership roles for two corporations, both nationally recognized for excellence in their fields.
- Enjoy making presentations that contribute to company goals through problem resolution, team building, and organizational development.
- Impressive reputation for building cohesion among disparate groups and individuals.

PROFESSIONAL EXPERIENCE

TEAM BUILDING

Fluor Corporation

- Recognized for consistently building productive teams in different departments, despite organizational problems such as re-engineering, downsizing, and internal conflict.

> *Employers have responded positively to the hybrid based on the functional resume since it clearly says where the applicant's experience took place.*

  - On behalf of CEO, currently administer a confidential program to identify Fluor's 200 top performing employees. Develop ranking criteria; monitor performance, write compensation guidelines; and oversee succession planning.
  - As Quality Management Team Leader, resolved power struggles and racial tension using a positive approach to conflict resolution and staff development.
  - Facilitated communication and cooperation among 12 service units, resulting in increased productivity and 33% reduction in overhead.
  - Supervised a group of 65 administrative personnel, building a strong work ethic and providing cross-training that improved work-flow significantly.

Foodmaker, Incorporated

- Turned around an unprofitable business unit, achieving a 10% profit margin in nine months by developing a crew of 30 part-time employees from socioeconomically diverse backgrounds.
  - Replaced 80% of staff and promoted 50% of remaining personnel into leadership positions.
  - Raised work standards through customer service, operations, and team building training.
  - Stopped internally organized theft of approximately $10K per year.

TRAINING

Fluor Corporation

- Taught 12-part listening and communication skills classes to enhance staff cooperation and productivity.
- Wrote technical procedures and provided one-on-one training to a major corporate client, instilling a level of confidence that led to a $3M increase in the contract value.
- Incorporated Myers-Briggs and organizational development material into weekly department meetings to break down interpersonal barriers and share job knowledge.

Foodmaker, Incorporated

- Due to exceptional performance, promoted to Training Supervisor after first year. Trained 50 new restaurant managers in all aspects of operations, personnel management, business procedures, and customer service.
- Performed quality inspections of chain restaurants and provided follow-up management and service crew training.

— Continued —

Darleen Collier
Page Two

WORK HISTORY

1981-present	Fluor Corporation, San Francisco, CA
	Executive Programs Manager, 1993-present
	Facilities Support Services Manager, 1990-1993
	Administrative Services Manager, 1988-1990
	Project Administrator, 1981-1988
1978-1981	Foodmaker, Incorporated, Hayward, CA
	Training Supervisor, 1979-1981
	Restaurant Manager, 1978-1979
1973-1978	Elementary School Systems, Pleasanton, CA and Athens, OH
	Teacher

EDUCATION AND CERTIFICATION

M.Ed., Public School Administration, Ohio University, Athens
B.A., Anthropology, minor in Psychology, University of California, Berkeley

Myers-Briggs Type Indicator Certification, Association for Psychological Type
Quality Management Team Leader Training, Bechtel Corporation

PROFESSIONAL AFFILIATION

American Society of Trainers and Developers (ASTD)

Resume written in 1995.

Francine Whiley

4429 Detroit Avenue • Oakland, CA 32011 • (510) 332-7430

JOB OBJECTIVE

Director of Civil Complaint Board, San Francisco Police Department

SUMMARY OF QUALIFICATIONS

- More than 20 years as an executive manager in the legal and business fields.
- Excellent researcher with ability to manage a heavy caseload.
- Skilled supervisor who knows how to build consensus among personnel.
- Exceptional technical and interpersonal problem solver.
- Strength in public relations. Experienced public speaker and spokesperson.

RELEVANT ACCOMPLISHMENTS

These achievement statements are credible since they are headed by the name of the organization where they took place.

MANAGEMENT / SUPERVISION

Polygram Records

- Served as one of five members on the Executive Management Committee, which resolved harassment, discrimination, labor relations, and public relations issues.
- Enhanced departmental and interdepartmental teamwork by fostering strong company-wide communication.
- Managed Business Affairs and Legal Department comprised of attorneys, paralegals, secretaries and contract administrators from diverse cultural backgrounds.

Marshall & Morris, Esqs.

- Trained and supervised paralegals in client relations, legal research and preparation of reports for this multi-million dollar law firm.

LEGAL

Marshall & Morris, Esqs.

- Conferred with and advised clients with respect to claims against them or their organizations.
- Researched and evaluated validity of claims.
- Conducted conciliation meetings and made concrete recommendations for disposition of claims.
- Scheduled and participated in hearings.

Polygram Records

- Served as legal advisor to management regarding claims by artists, distributors and employees.
- Conducted and supervised research of claims and prepared evaluations and recommendations.
- Provided statistical reports with respect to departmental operations.

WORK HISTORY

1993-present	Legal Consultant, Oakland, CA
1983-93	Attorney, New York, NY
1980-83	Vice President, Business Affairs and Legal Dept., Polygram Records, Inc., New York, NY
1971-80	Associate, 1977-80, Paralegal, 1975-77, Director, International Music Dept., 1971-75, Marshall & Morris, Esqs., New York, NY

EDUCATION

J.D., New York Law School, New York, NY, 1977

B.A., Hunter College, New York, NY, 1968

Resume written in 1994.

JOHN S. BOTT

490 Kansas Street • Santa Rosa, CA 91448 • (315) 527-8766

▬▬▬ Marketing/Sales Executive ▬▬▬

➤ Successful Marketing/Sales Manager at the corporate level.

➤ Goal-oriented, self-motivated, and persistent.

➤ Derive satisfaction in doing a job well while supporting others in their success.

PROFESSIONAL EXPERIENCE

MARKETING/SALES

As Regional Sales Manager for Research Holdings:

- Serviced over 200 public company accounts for this financial publication with circulation to over 62,000 stockbrokers.
- Expanded Northern California and Mid-west territories 21%, increasing revenue by over $300,000 in 1 year.
- Cultivated a loyal clientbase by providing security to clients within their market.
- Assisted clients in setting goals and developing successful marketing strategies.
- Made sales presentations in person and by phone to corporate decision makers, utilizing knowledge of the market, the product, and the client's financial and marketing positions.
- Generated quality leads/sales through research, cold calling, and persistent followup.

MANAGEMENT

As Regional Sales Manager for Research Holdings:

- Managed client accounts and 2 territories, consistently setting and achieving high quotas.
- Organized time and work efficiently to create a cost effective and productive environment.
- Coordinated sales with associate in Los Angeles to increase profit-loss ratio.
- Maintained a current inventory of products for cyclical demands.

For City of Ithaca:

- Quickly assessed situations, and delegated/performed tasks to relieve emergencies.

For Tashmoo Restoration:

- Co-managed construction projects from blueprints through completion.

(margin note:) John created a hybrid resume based on the functional format that emphasized his current sales position.

WORK HISTORY

1991-present	Regional Sales Manager	Research Holdings, San Francisco, CA
1990-91	Carpenter	Tashmoo Restoration, Vineyard Haven, MA

Concurrent with Education:

1988-90	Firefighter	City of Ithaca, NY
Summer '86,'87	Launch Operator/Marketing Rep	Edgartown Marine, Edgartown, MA

EDUCATION

Bachelor of Arts in English, minor in Economics, Ithaca College, Ithaca, NY, 1990

PERSONAL

Fundraiser, Youth At Risk, San Francisco
Fundraiser, Boys and Girls Club, San Francisco
Committee Member, Grace Cathedral Golf Classic, San Francisco
Licensed Small Passenger Vessel Operator, U.S. Coast Guard certified

Enjoy golf, hunting, sailing, biking, and fishing

(note:) Resume written in 1995.

Go For It

You've figured out which hybrid format to use, so it's time to put your thoughts on paper. Follow the step-by-step principles in Part 2, using the hybrid template you've chosen from this chapter. It's that simple!

The Least You Need to Know

➤ The hybrid based on the chronological resume emphasizes your career history while highlighting skills that are particularly relevant.

➤ The hybrid based on the functional resume de-emphasizes your work history and spotlights your transferable skills in a structure that looks like a chronological resume.

Chapter 15

What the Heck Is a Curriculum Vita?

In This Chapter

➤ What is a curriculum vita?

➤ What's the difference between a resume and a curriculum vita?

➤ Writing an interesting and dynamic vita

➤ When it comes to a curriculum vita, more is more

"Show me your curriculum vita!" You've probably heard this request in your job search travels. "My what?" you exclaim, hoping it's not a part of your body that's not in good enough shape to reveal, much less show off. The words "curriculum vita" may sound intimidating, but the "animal" itself isn't. Let's take a look at the nuts and bolts of creating one.

Definition
Curriculum vita (or *CV* or *vita* for short) is the term used by the academic and scientific communities to mean "resume."

Curriculum Vita or Resume?

If you're seeking a faculty, research, or leadership position at an academic or scientific organization, you've probably heard the term "curriculum vita." Just as some industries (such as engineering, sales, and the performing arts) have their own styles and requirements for a resume, so does the professional academic world.

A curriculum vita may sound like an intimidating formal document, but relax—there's no need to put on your evening gown or tux to write your CV! You've already learned the principles for creating an effective resume (remember the five resume commandments and the Top Ten Checklist?). To create a CV, there are only three exceptions to the guidelines you read about in Parts 1 and 2:

➤ Most CVs are more than two pages long.

➤ The information on a CV tends to be detailed, providing data such as publications, presentations, and academic work.

➤ Curriculum vitas do not necessarily contain job objective statements, although it's perfectly all right to include one.

Let's look at each of these exceptions more closely.

How Long Should a CV Be?

The length of a CV may vary. A CV for a recent Ph.D. graduate would normally be two to three pages long. For someone with extensive professional experience, it could run as long as seven or eight pages. That's a lot of paper, but the people reading them seem to live by the slogan "more is more." (That's the CV twist on the "more is less" theme I've been espousing all along.)

How Detailed Should a CV Be?

Your CV audience is more interested in facts than it is in hype (that is, language that sounds exaggerated in order to impress). Data such as reference information, dates, and exact titles are important, since they give a means for verifying information. Providing technical descriptions also gives you a chance to show that you know what you're talking about without sounding like a braggart.

Here's an example of what I mean. Instead of saying:

Prominent scientist who has been honored at universities around the world for ground-breaking discoveries

It's more appropriate to state:

Organic chemist who has presented discoveries and research at universities in Russia, Mexico, Canada, and the U.S.

Should I Include a Job Objective Statement?

Many CVs don't include job objectives, especially if the applicant intends to stay in the same field. Between the college degree and the work history, it's usually obvious what type of position is being sought. However, if you're planning to change careers (for example, from research to teaching), a job objective statement at the top of the CV is helpful to the reader.

Give Your CV Some Personality

Because the CV usually addresses a conservative reader, many assume that it needs to follow a rigid outline. Well, not if I can help it! You can use creativity to present your strengths while respecting the expectations of the academic, scientific, or institutional employer. That means you can consider using any one of the five formats I've suggested so far: chronological, functional, achievement, hybrid based on the chronological format, or hybrid based on the functional format.

Curriculum Vita Headings

Following are some headings you may want to include on your CV. If a category isn't applicable to you, disregard it or combine it with another heading.

Education

This section almost always appears near the top of page one. It should provide information about each degree you have achieved, including major, date received, institution, city, state, and titles of theses and dissertations. You can also include course titles if they demonstrate relevant knowledge. Internships may either be placed under this heading, in a section of their own, or under "Experience," depending on which strategy makes the most sense for your situation.

Experience

Assuming that you are staying in the same line of work, you can use the chronological format for your CV. In that case, your work experience is usually listed in reverse chronology, with descriptive statements and achievements under each heading.

If you're changing careers or have significant gaps in your employment history, you can use the functional format for your CV. To achieve a traditional look, follow the ideas for constructing a hybrid based on the functional format (see Chapter 14).

Publications, Presentations, and Workshops

Articles, monographs, books, chapters in books, and research papers that you have authored or co-authored should go under the heading "Publications."

State the titles of papers you presented, names of conferences, locations, and dates in the category termed "Presentations and Workshops." If it adds to your qualifications, elaborate on the roles you played.

Committees and Appointments, Professional Affiliations

List your titles, names of committees, locations, dates, and, if appropriate, what results were achieved under "Committees and Appointments."

In addition, list the associations that you belong to alphabetically or in order of relevance to your profession under "Professional Affiliations." If you hold an office, that should also be noted.

Additional Headings

Other headings that might appear on your CV include: "Exhibitions," "Awards and Honors," "Research," "Grants," "Symposia," "Lectures," "Teaching," and "Licenses."

Free Samples

Here they come—the CV samples used by real job seekers to get real live jobs. In the interest of space in this book, I selected CVs that are no more than three pages long. Keep in mind, however, that yours might very well run beyond three pages. That's perfectly fine. Remember the CV slogan: More is more.

Linda Rieker

429 Talbot Street • Corona Del Mar, CA 92753 • (714) 458-4910

OBJECTIVE   Fine Arts faculty position, teaching Creative Photography.
Other areas of competency:
- Artists' Books
- Contemporary Art Issues
- Digital Imaging
- Writing for Visual Artists

(Clear objective statement (an optional section for a CV but helpful in Linda's case)

EDUCATION

M.A.   English and American Literature, 1991
Claremont Graduate School, Claremont, CA

M.F.A.   Creative Photography, 1989
California State University, Fullerton, CA

B.A.   Fine Arts, 1972
University of Western Ontario, London, Canada

(Education near top of CV)

SUMMARY OF EXPERIENCE

FINE ARTIST

- Received the Frederick Weisman Foundation Purchase Award for photographic piece, currently in permanent collection of the Newport Harbor Art Museum.
- As accomplished fine arts photographer, exhibited nationally in museums, galleries and universities.
- Combined word and image through one-of-a-kind book-objects, exhibited at artists' books exhibitions.
- Photographed the influence of religion and ritual in world cultures. Work done while traveling throughout: Africa, India, Pakistan, Nepal, Thailand, Myanmar, Papua New Guinea, Japan, South America and the West Indies.
- Produced artwork for cover of *Mindscapes*, a national literary magazine.

(Strong accomplishments that earn Linda the reader's respect)

TEACHER

- Taught classes on techniques and aesthetics of black and white photography at Art Institute of Southern California, Saddleback College and Cypress College. Engaged students in critiques of their own work incorporating social, political, and ethical issues.
- Since 1993, developed and instructed seven arts and humanities courses at University of California, Irvine Extension.
- At several colleges and schools, presented slide-lectures of own photographic artwork, generating philosophical and analytical discussion.
- Gave lecture with visual presentation to Claremont·Graduate School students on the changing role of women as demonstrated through art, media and literature.
- As key note speaker at the Feminist Forum, heightened awareness of the lack of representation of women in visual art, resulting in an organized effort to increase visibility of women in the arts.

EXHIBITIONS COORDINATOR

- As independent curator, co-directed photography exhibitions that included conceptual and confrontational installations. Wrote press releases, designed announcements, organized exhibition space and installed artwork.
- Developed and coordinated all aspects of personal exhibitions from conception to installation.

- Continued on page 2 -

("Continued" at the bottom of pages 1 and 2)

Linda created additional categories to handle lists of information that support her career objective.

Page number at the top of pages 2 and 3

Linda Rieker
Page 2

RECENT WORK HISTORY

1994-present	**Adjunct Faculty Member, Photography**	Cypress College, Cypress, CA
1993-present	**Instructor, Arts and Humanities**	UC Irvine Extension, Irvine, CA
1988-present	**Professional Artist and Writer**	Laguna Beach, CA
1993	**Associate Faculty Member, Photography**	Saddleback College, Mission Viejo, CA
1990-92	**Associate Curator**	B.C. Space Gallery, Laguna Beach, CA
1989	**Lecturer, Fine Art Photography**	Art Institute of Southern California, Laguna Beach, CA
1981-89	**President, Equestrian, CEF Judge**	Equi Ventures, Inc., Aurora, Ontario, Canada

REPRESENTATIVE LECTURES

1995	"Memory and the Photographic Image"	UC Irvine, Irvine, CA
1994	"Contemporary Women Photographers"	Feminist Forum, Laguna Beach, CA
1993	"One-Of-A-Kind Books "	Cypress College, Cypress, CA
1993	Artist in Residence	St. Margaret's School, San Juan Capistrano
1992	"Creating the Artists' Book"	Art Institute of Southern California, Laguna Beach, CA
1992	"The Lack of Representation of Women in Visual Art"	Feminist Forum, Laguna Beach, CA
1992	"Interpretations of Non-Western Cultures through Art"	Cypress College, Cypress, CA
1991	"Photography as Art"	California State University, Fullerton, CA
1991	"Images of Diverse Cultures"	St. Margaret's School, San Juan Capistrano
1990	"Representations of the Body"	Claremont Graduate School, Claremont, CA
1990	"Manipulated Images"	Art Institute of Southern California, Laguna Beach, CA

AWARDS

1994	Juror's Award. "Alternatives '94," Ohio University, Athens, OH
1990	Juror's Award, Long Beach Art Association, Long Beach, CA
1990	Soho International Art Competition #10, New York, NY
1989	Soho International Art Competition #9, New York, NY
1989	Frederick Weisman Foundation Purchase Award, Los Angeles, CA

PERMANENT COLLECTIONS

Newport Harbor Art Museum, Permanent Collection, Newport Beach, CA
Club Post Nuclear, Laguna Beach, CA

EXHIBITIONS: PHOTOGRAPHY

1995	"Photropolis," San Diego, CA
1994	"Mind Mines," Cypress College, Cypress, CA
1994	"Alternatives '94," Ohio University, Athens, OH
1991-92	"The Alchemy of Gesture," SF Camerawork, San Francisco, CA
1991	Gallery 817, Los Angeles, CA
1991	"Alternatives '91," Ohio University, Athens, OH
1991	Long Beach Photography Exhibition, Long Beach, CA
1991	Ariel Gallery, Soho, NY
1990	"Cultural Codes," B.C. Space Gallery, Laguna Beach, CA
1990	Seven States Exhibition, Long Beach, CA
1990	Ariel Gallery, Soho, New York, NY

- Continued on page 3 -

EXHIBITIONS: PHOTOGRAPHY (Continued)

1989	"Alternatives '89," Ohio University, Athens, OH
1989	Long Beach Art Association, Long Beach, CA
1989	"New California Artists - Photographs from the Permanent Collection," Newport Harbor Art Museum, Newport Beach CA
1989	LACPS Annual Exhibition, Lindhurst Gallery, University of Southern California, Los Angeles, CA
1989	"Photograph as Document Exhibition," Downey Museum, Downey, CA
1989	Frederick Weisman Foundation Exhibition, California State University, Fullerton, CA
1989	"Journeys," West Gallery, California State University, Fullerton, CA
1988-90	Club Post Nuclear, Laguna Beach, CA
1988	LACPS Exhibition, Brand Library Art Galleries, Glendale, CA
1988	"Markings," Center Gallery, California State University, Fullerton, CA
1987	Martha Fuller, Photographs, Art Institute of Southern California, Laguna Beach, CA

EXHIBITIONS: ARTISTS' BOOKS

1993	"L.A. Biblioteca," Site Gallery, Los Angeles, CA
1992	"The Book is Art," Renee Fotouhi Fine Art, East Hampton, NY
1992	"Love & Romance," Center for Book Arts, New York, NY
1991	"Photographic Book Art in the U.S.," University of Texas at San Antonio, TX
1991	"War & Peace," Center for Book Arts, New York, NY
1990	"Books: Inside & Out," Anchorage Museum of History & Art, Anchorage, AK
1990	"A Southern California Decade: An Exhibition of Contemporary Books," University of California, Los Angeles, CA
1989	"Fifteenth Anniversary Exhibition," Center for Book Arts, New York, NY

PUBLICATIONS: CONTRIBUTIONS

1992	*Mindscapes*, Cover Artwork, Vol. 2, No. 1
1991	*Artweek*, Contributing Writer/Reviewer,
1988-89	*Artists' Liaison Catalogue*
1987&89	*Photographer's Forum Annual*, Santa Barbara, CA

PUBLICATIONS: REVIEWS OF ARTIST

1991	Howard Farber, *Artspeak*, February, 1991
1990	"Culture, Landscape & Memory," Cathy Curtis, *Los Angeles Times*, September 13, 1990
1990	David Battenburg, *Orange Coast Daily Pilot*, September 9, 1990
1990	Jan Ingram, *Anchorage Daily News*, June 17, 1990
1989	Cathy Curtis, *Los Angeles Times*, July 24, 1989
1989	David Battenburg, *The Laguna Coastline*, August 25, 1989
1989	Laura Tuckman, *The Orange County Register*, July 2, 1989

AFFILIATIONS

College Art Association
LACPS
SF Camerawork
Southern California Women's Caucus for Art

Resume written in 1996.

Dorothy K. Wagner

1137 Louisville Avenue • Oakland, California 94510 • (510) 435-6654

JOB OBJECTIVE

Teacher, Fulbright Commission in Cairo, Egypt

Subjects:	English	Art
	Literature	Social Sciences

Precise academic career objective that shows Dorothy is targeting this position

SUMMARY OF QUALIFICATIONS

Summary statements that support her objective specifically

- Five years teaching experience, students K-12 and adults.
- 18 years working in international/multicultural environments as a teacher, scholar, or professional international liaison.
- Particular strength in bridging cultural gaps among people through education and interpersonal relations.
- Independent travel and research in the Middle East and Europe.

EDUCATION AND CREDENTIAL

Mills College, Oakland, CA
  MA, Liberal Arts, 1987
  BA, English, 1979

California Teaching Credential, anticipated Spring 1994

Education appears on page 1

PROFESSIONAL EXPERIENCE

1989-present **Guest Teacher/Lecturer**
Public Schools: St. Martin's of Tours Elementary School, San Jose, CA
Downer Elementary School, Richmond, CA
Olinda Elementary School, Richmond, CA
Mission High School, San Francisco, CA

Interesting presentation of multiple jobs: Dorothy put several positions under one "umbrella" (Guest Teacher/Lecturer) to promote a stable image.

- Made classroom presentations to students K-8, demonstrating the importance of art in man's physical and mental survival.
- Tutored high school students of "Project Read," integrating reading and writing to offer new perspective and respect for their own life stories.
- Conducted cultural field trips to sites including businesses, performing arts centers, and museums.

Lecturer/Volunteer Teacher
de Young Art Museum, San Francisco, CA

- Lectured on "Art of Africa, Oceania, and the Americas" to groups ranging from 10-60 adults.
- As a teacher in the "View and Do" program, taught children ways of "looking" at art and motivated them to create art with museum artists.
- Managed groups of students from diverse multicultural backgrounds, including non-English speakers.
- Conducted museum tours for persons with physical and mental special needs.

— Continued —

232

Dorothy K. Wagner
Page 2

1982-1993   **International Liaison**
Concord Jazz Records, Concord, CA
- Served as International Liaison to well known visiting musicians from Africa, Europe, South America, and Asia.

1976-1987   **International and Domestic Hostess**
Ford Motor Company, Oakland, CA
- Served as hostess and cultural advisor on company trips for up to 200 winners of sales contests. International trip sites included:

Morocco	Caribbean
Spain	Hawaii
Mexico	Canada

Additional categories that support Dorothy's objective

INTERNATIONAL ACTIVITIES

Presenter, Conference on European Migration to the United States and Canada, 1783-1983. Conference to be held on board the "Queen Elizabeth 2," via England to New York, August, 1994.

Independent scholar/researcher focusing on the works of Charles Rennie Mackintosh, University of Glasgow Hunterian Art Museum, Scotland, and London, England, 1986.

Independent study and travel to most major art centers in Europe and the United States. Guided others and helped develop their interest, knowledge, and enjoyment.

Volunteer, Humanities West, an educational and cultural program funded by the National Endowment for the Arts.

PUBLICATIONS

Wagner, Dorothy, K., *Romantic Motifs in the Work and Life of Charles Rennie Mackintosh*, Mills College Publications, 1987.

Wagner, Dorothy, K., "Loi Fuller, Fairy of Light" and "Lucia Mathews, California Artist," *The Emerging New Woman* (textbook), Mills College Publications, 1985.

AWARDS

Honorable Mention, International photography and essay competition for the Glasgow, Scotland, European City of Culture Celebration, 1990.

Seattle Beautiful Award, Chamber of Commerce, Seattle, WA.

Resume written in 1994.

Natasha Peterson, Ph.D.

882 Clement Street, #17 • San Francisco, CA 94709 • (415) 993-0013

JOB OBJECTIVE

Staff Psychologist

> *Traditional chronological approach makes Natasha appear suitable for a mainstream position.*

EDUCATION

> *Natasha puts her best foot forward by placing her strong education section near the top of the resume.*

Ph.D., California School of Professional Psychology, Berkeley/Alameda, 1992
Doctoral Dissertation: An Examination of Personality Characteristics and Resilience
                           of Offspring of Alcoholics

M.A., California School of Professional Psychology, Berkeley/Alameda, 1987

B.A., Summa Cum Laude, Psychology, University of New Hampshire, Durham, NH, 1983

PROFESSIONAL EXPERIENCE

1994-present APOGEE, INC., Vallejo, CA
Staff Psychologist

- Provide individual and group psychotherapy for adults from diverse socioeconomic
  backgrounds with problems including:

Adjustment disorders	Anxiety disorders
Organic disorders	Character disorders
Mood disorders	Grief

- Collaborate with interdisciplinary team to coordinate psychological services for up to
  40 patients in three skilled nursing facilities.

1991-present PRIVATE PSYCHOTHERAPY PRACTICE, Santa Rosa and San Rafael, CA

- Offer individual, couple, and group psychotherapy, specializing in treatment of adult
  children of alcoholics.
- Conduct psychodiagnostic assessment.

1991-1993 KAISER PERMANENTE MEDICAL CENTER, Santa Rosa, CA
Contract Psychologist, 1993
Post-Doctoral Fellow, 1991-1992

- Conducted brief psychotherapy to a multi-ethnic population:
  - Individual psychotherapy with non-psychotic adults.
  - Group therapy with early adolescent children and adults.
  - Family therapy, focusing primarily on parenting training and couples counseling.
  - Individual play therapy with children experiencing:

Behavioral problems	Separation anxiety
Attention deficit disorders	Depression

- Consulted to medical staff, particularly pediatrics and family practice physicians.
- Performed up to 20 adult intake evaluations per week, as Contract Psychologist.

1988-1991 PACIFIC PRESBYTERIAN MEDICAL CENTER, San Francisco, CA
Staff Outpatient Therapist, 1989-1991
Pre-Doctoral Clinical Psychology Intern, 1988-1989

- Provided psychodynamic individual and group therapy to adults with a wide range of
  acute and chronic disorders.
- Conducted intake interviews, psychodiagnostic assessment, and crisis intervention.
- Participated in seminars, conferences, and grand rounds.

— Continued —

Natasha Peterson, Ph.D.
Page 2

1987-1988   CALIFORNIA STATE UNIVERSITY COUNSELING CENTER, Hayward, CA
Pre-Doctoral Intern
- Offered individual and group therapy, crisis intervention, alcohol and drug counseling, and vocational counseling to a multi-cultural student population.

1986-1987   ALAMEDA FAMILY SERVICE AGENCY, Alameda, CA
Psychology Intern
- Performed needs assessment of mental health services to adults, children, and families.
- Provided individual, marital, family, child, and group psychotherapy, working with a client base comprised largely of Filipino and Hispanic patients.

1984-1985   STRAFFORD GUIDANCE CENTER, Dover, NH
Case Manager
- Facilitated therapeutic/rehabilitative programming in an apartment complex for adults who had multiple psychiatric hospitalizations in the recent past.
- Offered individual therapy and case management for clients with diagnoses ranging from major mental illness to severe personality disorders.

1979-1983   UNIVERSITY OF NEW HAMPSHIRE, Durham, NH
Freshman Camp Counselor
- Organized and executed a freshman orientation program. Led discussion groups and activities to help young adults in their transition from home to independent living.

PROFESSIONAL TRAINING

> Long and impressive list made easy to read by grouping training sessions by type

Psychodynamic Seminars
A Dialogue Between Control Mastery and Self Psychology
Harold Searles, Psychological Forum

Chemical Dependency Training
Adult Children of Alcoholics Workshop
Addictions in the 1980s: Alcohol and Drug Problems and Treatment

Psychogeriatric Training
Skills Development in Psychogeriatrics: A Clinical Approach
Important Developments in the Treatment of Depression and Impulse Control Disorders

Psychological Assessment Workshops
Rorschach Workshop
Psychological Assessment Review Workshop
Psychodiagnostic Assessment Workshop

Family Therapy Workshops
Stepfamily Workshop
Paul and Ellen Wachtel: The Vital Interface: Family Therapy and Individual Therapy
The Family in Transition and Under Stress

Other Workshops
The Evolution of Psychotherapy Conference
Child Abuse Assessment and Reporting
Human Sexuality Workshop
Emergency Services Workshop

— Continued —

LICENSE

Licensed by State of California as Psychologist #PSY13359

PRESENTATIONS

Adult Children of Alcoholics Colloquium, California State University Counseling Center, Hayward, CA

Women and Anger Workshop, University of the Pacific, Stockton, CA

PROFESSIONAL MEMBERSHIPS

American Psychological Association

Redwood Psychological Association

Resume written in 1994.

Lyne Shankin

2677 Cedar Park Road, #203, San Francisco, CA 94118

E-Mail: ShankinL@slipnet.com

Phone: (415) 427-4418 • Fax: (415) 463-7512

Lyne's heading tells the reader she is at ease with three types of communication: e-mail, fax, and phone.

OBJECTIVE

A position as Human Interface Specialist

SUMMARY OF QUALIFICATIONS

- 15-year background in experimental design with recent experience in human interface engineering.
- Expertise in prototyping with MacroMedia Director.
- Organized teamplayer who communicates well with engineers, marketing professionals, graphic designers, and end-users.
- Recipient of UC Berkeley's Outstanding Graduate Student Instructor Award.

EDUCATION

Ph.D. Cognitive Psychology   1994
     University of California, Berkeley, CA

M.S. Audiology and Speech Pathology   1985
     Université de Montréal, Québec, Canada

B.S. Audiology and Speech Pathology   1981
     Université de Montréal, Québec, Canada

Additional Coursework
CCRMA (Center for Computer Research in Music and Acoustics)   1992
     Stanford University, Stanford, CA

Top-notch education that serves as a solid foundation for her objective

RELEVANT EXPERIENCE AND ACCOMPLISHMENTS

HUMAN INTERFACE ENGINEERING

Taligent , Inc.

Powerful achievements are presented in the hybrid based on a functional format. Smart!

- Collaborated with engineers, graphic designers, marketing staff, and psychologists to clarify needs of a thorough three-month usability study of a new operating system.
- Created an interface prototype, using MM Director.
- Led a team of four usability specialists who conducted a structured lab study involving 25 users who represented a wide range of computer literacy.
- Analyzed results and used a team approach to author 34 practical recommendations regarding conceptual, visual, and auditory aspects of the interface.

Streetlight Software, Inc.

- As the first usability study participant, tested navigation and entertainment software that uses the General Magic platform, to be released in early 1995.
- Recommended design improvements and worked with engineers to develop a more focused usability study.

— Continued —

"Continued" at the bottom of pages 1 and 2

Lyne Shankin

Page 2

(Lyne's name and page number at the top of pages 2 and 3)

EXPERIMENT DESIGN AND RESEARCH

Auditory Research Laboratory, University of California, Berkeley
- Designed and implemented several participant studies on:
  - Expectation and how it changes with familiarity of subject matter.
  - Pitch and music perception.
- Wrote several computer programs that synthesized complex auditory stimuli.
- Presented study results at two scientific conferences and numerous UC Berkeley and Stanford University seminars.

Psychoacoustics Laboratory, Northeastern University
- Developed a research strategy that achieved quantitative results in a highly subjective psychological study.

Dept. of Speech Pathology & Audiology, Université de Montréal
- Participated in a clinical study of the effect of general anesthesia on the middle ear system, which led to the development of an alternative technique for anesthesia.

WORK HISTORY

Human Interface Specialist — 1994
Streetlight Software, Inc., San Francisco, CA

Experiment Designer and Researcher — 1985-94
Auditory Research Laboratory, University of California, Berkeley, CA

Usability Specialist — 1993
Human Interface Team, Taligent, Inc., Cupertino, CA

Graduate Student Instructor — 1985-91
Psychology Department, University of California, Berkeley, CA

Lecturer — 1984-85
Dept. of Speech Pathology & Audiology, Université de Montréal, Québec, Canada

Research Assistant — 1980-82, 83-85
Dept. of Speech Pathology & Audiology, Université de Montréal, Québec, Canada

Research Assistant — 1982-83
Psychoacoustics Laboratory, Northeastern University, Boston, MA

COMPUTER EXPERIENCE

Systems: Apple Macintosh, IBM (DOS and Windows), NeXT
Prototyping: MacroMedia Director
Programming: Pascal

— Continued —

238

Lyne Shankin

Page 3

PUBLICATIONS

Shankin, L. (1993). Melodic expectancy in L.B. Meyer's theory of musical meaning. Proceedings of the *SMPC (Society for Music Perception & Cognition)*.conference, June 1993.

Hafter, E.R., Saberi, K., Schlauch, R.S., Shankin, L. & Tang, J. (1992). Use of stimulus pre-cues to study processing at various levels of auditory and musical processing. Program of the *Second International Conference on Music Perception and Cognition*, 8.

Hafter, E.R., Saberi, K., Shankin, L. & Jensen, E. (1991). Selective attention in auditory detection. *Bulletin of the Psychonomic Society*, 32 (4).

Shankin, L. & Hafter, E. (1990). Selective attention in absolute pitch listeners. *J. A. S. A.*, 88 (S49).

Shankin, L. (1988). The subjective size of musical intervals. *J. A. S. A.*, 83 (S51).

Hafter, E.R. & Shankin, L. (1986). Detection of specific periods in a random sequence. *J. A. S A.*, 80 (S92).

Perreault, L., Normandin, N., Shankin, L. et al. (1982). Tympanic membrane rupture after anesthesia with nitrous oxide. *Anesthesiology*, 57 (4).

Perreault, L., Normandin, N., Shankin, L. et al. (1982). Middle ear pressure variations during nitrous oxide and oxygen anaesthesia. *Can. Anaesth. Soc. J.*, 29 (5).

Normandin, N., Shankin, L. et al. (1981). Admittance of the middle ear system under general anesthesia. *J. Acoust. Soc. Am.*, 69 (S14).

Resume written in 1994.

239

Create Your CV!

Now that you've got your feet wet, it's time to jump in. Create strong sections in your CV by using the concepts presented in Part 2. With the additional sections mentioned in this chapter, your CV is likely to run several pages—all of which should be numbered and have a "Continued" at the bottom.

The Least You Need to Know

➤ "Curriculum vita" is the term used in academic and scientific communities to mean "resume."

➤ CVs are usually longer than two pages (and may be as long as seven pages), and frequently don't include a job objective statement.

➤ You can use either a chronological, functional, achievement, hybrid based on a chronological, or hybrid based on a functional format, but keep it conservative in presentation and language for most uses.

➤ Additional sections that might work well on your CV include "Publications" and "Awards and Honors."

➤ Be sure to number all pages and include "Continued" at the bottom of all except the last page.

Chapter 16

Spread Your Net Far and Wide

In This Chapter

➤ What is a networking card?

➤ Using networking cards to beat the business card strategy

➤ Educate your friends and associates about your job search

➤ How to create dynamite networking cards

You've done a lot of work putting together your resume. You've defined your job objective, articulated your professional qualifications, and brainstormed your relevant achievements. Doesn't it feel great to see your best attributes laid out on paper? Now you can take all that information and turn it into another terrific marketing tool—the *networking card*.

In this chapter, you discover how simple it is to create a networking card, and how to use this card to help spread the word about your job search.

Beat the Business Card Strategy With Networking Cards

How many times have you gotten home from a party, professional meeting, or other networking event, pulled a bunch of business cards out of your pocket, and couldn't figure out for the life of you who most of them represented? That's what happens to me. I throw them all away except the few that conjure up an image of someone. Now, if *your* business card had been in my pocket, it very well could have gotten tossed, unless you'd put something on it to jog my memory. And that's the idea behind a networking card.

A networking card is a hybrid between a resume and a business card. It's an ideal marketing tool when a resume is too long and a business card doesn't say enough. You can design it to fit your special purpose, whether that's to find a particular job or to explore career options.

Educate Your Network

> **Warning**
> A networking card is not a substitute for a resume. It's a marketing tool in its own right. When asked to submit a resume, send the real thing, not a networking card. And when sending out your resume, there's no need to include a networking card.

Remember the networking story I was telling you way back in Chapter 1? (The guy comes out of his house one morning and tells the garbage collector he got laid off. The garbage collector then puts him in touch with someone who lives around the corner, and our lead character gets the perfect job.) Networking really *does* work—sometimes in the most unexpected ways. Capitalize on every word-of-mouth opportunity by arming your friends, relatives, and allies with your networking cards so that when someone asks them a tricky question like "What exactly does your friend do?" your spokesperson can look at your networking card and respond intelligently. You got it: it's a cheat sheet!

Creating Your Network Card

Here's how to make your networking card: After writing your resume, decide what your most marketable information is and transfer it onto a 5-1/2 × 4-inch (or smaller) format. Information can include your job objective, education, work history, or highlights of qualifications, depending on what is most relevant. Print on card stock and they're ready to go!

In the first example that follows, Terri wasn't sure exactly what type of marketing position she wanted. So she wrote a resume and networking card that emphasized the skills she wanted to use, rather than a job objective. She got many interviews and landed a job that an employer created just for her.

Terri's resume is followed by five resumes for other job seekers and their matching networking cards and letterhead. Notice that the topics for each card are not all the same. The headings were selected according to the job seeker's particular qualifications.

> **YOU'RE HIRED.** **Tip**
> A nice touch to your resume presentation is matching letterhead. Letterhead is easy to create. If you're working on a computer, duplicate your resume and delete all the text except the heading. If you're not working on a computer, cut the heading off your finished resume and paste it onto a blank sheet, then have it printed or copied.

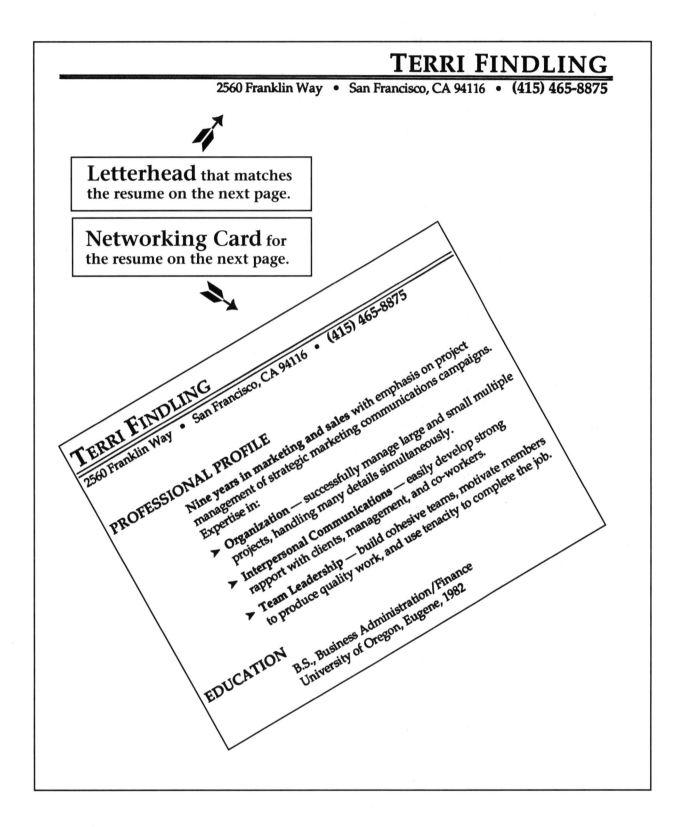

Letterhead that matches the resume on the next page.

Networking Card for the resume on the next page.

TERRI FINDLING

2560 Franklin Way • San Francisco, CA 94116 • **(415) 465-8875**

PROFESSIONAL PROFILE

Nine years in marketing and sales with emphasis on project management of strategic marketing communications campaigns. Expertise in:

➤ **Organization** — successfully manage large and small multiple projects, handling many details simultaneously.

➤ **Interpersonal Communications** — easily develop strong rapport with clients, management, and co-workers.

➤ **Team Leadership** — build cohesive teams, motivate members to produce quality work, and use tenacity to complete the job.

EXPERIENCE

1991-1992 **Marketing Communications Consultant**
HEWLETT-PACKARD COMPANY, Mountain View, CA

- Managed marketing communications projects for the $3 billion Worldwide Customer Support Division.
- Oversaw collateral development, direct marketing campaigns, and testimonial programs.

Accomplishments
➤ Developed creative strategy for dealer end-user literature accompanying the "Certified Workstation Reseller" program rollout.

➤ Produced analysis of the market position of key competitors (DEC, IBM, EDS), used as a guideline for sales brochure for major program launch.

➤ Drove development of *The Competitive Support Field Guide*, a 150-page compendium of 32 competitors, detailing support services and key selling points.

1988-1990 **Account Manager**
ORACLE CORPORATION, Redwood Shores, CA

- Drove entire process for creation of sales and collateral materials for this $1 billion software company.
- Managed 20 projects simultaneously, including: brochures, logos, and signage.

Accomplishments
➤ Co-developed strategy and directed production of *Distributed Solutions Guide*, a $250,000 brochure which successfully targeted select Fortune 500 senior managers.

➤ Enhanced Oracle's public image by serving as company liaison to "The Human Race," a non-profit fundraiser. Collaborated with government officials, culturally diverse volunteers, and internal staff to promote the event.

1983-1988 **Senior Account Executive**
CPG INTERNATIONAL (a Times-Mirror subsidiary), San Francisco, CA

- Managed public relations for this $80 million art materials manufacturer.
- Directed company services for a seven-state territory billing $2.75 million.

Accomplishment
➤ Planned and implemented "Bay Area Blitz" campaign. Result: sales increased 15%.

EDUCATION

B.S., Business Administration/Finance, University of Oregon, Eugene, 1982

Resume written in 1994.

HAROLD BUZWELL

(443) 826-9937 • 6625 Sandlewood Street • Oakmont, CA 99832

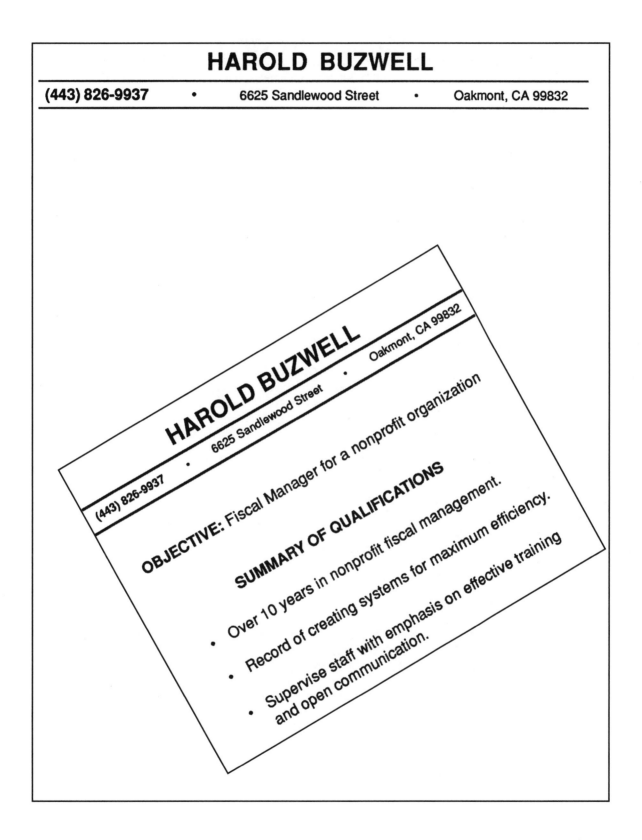

HAROLD BUZWELL   Oakmont, CA 99832

(443) 826-9937 • 6625 Sandlewood Street

OBJECTIVE: Fiscal Manager for a nonprofit organization

SUMMARY OF QUALIFICATIONS

- Over 10 years in nonprofit fiscal management.
- Record of creating systems for maximum efficiency.
- Supervise staff with emphasis on effective training and open communication.

HAROLD BUZWELL

(443) 826-9937	•	6625 Sandlewood Street	•	Oakmont, CA 99832

OBJECTIVE: A position as Fiscal Manager for a nonprofit organization

SUMMARY OF QUALIFICATIONS

- More than 10 years experience in nonprofit fiscal management.
- Record of creating, implementing, and maintaining systems for maximum efficiency and accuracy.
- Cooperative spirit that contributes to the organization's goals.
- Ability to supervise staff with an emphasis on effective training and open communication.
- B.S. degree in Business Administration.

PROFESSIONAL EXPERIENCE

1986-present *FISCAL MANAGER / FINANCIAL CONSULTANT*

- Provided bookkeeping and accounting services to nonprofit organizations and small businesses. Services included:
  - All phases of bookkeeping through financial statements.
  - Budget preparation/monitoring and cash flow management.
  - Reporting to government and private funding agencies.
  - Evaluation and upgrading of financial systems.
  - Accounting software selection and installation.
  - Development and maintenance of internal controls.
  - Payroll, A/R, A/P, and tax preparation.
- Clients included:

Oakmont Community Music Center	St. Francis Center
Pleasanton Community Counseling	Health Care Works
Make-A-Theatre	Pacfic West Restaurant

1980-85 *FINANCIAL MANAGER / ADMINISTRATOR*
THE MISSION FOUNDATION, San Diego, CA

- Managed all internal financial and administrative functions including:
  - Grants program and loan fund administration.
  - General finance and accounting.
  - Staff supervision.
- Developed policies and procedures that facilitated smooth operations.

1979-80 *FULL CHARGE BOOKKEEPER*
ANSEL POWELL, C.P.A., San Diego, CA

- Performed all phases of bookkeeping for a clientele of small businesses.

EDUCATION

B.S., Business Administration, Golden West University, 1991
Accounting Program, San Diego State University

Workshops for Nonprofit Organizations:

Budgeting	Accounting Software	Insurance Requirements
Cash Management	Fundraising Software	Legal Requirements

Resume written in 1995.

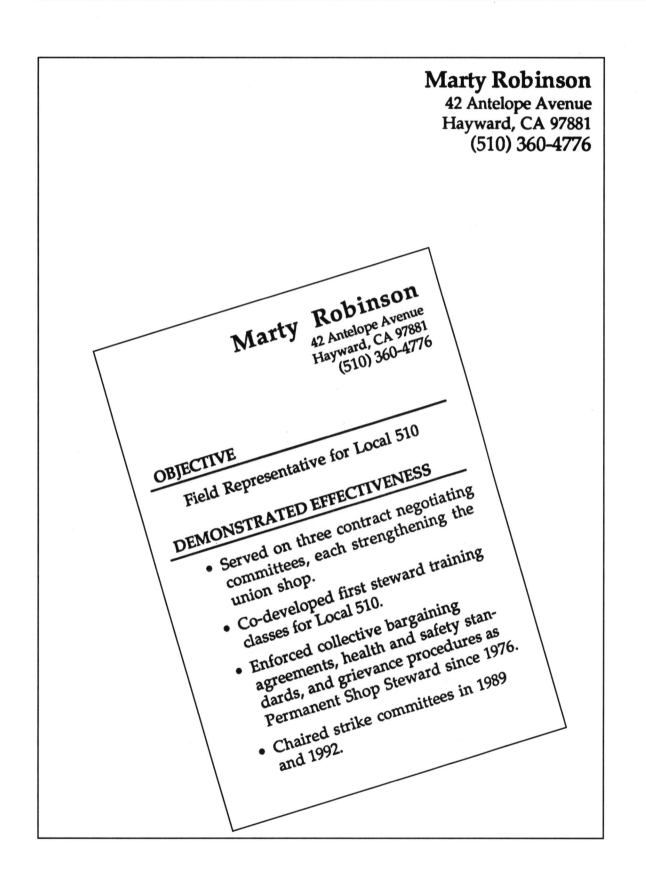

Marty Robinson
42 Antelope Avenue
Hayward, CA 97881
(510) 360-4776

Marty Robinson
42 Antelope Avenue
Hayward, CA 97881
(510) 360-4776

OBJECTIVE

Field Representative for Local 510

DEMONSTRATED EFFECTIVENESS

- Served on three contract negotiating committees, each strengthening the union shop.
- Co-developed first steward training classes for Local 510.
- Enforced collective bargaining agreements, health and safety standards, and grievance procedures as Permanent Shop Steward since 1976.
- Chaired strike committees in 1989 and 1992.

Marty Robinson
42 Antelope Avenue
Hayward, CA 97881
(510) 360-4776

OBJECTIVE

Field Representative for Local 510

DEMONSTRATED EFFECTIVENESS

- Effectively negotiated and arbitrated grievances and contracts.
  - Served on three contract negotiating committees, each strengthening the union shop.
  - Co-developed first steward training classes for Local 510.
  - Enforced collective bargaining agreements, health and safety standards, and grievance procedures as Rotating Floor Steward or Permanent Shop Steward since 1976.
- Chaired strike committees in 1989 and 1992, developing picketing plans, choosing picket captains, and informing membership of legal behavior on the picket line.
- Co-developed and led Local 510 affirmative action workshops, using bilingual and biculturals skills to stress commonalties among people.
- Conducted training and strategy sessions for U. C. labor and academic professionals, resulting in Partnership Programs.

WORK HISTORY

1973-present **Journeyman Installer**
SIGN, DISPLAY, AND ALLIED CRAFTS, LOCAL 510, I.B.P.A.T.

1990 **Primary Campaign Manager**
WILSON RILES, JR., MAYORAL CANDIDATE, OAKLAND

1987-90 **Teacher,World Cultures/Spanish/Bilingual**
OAKLAND UNIFIED SCHOOL DISTRICT

EDUCATION

B.A., Comparative Culture, University of California, Irvine, 1973

Graduate Studies, Latin American Culture, Stanford University

MEMBERSHIPS

Alameda County Central Labor Council
Local 510 Political Action Committee
Oakland Direct Action Committee
Former Member, A.P.R.I & C.B. T.U.

Resume written in 1995.

Marilyn P. Jenkins
1075 Fransisco Place, Apt. 4
San Diego, CA 93021
(883) 429-7406

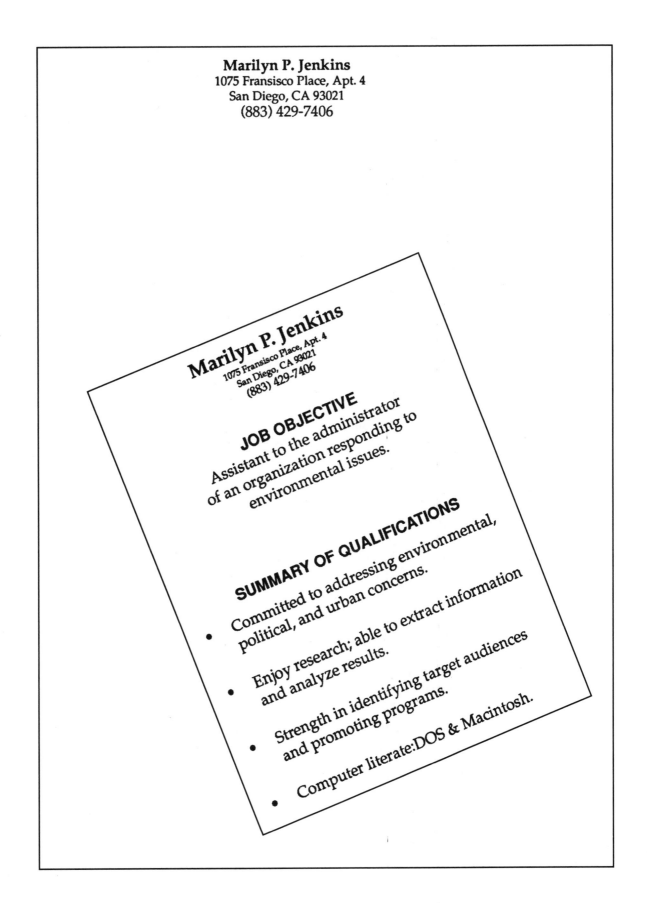

Marilyn P. Jenkins
1075 Fransisco Place, Apt. 4
San Diego, CA 99021
(883) 429-7406

JOB OBJECTIVE

Assistant to the administrator of an organization responding to environmental issues.

SUMMARY OF QUALIFICATIONS

Committed to addressing environmental, political, and urban concerns.

- Enjoy research; able to extract information and analyze results.

- Strength in identifying target audiences and promoting programs.

- Computer literate:DOS & Macintosh.

Marilyn P. Jenkins
1075 Fransisco Place, Apt. 4
San Diego, CA 93021
(883) 429-7406

JOB OBJECTIVE
An assistant to the administrator of an organization responding to environmental issues.

SUMMARY OF QUALIFICATIONS
- Committed to addressing environmental, political, and urban concerns.
- Enjoy research; able to extract information and analyze results.
- Strength in identifying target audiences and promoting programs.
- Record of maintaining professional relations through consistent follow up.
- Computer literate in DOS & Macintosh.

RELEVANT ACCOMPLISHMENTS

RESEARCH
Forest Island Project:
- Successfully used resources and interviewing techniques to research the health food industry in respect to ecological issues.
- Researched the effects of tourism on the environment and the benefits of sustainable tourism.

Orlie, Hill and Cundall:
- Conducted market research and presented a successful marketing plan for client's hotel/restaurant.

PROMOTIONS
- Developed national distribution network and coordinated promotion schedule for Old Chicago Foods (health food manufacturer).
- Organized Resta Studio's art exhibitions in San Francisco; handled promotions including local media contacts and mailings.
- Traveled nation-wide to trade shows and prospective market areas for both Old Chicago Foods and Resta Studio.
- As Chairperson of Public Relations Committee, doubled the previous year's attendance of Golden Gate University Marketing Career Day.

ENVIRONMENTAL INVOLVEMENT
- Photographed the United Nations Conference on Environment and Development (UNCED) in San Francisco for the U.S. Citizen Network.
- Currently working on photo documentary defining the political imbalance between business and environmental interests.

RELEVANT WORK HISTORY
Concurrent with Education:

1996	Intern	Forest Island Project (environmental project), Berkeley, CA
1993-1995	Artist Representative	Resta Studio Maui, San Francisco, CA
1992	Intern	Orlie, Hill and Cundall (direct marketing), Sausalito, CA

Previous Experience:

1988-92	Sales Representative	Old Chicago Foods, Petaluma, CA

EDUCATION
B.A., Business and Humanities, Golden Gate University, San Francisco, CA, June 1992

Resume written in 1996.

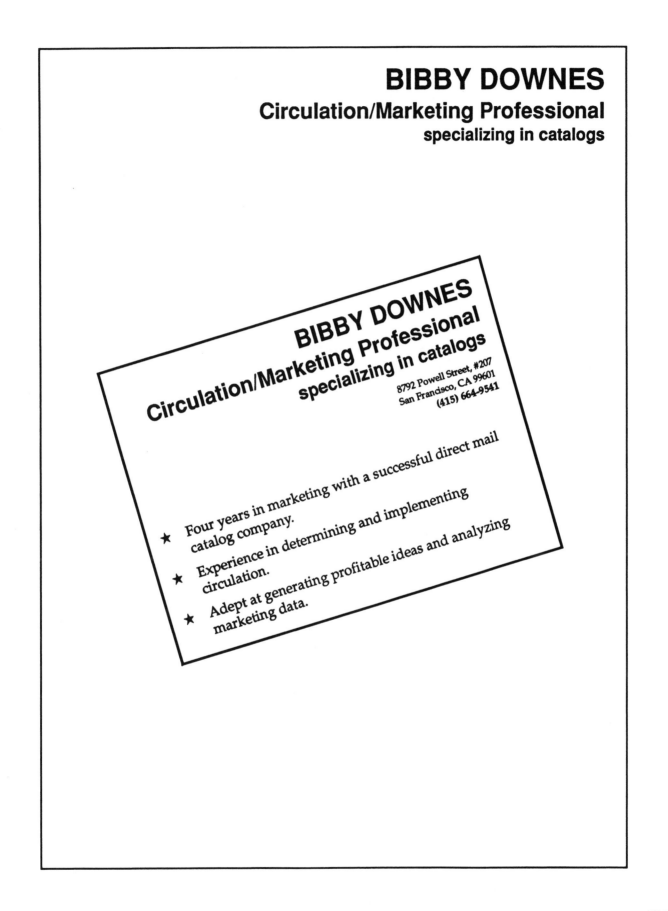

BIBBY DOWNES
Circulation/Marketing Professional
specializing in catalogs

BIBBY DOWNES
Circulation/Marketing Professional
specializing in catalogs

8792 Powell Street, #207
San Francisco, CA 99601
(415) 664-9541

★ Four years in marketing with a successful direct mail catalog company.

★ Experience in determining and implementing circulation.

★ Adept at generating profitable ideas and analyzing marketing data.

BIBBY DOWNES
Circulation/Marketing Professional
specializing in catalogs

8792 Powell Street, #207
San Francisco, CA 99601
(415) 664-9541

★ Four years in marketing with a successful direct mail catalog company.

★ Experience in determining and implementing circulation.

★ Adept at generating profitable ideas and analyzing marketing data.

PROFESSIONAL ACCOMPLISHMENTS
As Marketing Coordinator at Backroads Bicycle Touring

MARKETING

- Designed a media campaign which, in one year, increased coverage from 218 to 500 free placements.
- Supervised photographers and edited photographs for 64-page color catalog that won eight catalog awards including two CATALOG AGE Gold Awards and one Caples Award.
- Developed targeted marketing program that increased annual travel agency bookings from 300 to 1000 in two years.
- Analyzed marketing data using Lotus 1-2-3, which helped decrease cost per order by 20%.
- Assisted in developing a computer program that tracked demographics of the customer base.
- Supervised advertising program; researched media options, worked with designers, placed ads, and tracked results.

CIRCULATION

- Directed service bureau.
- Selected lists to rent; tracked results and analyzed effectiveness.
- Assisted in determining literature projections.
- Served as liaison to outside list manager.

WORK HISTORY

1988-present	Marketing Coordinator	BACKROADS BICYCLE TOURING, INC., Berkeley
1986-88	Sales Consultant	CHICAGO BOARD OF TRADE TRAVEL, Chicago
1983-86	Computer Programmer Analyst	FIRST NATIONAL BANK OF CHICAGO, Chicago

PROFESSIONAL AFFILIATIONS

• Northern California Catalog Club   • DirectNet   • Toastmasters

EDUCATION

B.A., Business Administration, Dean's List, GPA 3.6, 1982
Colorado College, Colorado Springs, CO

Computer Career Program (Completed with distinction), 1983
De Paul University, Chicago

Resume written in 1993.

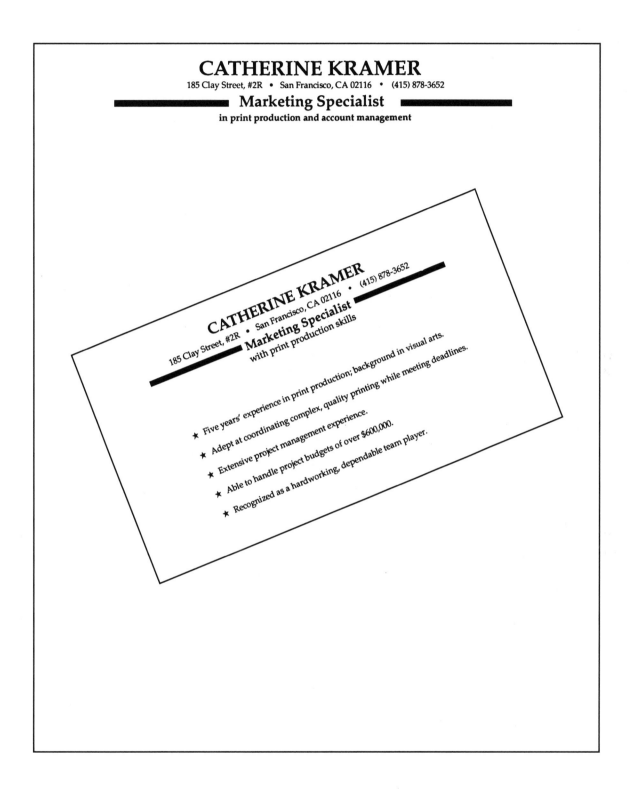

CATHERINE KRAMER
185 Clay Street, #2R • San Francisco, CA 02116 • (415) 878-3652
Marketing Specialist
in print production and account management

CATHERINE KRAMER
185 Clay Street, #2R • San Francisco, CA 02116 • (415) 878-3652
Marketing Specialist
with print production skills

★ Five years' experience in print production; background in visual arts.

★ Adept at coordinating complex, quality printing while meeting deadlines.

★ Extensive project management experience.

★ Able to handle project budgets of over $600,000.

★ Recognized as a hardworking, dependable team player.

CATHERINE KRAMER

185 Clay Street, #2R • San Francisco, CA 02116 • (415) 878-3652

■ Marketing Specialist ■

with print production skills

★ Five years' experience in print production with a background in visual arts.
★ Adept at coordinating complex, quality printing while meeting deadlines.
★ Extensive project management experience.
★ Able to handle project budgets of over $600,000.
★ Recognized as a hardworking, dependable team player.

EXPERIENCE

1992-95   *Production Coordinator*, **Corporate Communications Department**
THE CHICAGO CONSULTING GROUP, INC., Chicago, IL
Supervised the print production of all marketing materials for this worldwide management consulting firm.
• Oversaw the research, design, production, and implementation of new logo, establishing corporate identity among all 19 international offices ($600,000 project).
• Managed the production of a six-color brochure containing illustrations, debossing, embossing, and foil stamping ($100,000 project).
• Hired and managed designers and print vendors, ensuring both quality and cost-effectiveness.
Projects included: Brochures   Monthly Perspectives
                      Press Kits   Publication Reprints
                      Monthly Newsletters Advertisements
• Supervised and signed-off on press runs to be sure exact specifications were met.
• Managed large conference mailings of up to 20,000 pieces.
• Utilized Microsoft Word and Aldus Pagemaker for preliminary layout work.

1990-92   *Publications Coordinator*
HILLS COUNTRY DAY SCHOOL, Evanston, IL
Oversaw all print production in the Alumni/Development Office.
• Designed the Alumni Newsletter, promoting an image of active, contributing alumni.
• Photographed parent-student and trustee activities for the newsletter.
• Created the school calendar, incorporating my photography and design.
• Produced event invitations, contribution requests, flyers, and posters.

1989-90   *Sales Representative, Sport Division*
THE GAP ., Chicago, IL
Handled sales/marketing of Gap clothing in 32 specialty stores.
• Presented seasonal lines, promoting multiple units that increased sales.
• Followed through on deliveries and displays to maximize sales.
• Conducted seminars for store managers on profitable merchandising.

1988   *Media Coordinator*
THOMAS, WILDS & FREEDMAN (advertising agency), Chicago, IL
• Prepared magazine and newspaper cost studies and surveys used to develop advertising strategies for clients such as Converse and Ocean Spray.

EDUCATION

BA, Government, minor in Visual Arts (photography)
Bowdoin College, Brunswick, ME, 1987
Senior year internship with graphic artist
Photography and Painting Courses
California College of Arts and Crafts, Oakland, CA, Summer '84

Resume written in 1995.

The Least You Need to Know

➤ A networking card is a hybrid between a resume and a business card.

➤ Your networking card gives friends and relatives a way to pass along information about you, even if they don't understand exactly what you do.

➤ Your networking card should contain only the absolutely most marketable information you have to offer a potential employer.

Part 4
Keeping Up With Technology

Seems like once there's momentum, there's no stopping a speeding object. (Isn't there a physics law that runs something like that?) In your case, that object is your resume. It's time for your fabulous marketing tool to get out there and reap results!

You probably already have a plan for getting your resume plastered all over town using the U.S. postal service. But you may not know that there's another exciting way to get your resume to prospective employers faster than ever—through the Internet. That's right, you can get your resume to prospective employers from the comfort of your cozy home!

So sit down at your computer and let your cyberfingers do the walking through the career section of your on-line directory. In Part 4 you learn how to prepare a resume for your cyberspace job search. You also learn about resume scanning technology that your resume may encounter once it reaches the employer's desk.

Chapter 17

Resume Scanning: Who's Reading Your Resume?

In This Chapter

➤ What is resume scanning?

➤ Identifying companies that use resume scanning

➤ Understanding the employer's side of resume scanning

➤ The pros and cons of resume scanning

It may seem Orwellian, but it's here: resume scanning software to help personnel departments manage their flood of resumes. The software "reads" each resume in a few minutes, identifies key words, and stores the resume electronically as a database file. Wait a minute, what happened to the humans in the Human Resources department? Well, that's just the point—now there don't have to be as many people to process the resume stacks each day.

Know What You're Getting Into

Because resume scanning systems are expensive, only very large companies use them. (Usually a company has to be 1,000 employees-strong before the scanning software is cost-effective.) So if you're applying to a large company, you may need to know how to adapt your resume to be scanned.

How do you know if you need to adjust your resume for a scanning encounter? Just call the Human Resources department of the company where you'd like to work and

Warning
Don't underline words on your electronic resume. A scanner can't interpret a word if any letter in that word intersects with a line. For example, notice how the letter "y" touches the line that underlines "<u>day</u>." If that happens on your resume, you lose, since the computer won't "understand" the "y" character.

ask if they use resume scanning. If they say "no," the resume you've created using this book will work great. If they say "yes," ask them if they can mail, fax, or e-mail you a set of guidelines so you can create your resume for their system.

> **Warning**
>
> Resume scanners have a tendency to interpret dates in the Education section in a rather peculiar way. They assume that if there are two dates given for a degree (for example, B.A., 1989–1993), you did not receive your degree. To make sure you get credit for your degree accomplishment, put only the year of completion, (for example, B.A., 1993), and the scanner will "understand" that you have your degree.

The Inside Scoop

Here's how it works on the employer's end: When your resume arrives in the mail, it won't be read by human eyes—instead, it'll be placed facedown in a scanner (which looks sort of like a photocopier). The resume will be "scanned" with software that can transform your resume text into a form-like document that slips into its database. By the time the scanner is done, your information will no longer look anything like the resume you sent. In fact, the paper resume you sent will most likely be taken out of the scanner and thrown away.

Once your "resume" is in the company's database, your information can be accessed by hiring managers throughout the organization (and in some cases that means nationwide). A manager can ask the scanning application to look for up to 60 key words for each available position. Key words might indicate job title, technical expertise, education, geographic location, and employment history. The computer then goes through its database, matches resumes with the designated key words, and even ranks the selected candidates against each other.

Listing Key Words

Brainstorm what key words the employer would likely program into the software, then insert those words into the text appropriately. Since it's unlikely that you'll be able to find out exactly what key words are being programmed into the computer to search for a candidate, just try to create a list of words that you think the hiring manager will select. The following examples may help:

➤ A list of key words for a systems analyst might look like this:

Systems: Novell networks and telecommunications. Retail point-of-sale. Manufacturing. Wholesale and distribution. Inventory management. Bar code and data collection technology. Imaging. Database management.

Payroll. Accounting. **Software:** UNIX. MS-DOS. Novell. Thoroughbred O/S. Business Basic. Lotus 1-2-3. WordPerfect. Windows. dBase/FoxPro. ACT. **Nontechnical:** Team. Communication. Presentations. Project management. Spanish. Writing.

➤ A resume for a staff nurse might be scanned for these key words:

Units: Geriatrics. MCH. Med./Surg. Psychiatric. OB/GYN. High-risk OB/GYN. **Diseases:** Diabetes. Cancer. ESR. Hypertension. Pneumonia. Ulcerative colitis. Arthritis. CVA. Angina. AIDS. **Post-operative care:** GYN. Orthopedic. Medical. **IV therapy:** Central line. Peripheral. **Medication administration:** PO. SQ. IM.

Pros and Cons of Scanning

Your mind is probably already racing ahead to the pros and cons of going through a resume scanning system. Here are my thoughts on the subject.

Advantages

➤ As long as your resume contains the key words the employer has asked the scanner to find, you will be considered for the job. For example: If you don't have the required B.A., but you have the equivalent or are about to complete a B.A., you can state it in those terms: "B.A. equivalent," or "Currently enrolled in B.A. program," or "20 units toward B.A." As long as "B.A." is there, it will pass the scanner's test and give you a chance for human consideration.

➤ Even if you haven't used the exact title the employer is looking for in the job objective statement, you can still be considered for a position if the right skills (that is, the right key words) are represented in the content of your resume.

➤ Resume scanning ensures that all resumes are evaluated consistently. Some human resources personnel look at only the first 50 resumes in a stack of 200 and throw the rest away. By using the scanner, all resumes are evaluated impartially.

➤ Since resumes are in a database, all company departments can access them to find candidates. This increases your chances of being considered for more than one job.

➤ Employers are less likely to misplace your resume when it has been stored in a computer.

➤ Longer resumes are acceptable—up to three pages. Having more pages enables you to include as much information as possible to catch the scanner's attention and to use larger type to ensure scannability.

Disadvantages

➤ Some feel resume scanning dehumanizes the hiring process for both you and the employer. Before the resume can be seen by a person, it first has to pass the test of a computer—a cold approach to "human" resources.

➤ If particular key words aren't in the resume, it won't prompt a positive response, even if the text contains the meaning behind those words. For instance, if the computer is asked to find a particular acronym (such as CPA) and you have written out the full name for the acronym (Certified Public Accountant), the scanning program won't pick it up. You need to use the terminology the employer is likely to ask for.

➤ Since resumes are stored electronically, not in hard copy, appealing graphics won't matter. By the time a living, breathing employer reads your resume, it will have been scanned and reproduced by the computer, using its own fonts and formats.

➤ Scanners have trouble reading type on colored paper (even gray), and easily misinterpret unusual type faces, italics, and underlined words. They also have difficulty with dot-matrix printing.

➤ Scanning programs are used to read cover letters. So even your finest efforts to create a personal touch may be in vain.

Go For It

If you decide you need to create an electronic resume, turn to the next chapter where I've written a step-by-step guide for creating a resume for scanner and on-line channels.

But first, take a look at the following resumes that have been designed specifically to be scanned.

John Adelman

134 Post Road • Burlingame, California 99378   Home: (312) 870-3195 • Work: (312) 006-8295

JOB OBJECTIVE: A position in Human Resources with a focus on Benefits Administration.

SUMMARY OF QUALIFICATIONS

- Eight years experience in human resources-related positions.
- Two years in benefits administration.
- Designer and director of highly successful corporate wellness program.
- Currently enrolled in SFSU Human Resources Management Certificate Program.

John's scannable resume uses Palatino font—one of the easier fonts for a scanner to decipher.

PROFESSIONAL ACCOMPLISHMENTS

EMPLOYEE BENEFITS

White & Johnson

- Designed and produced firmwide Wellness Program including a 14-vendor Health Fair, health education newsletters and speakers, health risk assessments, and blood pressure and cholesterol testing. Created and chaired 12-member Wellness Committee.
- Played key role in restructuring insurance benefits, as member of Insurance Advisory Committee. Co-developed employee communications regarding program changes.
- Wrote and produced quarterly benefits newsletter, which increased employee awareness of preventive medicine and cost-effective utilization of health coverage.
- Analyzed childcare needs and presented findings that resulted in firm's participation in pilot emergency childcare program.

Nellson Enterprises

- Successfully handled complex insurance claims and appeals.

PERSONNEL ADMINISTRATION

White & Johnson

- Co-developed new vacation leave policy and introduced options through large staff presentations and written communications.
- Served on Quality Awareness Team and developed telephone skills training series.
- Assisted in organizing safety awareness programs and staff CPR/First Aid training.

Nellson Enterprises, Sanders Realty, and Center for Teacher Education

- Hired and supervised teams of up to 20 professionals, involving performance evaluations and employee relations.

PROGRAM COORDINATION

- Designed and produced educational programs and events for St. Paul's Episcopal Church, Paramount Middle School, and Los Alamo Primary School.

WORK HISTORY

1987-present Wellness Program Administrator/Legal Secretary, White & Johnson, Tiburon, CA
1984-1986   Staffing and Insurance Claims Manager, Nellson Enterprises, Santa Fe, NM
1982-1983   Executive Secretary, State Bar of California, San Francisco, CA
1978-1982   Personnel and Sales Manager, Sanders Realty, San Francisco, CA
1975-1978   Administrator and Teacher, Center for Teacher Education, San Francisco, CA

EDUCATION AND AFFILIATION

San Francisco State University
Human Resources Management Certificate Program, currently enrolled
B.A., 1976   Graduate Studies, 1977
Member, Northern California Human Resources Council

To indicate that John received his degree, he wrote only the date of completion.

Resume written in 1994.

263

J. Thomas Boris

2088 Telegraph Ave. • Berkeley, CA 94707 • (510) 443-5462

> Thomas learned that the university he had in mind uses resume scanning, so he created a resume to suit their scanning system.

JOB OBJECTIVE: University Registrar

SUMMARY OF QUALIFICATIONS

- Thorough understanding of Admissions and Records from more than 10 years in Office of Registrar positions reaching from clerical to administrative levels.
- Experienced with a number of college/university database systems.
- Skilled at building rapport with interdepartmental constituents.

PROFESSIONAL EXPERIENCE

1993-present OHLONE COLLEGE, Fremont, CA
Director of Admissions and Records (Registrar)
- Manage the Office of Admissions and Records for this community college with student enrollment of 10,000.
- Monitor and report changes in enrollment to State Chancellor's Office to determine level of college funding.
- Provide database management for admissions, touch-tone and in-person registration, permanent records, transcripts, and degree/graduation audits.
- Direct the consolidation of user access to student academic data, in keeping with federal privacy provisions.
- Serve on several committees and act as resource to college committees, administrators, faculty, and staff.
- Publish the course directory for the fall and spring semesters and summer session.
- Advise students of diverse populations regarding academic options.

1992-1993 LAS POSITAS COLLEGE, Livermore, CA
Registrar
- As the first registrar, created and managed Office of Admissions and Records for this community college with 5,000 students.
- Participated in college-wide decision-making, as member of the administrative committee comprised of the president, dean of instruction, dean of student services, and associate deans.
- Coordinated the conversion of existing management information system to on-line integrated database system to coincide with change to semester calendar.
- Implemented a successful international student program.

1988-1991 REGIS UNIVERSITY, Denver, CO
Assistant Registrar, 1990-1991
Learner Relations Coordinator, 1989-1990
Transfer Credit Evaluator, 1988-1989
- Established and managed a fully functioning Registrar's Office on a new satellite campus composed entirely of international students.
- Coordinated the development of a computer link between satellite and main campuses.
- Managed class scheduling and publication of course directory and college bulletin.
- Generated college and federal enrollment reports.
- Trained and supervised staff on college transfer policies and evaluations.
- Revised the Regis University Transfer Guide.
- Certified students for athletic eligibility.

— Continued —

J. Thomas Boris
Page 2

1985-1987   **FRESNO PACIFIC COLLEGE**, Fresno, CA
               Transcript Clerk, Office of the Registrar

1982-1985   **PORTERVILLE COLLEGE**, Porterville, CA
               Office Clerk, Office of Admissions and Records

> "MBA in progress"—a good thing to be on Thomas' resume since he wants to be considered for a job requiring an MBA.

EDUCATION

M.B.A. Program in progress, Liberty University, Lynchburg, VA

B.A., Business Administration, *Cum Laude,* Fresno Pacific College, Fresno, CA, 1987

AACRAO Seminars: Enrollment Management
                      International Student Services
                      Records Management

PROFESSIONAL AFFILIATIONS

NAFSA, Association of International Educators, 1991-present

California Association of Community College Registrars and Admissions Officers, 1991-present

Rocky Mountain Association of Collegiate Registrars and Admissions Officers, 1988-1990

> Resume written in 1995.

265

P e d r o   V a l e n c i a

6 Main Drive, #449 • Oakland, CA 94808 • (510) 876-4654

Pedro used a hybrid based on a chronological resume to market himself. He used 12 pt. Palatino font with minimal formatting.

JOB OBJECTIVE

Process or Device Engineer

EDUCATION

1991 - 1994   University of California, Berkeley
B.S., Electrical Engineering and Computer Science, August 1994
B.S., Materials Science and Engineering, August 1994

1989 - 1991   Foothill College, Los Altos Hills, CA
Engineering Major

He placed his Education section near the top of his resume to indicate that he has been a full-time student since 1989 when his work history stopped.

PROFESSIONAL EXPERIENCE

1975 - 1989   Intel Corporation, Folsom, CA and Santa Clara, CA
Line Maintenance Supervisor, 1988 - 1989
Senior-Level Electronics Technician, 1984 - 1988
Wafer Fab Engineering Technician, 1978 - 1984
Test Operator / Assistant Supervisor, 1975 - 1978

WAFER FABRICATION

- Conducted process characterizations to improve product yield and process repeatability.
- Performed failure analysis and dispositioned lots.
- Gained skill in working with the following equipment while monitoring product manufacturing.
   Ion implanters
   EPI reactors
   Diffusion furnaces
   Scanning electron microscope (SEM)

TESTING

- Received formal factory training in:
   Trillium VLSI testers
   LTX analog systems
   Teradyne systems
   Various automated test handlers
- Supported, maintained, and calibrated test equipment; updated maintenance documentation.
- Performed troubleshooting to component level.
- Developed and implemented circuit designs to increase reliability and compatibility between test equipment and tester interface hardware.

— Continued —

Pedro Valencia
Page 2

TEAM LEADERSHIP

- Supervised a technical team of 10, responsible for supporting Test / Burn-in manufacturing operations.

- Ensured technicians were involved in problem ownership, definition, and resolution to enhance their job satisfaction and personal growth.

- Led three task forces that achieved reliability, standardization, and cost-effectiveness of test systems and handlers.

- Interfaced extensively with the vendors and field service engineers to implement factory modifications.

- Served as an active member of the Quality Improvement Process (QIP), a forum for discussing manufacturing / engineering ideas and strategies.

- Trained technicians and provided technical support on related manufacturing test systems.

Resume written in 1994.

John L. Stine
354 East 56th Street
New York, NY 10012
Tel: 212-226-8456
E-mail: jlstine@ix.netcom.com

John's e-mail address is critical to his heading since this is the primary means of communication with his potential employer.

John created this resume in text-only format (no indents, bold, or special effects) so that he could e-mail it directly to employers.

JOB OBJECTIVE: Product manager of switched and dedicated circuit access.

KEY WORDS: Telecommuting. ISDN. Frame Relay. DS0. T-1. Novell. AppleTalk. Macintosh. UNIX. DOS. Windows. Routers. Bridges. Cabling. WAN. Microsoft Word. Excel. Microsoft Project. Aldus PageMaker. dBASE IV. Pascal. C. RBOC. On-line. BBS. Proposal and Article Writing. Sales. Negotiation. Presentations. Implementation. Product Development. Planning. Administration. Scheduling. Vendor Negotiations. Press Relations. Media Kits. French.

Notice the use of periods in John's Key Word section to indicate the completion of an item on his list.

SUMMARY OF QUALIFICATIONS
• Experienced in project management of switched and dedicated circuit WANs. Designed, sold, and maintained ISDN-based telecommuting systems for the NY investment banking community.
• Built relations with ISDN equipment vendors and ISDN sales/support departments in RBOCs and Bellcore.
• Successfully nurtured markets in new technology.

PROFESSIONAL EXPERIENCE
Product Manager, DCi/Data Net, 1994 - 1995
• Designed and oversaw the product development of ISDN-based telecommuting. Product sold to three major investment banks. Increased revenues 20% in first three months.
• Worked with customers, vendors, telcos, salespeople, field engineers, and management to create a scalable method for deploying and maintaining ISDN-based telecommuting.
• Oversaw the daily administration of product sales and implementation.
• Gave regular presentations on product development.
• Negotiated more than $375K in compensation from telcos.
• Contributed to the creation of promotional and sales presentation materials.
• Wrote a comprehensive plan to carry through several iterations a service model for telecommuting via ISDN. Worked around obstacles (e.g., two accounting systems) and optimized resources.
• Deployed more than 300 remote nodes and 15 pilot projects.

Sales/Product Manager, I-3 Telecom, Inc., 1993 - 1994
• Collaborated in the startup of I-3 Telecom, which sold and maintained turnkey ISDN-based file transfer and WAN systems to advertising, media, and digital imaging companies.

Even a very long document can be e-mailed or scanned as one "page." So page numbers don't need to appear as they would on a hardcopy document.

• Developed relations with equipment manufacturers, local businesses, and telcos. Participated in joint promotional activities with Apple Computer, NYNEX, and ISDN equipment suppliers.
• Negotiated with NYNEX for special technical assistance on major accounts.
• Key clients: Associated Press, Time Magazine, NBC, FCB Leber Katz, Stern Magazine, and Ammirati & Puris.

C Programmer in UNIX, Leveraged Technologies, Inc., 1992 - 1993
• Designed and coded modules of an options analysis system for Kidder Peabody & Co.
• Assisted in the scheduling and allocation of coding responsibilities for a spot market currency trading system for Telerate, a subsidiary of Dow Jones & Co.

Account Executive, Marketing/Sales, International Forms Corp., Inc., 1991 - 1992
• Established and maintained over 30 new accounts. Successes included:
- A cooperative advertising agreement with WordPerfect.
- The sale of 90% of the posters used in the 1992 Democratic National Convention.

EDUCATION
B.A., Mathematics (Minor: History), University of Virginia, Charlottesville, 1989.
Education Abroad:
University of Grenoble, Grenoble, France, 1990, Student: Intensive French.
Professor's Assistant: Taught English to French students.
Full scholarship, Hurstpierpoint College (public school), West Sussex, England, 1985.

ACTIVITIES
• Co-headed campaign that saved Naumburg Bandshell, Central Park. Personally collected over 4,000 signatures, recruited a lawyer (pro bono), and contacted public officials, community leaders, and the media.
• Personal interests: backgammon, bridge, bicycling, tennis, horseback riding, and photography.

Resume written in 1995.

Brian A. Ariel

33 Claremont Street • Berkeley, California 94731 • (510) 221-8634

JOB OBJECTIVE: Government Affairs Manager

This resume is scannable by most resume scanning systems since it employs minimal formatting.

SUMMARY OF QUALIFICATIONS

- Six years as a professional consultant providing corporate clients with research and analyses necessary to comply with governmental regulations.
- Comprehensive knowledge of state and local governmental affairs.
- Ability to advocate positions before diverse audiences.
- Spanish: speaking, reading, and writing competence.

EDUCATION

Ph.D., Political Science, 1994
University of California, Berkeley

M.A., Political Science, 1984
University of California, Berkeley

B.A, Politics, 1981
Princeton University, Princeton, NJ

PROFESSIONAL ACCOMPLISHMENTS

RESEARCH AND ANALYSIS

University of California

- Conducted research and authored dissertation on political responsibility, using case studies (Native American land claims and Reparation to Japanese-Americans) to justify national apologies.
- As university lecturer, crafted and presented analyses of contemporary political, legal, and ethical issues, addressing up to 100 students from diverse socioeconomic and cultural backgrounds.

Xenergy, Inc.

- Gathered and analyzed information using qualitative and quantitative research techniques such as interviews and primary and secondary source studies.

PUBLIC POLICY

Xenergy, Inc.

- Contributed to the development of the World Bank's energy policy by presenting research and analysis of governmental strategies to encourage energy efficiency.
- Served as research/public policy consultant to corporate clients regarding their relationship to governmental agencies such as state public utility commissions.
- Rewrote marketing and implementation strategies to increase customer participation in a recycling program for the Los Angeles Department of Water and Power.

WORK HISTORY

1989-present	Energy Consultant	Xenergy, Inc., Oakland, CA
1992-1994	Visiting Professor	Political Science Dept., University of California, Davis, CA
1984-1990	Instructor	Political Science Dept., University of California, Berkeley
1981-1983	Teacher	Westlake School for Girls, Los Angeles, CA

Resume written in 1995.

This resume is ready to be sent as a document attached to e-mail or as hard copy to a resume scanner.

Michael Schoolnik
300 East 34th Street, Apt. 7B • New York City, NY 10016
Tel: 212-683-6082 • E-mail: pp001066@interramp.com

Having the name on the first line all by itself is an important feature for all resumes that will be scanned.

Business Development Professional
for High Speed Online Services and Solutions

The Key Word section details Michael's technical and managerial expertise.

KEYWORDS

Integrated Switched Digital Network. Regional Bell Operating Company. Internet. Mosaic. World Wide Web. Adobe Acrobat. Multimedia. Interactive. Digital Delivery of Advertising to Publishers. On Line Delivery. On Line Subscription. Bulletin Board Service. Client Server. Groupware. Integration. Japanese. Tenacious. Competitive. Adaptable. Creative. Self Managing. Ability to Plan. Problem Solving. Accurate. Detail Minded. Takes Initiative. Supportive. Ethic. Follow Through. Communication Skills. Multitasking.

SUMMARY OF QUALIFICATIONS

- Expertise in the creation and marketing of ISDN fulfillment services including hardware, software, and support service packages.
- Innovator of product solutions to fill the public demand for:
  - Conducting private business via Switched Digital Services
  - High-speed Internet access
  - Accessing other stand alone online services
- Interested in developing information provider services to be accessed by the public via Internet, BBS, or other means.
- Recent success in business development for U.S. and Japanese online service companies.
- Conversant in Japanese language, business customs, and culture. Japan Working Visa.

PROFESSIONAL EXPERIENCE

1993-present   Business Link Communications Inc., New York, NY
VICE PRESIDENT, BUSINESS DEVELOPMENT

- Collaborated with president in building sales 400% through development of new ISDN integration business unit that creates and markets solutions for companies wanting to connect LANs at high speeds. ISDN solutions include:
  - High speed digital delivery of advertising to newspapers (DDAP). Clients: New York Times, McCann Erickson, Grey Advertising.
  - Distribution of syndicated news materials. Clients: Newscom and Los Angeles Times Syndicate.
  - Implementation of national pre-press networks. Clients: Applied Graphics Technology, RR Donnelly, Ziff Davis.
- Integrated hardware and software from Adtran, Transware, 4-Site, and SoftArc into one package to facilitate wide area network connections and file management.
- Deemed Authorized ISDN Sales Agent for NYNEX and Pacific Bell.
- Managed client ISDN projects including workflow evaluation, installation, training, and development of support packages for hardware and software.
- Advised president regarding strategic business agreements including a co-marketing contract with Scitex USA.
- Managed company endorsement of Adobe's Acrobat 1.0 and 2.0 for viewing and sending documents over ISDN. Handled press relations and participated in product rollouts.
- Planned and executed marketing tools, trade shows, and promotional events.

(Continued)

Michael Schoolnik
Page 2

1989-93   Koyosha Ltd., Tokyo, Japan
             MANAGER, BUSINESS DEVELOPMENT, Graphics Division, 1991-93
- Served as advisor to the Vice President of Corporate Planning of this company with $120MM in annual sales.
- Expanded sales 300% by researching and initiating dialogues with American software manufacturers for localization and resale of products in Japan.
- Developed Japanese and Foreign Information Providers photography and graphic packages sold via Knight Ridder's PressLink network.
- Established links between Tokyo and New York for producing The Economist in Japan in Japanese. This was the first time magazine pages were transmitted from Mac to Mac over ISDN in Japan.
- Represented Japanese company in contract negotiations with American firms, bridging cultural and language barriers to ensure strong business relations.
- Planned and developed first ever Japanese stock photography CD-rom products, a line that has since expanded 400%.
- As project leader, organized multimedia presentations, exhibitions, and marketing materials.

             CREATIVE DIRECTOR, Computer Publishing Laboratory, 1989-91
- Principally involved in the start up of this desktop publishing unit which in one year reduced production expenses 35%. Reported to Vice President of Corporate Planning.
- As leader of team comprised of Japanese nationals and Americans, directed the Infini-D software localization project which re-designed the original packaging to appeal to Japanese market.
- Conceived, designed, and produced $200,000 theme booths for participation in MacWorld Tokyo. Utilized bi-cultural skills to introduce new products to a foreign market.
- Directed creative teams in the production of print and interactive presentations.

1982-88   Dish Is It, San Francisco, CA
             GENERAL MANAGER
- Achieved 250% annual sales growth for this company that sold site-specific tile products to designers and architects.
- Partnered with manufacturers' representatives in 15 U.S. cities.
- Developed production and fulfillment processes that enabled an average gross profit margin of 60%.
- Negotiated large contracts with Bear Stearns, Banana Republic, and San Francisco Airport.

EDUCATION
BFA (Bachelor of Fine Arts), 1979, Rhode Island School of Design, Providence, RI

AFFILIATIONS
Certified SoftArc Consultant
NYNEX and Pacific Bell Sales Agent
Member, Picture Agency Council of America
Member, Newspaper Association of America

Resume written in 1994.

The Least You Need to Know

➤ If you're applying to a large-sized company, call first to ask if they use resume scanning in their applicant review process.

➤ If the company does use resume scanning, ask what their guidelines are so that you can create a resume for their particular system.

Chapter 18

Making This High-Tech Stuff Work for You

In This Chapter

➤ On-line resume distribution

➤ Creating your "electronic" resume

I remember how terrified most of us were when answering machines first moved into our homes. I hated recording my voice on someone's machine, knowing it would be spewed out of a speaker on the other end! Now that we've finally gotten used to them, another vehicle of communication is sneaking into our lives like the answering machine did, and may eventually assume the same status as our easy chair.

I'm referring to on-line technology—the proverbial Information Superhighway. And superhighway it is! It's speeding along so fast, even experienced on-liners have trouble keeping up with the latest.

Getting Up and Going On-Line

As a job seeker using on-line capabilities, you don't have to master the whole Internet; you only need to know enough to use it in your job search. If you haven't already, sign up with an on-line service that suits your level of computer competency (you may want to jump into one of the slower-paced lanes of the superhighway like America Online or CompuServe if you're a beginner), and start poking around.

Once on-line, you can take advantage of some great ways to learn about job openings, apply for positions, and even deposit your resume into resume databases where companies and recruiters look. Imagine, a job search conducted almost completely from that comfy chair at your desk!

Since the Internet and other on-line services are expanding so fast, it would be impossible to list all the services available now (since such a list would inevitably be outdated by the time you read this book). Instead, use the search engines available to you through whatever on-line avenue you travel. Look up key words such as *career, employment, jobs,* and *resumes*. You're bound to come up with a plethora of opportunities to explore!

Creating an "Electronic" Resume

To craft a resume that's ready for e-mailing, on-line resume banking, and scanning, you need a computer. The following "electronic" templates will be useful for giving you a structure in which to work. These templates are stripped of all formatting such as bold type and indents. If you're sending your resume on-line, use one of the templates as-is. If you're sending your resume via the U.S postal service to a resume scanner, you may choose to include some formatting once you understand the requirements of the particular scanning software used by your potential employer. (As we discussed in Chapter 17, call the company to which you're applying to inquire about their guidelines for creating a resume for their particular scanning system.)

Notice that each of the five electronic templates represents one type of resume I've talked about in this book: chronological, functional, achievement, hybrid based on a chronological, and hybrid based on a functional. Since a resume submitted on-line is susceptible to resume scanning, the following guidelines are written with scanning in mind.

Step One

All five formats mentioned above are acceptable to the resume scanner, so your first step is to decide which format is best for your situation. For help making that decision, review Parts 2 and 3.

Step Two

Place your name at the top of your resume, making sure that it is the only thing that appears on the first line. Here's why: the resume scanner interprets the first line (no matter what is written on the first line) as your name and will input it into the resume database as such. By the way, that means *everything* in the first line, so be sure you put only your name there.

Step Three

Make a list of at least 20 key words you think the hiring manager will use when asking the scanning software to perform a search for the position mentioned in your Job Objective. These key words can be technical or non-technical, and can be nouns, verbs, or adjectives.

Having an official Key Word section near the top of your resume is optional. I think it's helpful and can only ensure that the scanner finds the necessary information quickly. However, it's not required since even without a Key Word section, the scanner will search your document for relevant words.

If you decide to use the Key Word section on your resume, insert your list of words now. If you are not using a Key Word section, keep your list handy as you compose your text and be sure you integrate those terms into your resume.

Step Four

Clarify your job objective and insert that into your resume template. See Chapter 5 for help.

Step Five

Continue writing your resume, using the electronic template you have chosen, and following the guidelines discussed in Parts 2 and 3.

For even more ideas, browse through the five sample scannable resumes in Chapter 17. Notice that some of these samples have Key Word sections, others do not; some have formatting, while others do not.

Definition
Documents that do not have formatting are sometimes referred to as *ASCII* (pronounced "askey") or text-only documents. ASCII documents are ideal for resume scanning, e-mailing, and on-line distribution.

(Chronological Resume in Electronic Format)

NAME
Street • City, State Zip • phone

SKILLS SUMMARY
List 20 or more technical and interpersonal skills that would give the reader a quick overview of who you are and what you have to offer.

JOB OBJECTIVE
The job you would like to have next

SUMMARY OF QUALIFICATIONS
• Amount of experience you have in the field of your job objective, in a related field, or using the skills required for your new position.
• An overall career accomplishment that demonstrates you would be good at this job objective.
• What someone would say about you as a recommendation.

PROFESSIONAL EXPERIENCE
19xx-pres.   Company Name, City, State
              Job Title
• An accomplishment you are proud of that supports this objective.
• A problem you solved that leads the reader to believe you are valuable.
• A time when you positively affected the organization, the bottom line, your boss, your co-workers, your clients.
• Awards, commendations, publications, etc. you achieved that required this skill and relate to your job objective.

19xx-xx   Company Name, City, State
              Job Title
• A project that demonstrates how good you are at this type of work.
• Another accomplishment that shows you have the necessary skills.
• Quantifiable results that point out your skill.
• An occasion when someone "sat up and took notice" because of your skill.

19xx-xx   Company Name, City, State
              Job Title
• An accomplishment you are proud of that shows you will be valued by your next employer.
• A project that demonstrates how skilled you are.

EDUCATION
Degree, Major (if relevant), 19xx
School, City, State

(Functional Resume in Electronic Format)

NAME
Street • City, State Zip • phone

SKILLS SUMMARY
List 20 or more technical and interpersonal skills that would give the reader a quick overview of who you are and what you have to offer.

JOB OBJECTIVE
The job you would like to have next

SUMMARY OF QUALIFICATIONS
• Amount of experience you have in the field of your job objective, in a related field, or using the skills required for your new position.
• An overall career accomplishment that demonstrates you would be good at this job objective.
• What someone would say about you as a recommendation.

RELEVANT ACCOMPLISHMENTS

A KEY SKILL REQUIRED FOR YOUR JOB OBJECTIVE
• An accomplishment you are proud of that shows you're good at this skill.
• A problem you solved using this skill, and the results.
• A time when you used this skill to positively affect the organization, the bottom line, your boss, your co-workers, your clients.
• Awards, commendations, publications, etc. you achieved that required this skill and relate to your job objective.

A KEY SKILL REQUIRED FOR YOUR JOB OBJECTIVE
• A project you are proud of that used this skill and supports your job objective.
• Another accomplishment that shows you have this skill.
• Quantifiable results that point out your skill.
• An occasion when someone "sat up and took notice" because of your skill.

WORK HISTORY
19xx-present	Job Title	Organization, City, State
19xx-xx	Job Title	Organization, City, State
19xx-xx	Job Title	Organization, City, State

EDUCATION
Degree, Major (if relevant), 19xx
School, City, State

(Achievement Resume in Electronic Format)

NAME
Street • City, State Zip • phone

SKILLS SUMMARY
List 20 or more technical and interpersonal skills that would give the reader a quick overview of who you are and what you have to offer.

JOB OBJECTIVE: The job you would like to have next

SUMMARY OF QUALIFICATIONS

• Amount of experience you have in the field of your job objective, in a related field, or using the skills required for your new position.

• An overall career accomplishment that demonstrates you would be good at this job objective.

• What someone would say about you as a recommendation.

RELEVANT ACCOMPLISHMENTS

• An accomplishment you are proud of that supports this objective.

• Another accomplishment that shows you have the necessary skills.

• Awards, commendations, publications, etc. you achieved that relate to your job objective.

• A time when you positively affected the organization, the bottom line, your boss, your co-workers, your clients.

• A problem you solved that leads the reader to believe you are valuable.

• A project that demonstrates how good you are at this type of work.

WORK HISTORY
19xx-present	Job Title	Organization, City, State
19xx-xx	Job Title	Organization, City, State
19xx-xx	Job Title	Organization, City, State

EDUCATION
Degree, Major (if relevant), 19xx
School, City, State

(Hybrid Based on Chronological Resume in Electronic Format)

NAME
Street • City, State Zip • phone

SKILLS SUMMARY
List 20 or more technical and interpersonal skills that would give the reader a quick overview of who you are and what you have to offer.

JOB OBJECTIVE: The job you would like to have next

SUMMARY OF QUALIFICATIONS
• Amount of experience you have in the field of your job objective, in a related field, or using the skills required for your new position.
• An overall career accomplishment that demonstrates you would be good at this job objective.
• What someone would say about you as a recommendation.

PROFESSIONAL EXPERIENCE
19xx-pres.   Company Name, City, State
                      Job Title
A key skill required for your job objective
• An accomplishment you are proud of that shows you're good at this skill.
• A problem you solved using this skill, and the results.
• A time when you used this skill to positively affect the organization, the bottom line, your boss, your co-workers, your clients.

A key skill required for your job objective
• A project you are proud of that used this skill and supports your job objective.
• Another accomplishment that shows you have this skill.
• Quantifiable results that point out your skill.

19xx-xx   Company Name, City, State
                      Job Title
A key skill required for your job objective
• A time when you used this skill to positively affect the organization, the bottom line, your boss, your co-workers, your clients.
• Awards, commendations, publications, etc. you achieved that required this skill and relate to your job objective.

A key skill required for your job objective
• Quantifiable results that point out your skill.
• An occasion when someone "sat up and took notice" because of your skill.

EDUCATION
Degree, Major (if relevant), 19xx, School, City, State

(Hybrid Based on Functional Resume in Electronic Format)

NAME
Street • City, State Zip • phone

SKILLS SUMMARY
List 20 or more technical and interpersonal skills that give the reader a quick overview of who you are and what you have to offer.

JOB OBJECTIVE: The job you would like to have next

SUMMARY OF QUALIFICATIONS
• Amount of experience you have in the field of your job objective, in a related field, or using the skills required for your new position.
• An overall career accomplishment that demonstrates you would be good at this job objective.
• What someone would say about you as a recommendation.

RELEVANT ACCOMPLISHMENTS

A KEY SKILL REQUIRED FOR YOUR JOB OBJECTIVE
The organization where you achieved the following set of accomplishments
• An accomplishment you are proud of that shows you're good at this skill.
• A problem you solved using this skill, and the results.

The organization where you achieved the following set of accomplishments
• A time when you used this skill to positively affect the organization, the bottom line, your boss, your co-workers, your clients.
• Awards, commendations, publications, etc. you achieved that required this skill and relate to your job objective.

A KEY SKILL REQUIRED FOR YOUR JOB OBJECTIVE
The organization where you achieved the following set of accomplishments
• A project you are proud of that used this skill and supports your job objective.
• Another accomplishment that shows you have this skill.

The organization where you achieved the following set of accomplishments
• Quantifiable results that point out your skill.
• An occasion when someone "sat up and took notice" because of your skill.

WORK HISTORY
19xx-present	Job Title	Organization, City, State
19xx-xx	Job Title	Organization, City, State
19xx-xx	Job Title	Organization, City, State
19xx-xx	Job Title	Organization, City, State

EDUCATION
Degree, Major (if relevant), 19xx, School, City, State

Uploading Your Resume On-Line

Now that you've created your resume, you're ready to send it electronically to employers around the world. But how will you know what it looks like when the employer downloads (receives) it on the other end?

Here's one way to find out: After you've uploaded (sent) your resume into an on-line database, download it as if you were an employer. When it appears on your screen after being downloaded, check to see that all the information has transferred accurately and legibly. If something went wrong during the transfer, work with your original document to remedy the situation, or call on an experienced on-liner to help you fix the problem. Once it's straightened out, send your resume back into cyberspace, where it may well land at your next place of employment!

The Least You Need to Know

➤ Explore your on-line service for career-related forums where you can get job listings, post your resume, meet recruiters, and get helpful job search tips.

➤ Network on-line by creating and submitting a resume that is in ASCII or text-only format.

➤ Once you have uploaded your resume, download it as if you were an employer. This will enable you to check that it has been sent completely and accurately.

Index

When You're Smart Enough to Know
That You Don't Know It All

For all the ups and downs you're sure to encounter in life, The Complete Idiot's Guides give you down-to-earth answers and practical solutions.

Lifestyle

The Complete Idiot's Guide to Learning French on Your Own
ISBN: 0-02-861043-1 ▪ $16.95

The Complete Idiot's Guide to Learning Spanish on Your Own
ISBN: 0-02-861040-7 ▪ $16.95

The Complete Idiot's Guide to Successful Gambling
ISBN: 0-02-861102-0 ▪ $16.95

The Complete Idiot's Guide to Hiking and Camping
ISBN: 0-02-861100-4 ▪ $16.95

The Complete Idiot's Guide to Choosing, Training, and Raising a Dog
ISBN: 0-02-861098-9 ▪ $16.95

The Complete Idiot's Guide to Trouble-Free Car Care
ISBN: 0-02-861041-5 ▪ $16.95

The Complete Idiot's Guide to Trouble-Free Home Repair
ISBN: 0-02-861042-3 ▪ $16.95

The Complete Idiot's Guide to Dating
ISBN: 0-02-861052-0 ▪ $14.95

The Complete Idiot's Guide to Cooking Basics
ISBN: 1-56761-523-6 ▪ $16.99

The Complete Idiot's Guide to the Perfect Wedding
ISBN: 1-56761-532-5 ▪ $16.99

The Complete Idiot's Guide to the Perfect Vacation
ISBN: 1-56761-531-7 ▪ $14.99

The Complete Idiot's Guide to Getting and Keeping Your Perfect Body
ISBN: 0-02-861051-2 ▪ $14.95

The Complete Idiot's Guide to First Aid Basics
ISBN: 0-02-861099-7 ▪ $16.95

Personal Business

The Complete Idiot's Guide to Getting Into College
ISBN: 1-56761-508-2 ▪ $14.95

The Complete Idiot's Guide to Terrific Business Writing
ISBN: 0-02-861097-0 ▪ $16.95

The Complete Idiot's Guide to Surviving Divorce
ISBN: 0-02-861101-2 ▪ $16.95

The Complete Idiot's Guide to Managing Your Time
ISBN: 0-02-861039-3 ▪ $14.95

The Complete Idiot's Guide to Speaking in Public with Confidence
ISBN: 0-02-861038-5 ▪ $16.95

The Complete Idiot's Guide to Winning Through Negotiation
ISBN: 0-02-861037-7 ▪ $16.95

The Complete Idiot's Guide to Managing People
ISBN: 0-02-861036-9 ▪ $18.95

The Complete Idiot's Guide to Starting Your Own Business
ISBN: 1-56761-529-5 ▪ $16.99

The Complete Idiot's Guide to a Great Retirement
ISBN: 1-56761-601-1 ▪ $16.95

The Complete Idiot's Guide to Protecting Yourself From Everyday Legal Hassles
ISBN: 1-56761-602-X ▪ $16.99

The Complete Idiot's Guide to Getting the Job You Want
ISBN: 1-56761-608-9 ▪ $24.95

Personal Finance

The Complete Idiot's Guide to Buying Insurance and Annuities
ISBN: 0-02-861113-6 ▪ $16.95

The Complete Idiot's Guide to Doing Your Income Taxes 1996
ISBN: 1-56761-586-4 ▪ $14.99

The Complete Idiot's Guide to Getting Rich
ISBN: 1-56761-509-0 ▪ $16.95

The Complete Idiot's Guide to Making Money with Mutual Funds
ISBN: 1-56761-637-2 ▪ $16.95

The Complete Idiot's Guide to Managing Your Money
ISBN: 1-56761-530-9 ▪ $16.95

The Complete Idiot's Guide to Buying and Selling a Home
ISBN: 1-56761-510-4 ▪ $16.95

You can handle it!
Look for The Complete Idiot's Guides at your favorite bookstore, or call 1-800-428-5331 for more information.